THE KEYS OF HEAVEN

David Sutcliffe

Jesus said to Peter: 'And I will give unto thee the keys of the kingdom of heaven' (Matthew 16:19). Christian Socialists like Charles often spoke of a new kingdom on earth.

The folk song 'The Keys of Heaven' was collected by Charles Marson and Cecil Sharp from Mrs Emma Welsh of Isle Brewers on September 6th 1904. Another version was collected from my relative Charles Neville in East Coker in 1908.

THE KEYS OF HEAVEN

The Life of Revd Charles Marson

Socialist Priest and Folk Song Collector

by

David Sutcliffe

THE KEYS OF HEAVEN
The Life of Revd Charles Marson
Socialist Priest and Folk Song Collector
by
David Sutcliffe

Published by Cockasnook Books
22 Whernside Road, Nottingham NG5 4LD
www.cockasnook.co.uk

ISBN 978-0-9557460-7-9

First published 2010
Printed by The Russell Press,
Russell House, Bulwell Lane, Basford, Nottingham NG6 0BT

This book is available through
www.charlesmarson.co.uk

For my wife Lesley and children Amy and Thomas,
who have been so patient

And in memory of my father Canon Tom Sutcliffe,
who overcame sixty years of deafness and taught me
the secrets of communication

CONTENTS

Family Trees: Marson & Bayne
Preface

Marson's Literary Output
Acknowledgements
Bibliography and Sources
About the Author
Index

Descendants of Charles Marson

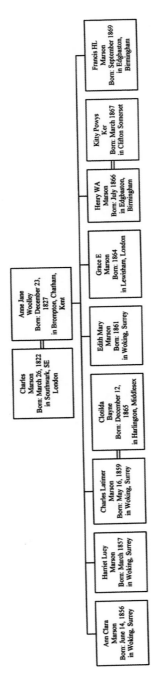

Charles Marson
Born: March 26, 1822
in Southwark, SE
London

Anne Jane Woolley
Born: December 23, 1827
in Brompton, Chatham, Kent

Ann Clara Marson
Born: June 14, 1856
in Woking, Surrey

Harriet Lucy Marson
Born: March 1857
in Woking, Surrey

Charles Latimer Marson
Born: May 16, 1859
in Woking, Surrey

Clotilda Bayne
Born: December 12, 1865
in Hartington, Middlesex

Edith Mary Marson
Born: 1861
in Woking, Surrey

Grace E Marson
Born: 1864
in Lewisham, London

Henry WA Marson
Born: July 1866
in Edgbaston, Birmingham

Kitty Powys Ker
Born: March 1867
in Clifton Somerset

Francis HL Marson
Born: September 1869
in Edgbaston, Birmingham

Descendants of Peter Bayne

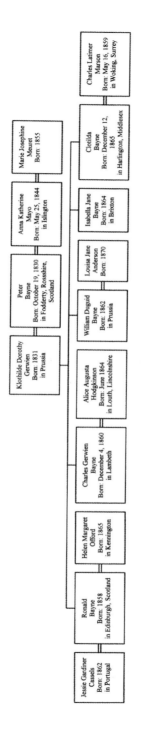

Preface

This is the story of a man, Charles Marson, who was far-sighted enough in the midst of the Victorian slums to imagine a post-industrial society that would be gloriously free and fair, if people could only curb their greed and materialism; brave enough to speak up for the 'Have-nots', because the 'Haves' would look after themselves; foolish enough to support unpopular causes like Socialism and Church Reform, even at the expense of his own career; and smart enough to make children and cynics alike laugh at his jokes and stories. He was a member of several of the important socialist groups of the time and edited an influential newspaper for them. He kicked out at a complacent and conservative Church that did not wish nor know how to use his considerable talents. Indeed he was sacked from five curacies and rejected by six Bishops, so his deeds are not recorded in church annals.

As a young man, he rebelled against the strict evangelical discipline of his parents and was exposed instead to a whole set of new ideas about lifestyle and beliefs – from sexual freedom and the status of women to the 'Simpler Life' and early socialism; from Hinduism and Spiritualism to the 'Arts and Crafts' movement and communal living. It was a modern agenda in many ways. As he once wrote disappointedly, 'I could find nothing to be enthusiastic about and I believe I shall have to fall back upon religion for comfort.' He was, however, impressed by Bishop John Colenso, who was 'the first man who suggested to me that it is possible to be a Christian without being intellectually a coward or a shuffler'.

Charles went to work as a volunteer in Whitechapel with Canon Samuel Barnett, who famously said: 'He who has, even for a month, shared the life of the poor, can never rest again in his old thoughts.' Charles was never complacent and continued to work among the poorest parishes in London. When he worked in South Australia, he spoke up for Aboriginal rights and on his return was prominent in the London cabbies' strike in 1894. In his ministry to the poor, he developed a style that highlighted the drama and mystery of High Church ritual and he was known for his lively (but short) sermons.

In his contact with the early socialists, he was wary of middle-class intellectuals and was adamant that socialism would not

11

succeed without the moderating values of Christianity to restrain personal greed and lust for power. He demanded that the Church and the State together should abandon laissez-faire capitalism and inefficient charity, and intervene directly to improve the life of the poor. Distrusting the Liberals, he boldly advocated the birth of a Labour Party.

In addition to his Christian Socialism, he had a life as a successful journalist, supplementing his meagre stipend with literary reviews and articles in national newspapers. In another venture he launched Cecil Sharp on his particular journey to record and revive English folk song in 1903 but received little credit for his efforts.

His books are out of print and his trail seemed nearly cold but his recently discovered letters reveal a fascinating life. They are full of ideas about how we should live and they are candid about his personal struggles – his engagement to Lady Agatha Russell and his infatuation with Edith Nesbit in her early days of writing; his marriage to Clotilda Bayne, 'blue-stocking' and women's activist; and his support for his drug addict brother Frank.

His final days were spent in Hambridge village in Somerset, where he indulged in his favourite pastime of fishing but he was no recluse – his humour and good fellowship meant that he felt at home as much in the pub as in the pulpit. He was <u>not</u> your average vicar!

1

First Impressions

RMS Austral
26th May 1889

'Dearest Chloe,

We got to Suez on Friday afternoon and such a crew came round in their dhows. The minute we landed, a crowd of donkey drivers seized us to ride to Suez, which is distant a mile and a half. We rode on large pommelled saddles, whew! How the beasts galloped and Arabs ran! Outside Suez we dismounted as the sun was setting, such a grand town. We got a guide and a large party of us went together through narrow streets lighted with hanging oil lamps like Old London. Everything was beautiful, benches, shop pillars, counters, candlesticks, jars.

We soon came out, about forty of us, and went down dark streets, surrounded by a crowd of Arabs to the boats. We got aboard a dhow with seven Arabs, at least some 15 of us did. We agreed to pay 6d per head. No sooner were we out to sea than the Arabs demanded 1/- a head. We of course refused, and they put out to sea and held the sheet until the boat rocked. There was a storm of angry voices, "We'll throw you overboard and work the ship ourselves", our men cried. I saw the dragoman (*interpreter*) aboard and told him quietly that our men meant to do it. He told his brethren and they quieted down and by a great detour we made the Austral. The Arabs carry great knives and are formidable customers but we were 11 men and might have given them some knocking about.

But imagine the excitement on board, as several parties were still out and we heard ugly stories. Two men were set upon and delivered from the crowd by a bold Roman priest, who saw and rushed up with a revolver, which he fired over the heads of the crowd and brought off the victim. One man got robbed of £3.10.0d and had a vicious crack made at his head with a bludgeon. A lady had her pocket picked with us; and two fellows were lured away.

Next day there was a crowd of Arabs in boats, selling all sorts of things. At last it came to a bit of a row, and a few things were thrown on each side. Our people behaved badly, after the Arabs had provoked them on Friday.'

Charles Marson was 30 when he wrote this letter to his fiancée Clotilda Bayne. He was on his way to Australia – a long and hazardous journey of six weeks by steamship. The letter neatly encapsulates much of what you need to know about Charles – he had courage, leadership, moral sense and good humour too. He had never put to sea before in his life, so showed great presence of mind to disregard his personal safety and defuse the tricky situation with the Arab sailors. In the cultural clash of those early days of tourism, he could see the funny side of things but disapproved of the European behaviour on the second day, when a mild retribution occurred. Two wrongs didn't make a right, as far as he was concerned.

Above all, the letter shows his great zest for life and the ability to share this with others. His outspoken nature handicapped his career within the Church, however, and made for a very unsettled life but he wouldn't have had it any other way.

☞━☗

He was born on May 16th 1859 at St John's Vicarage, Woking, Surrey. His mother Ann was thrilled that after two girls, this one was a boy. She was not usually given to sentimentality, having had a hard life herself but she couldn't suppress an onrush of excitement and hope that this little boy might achieve more than her God-fearing father and four hard-working brothers had ever done. Her husband Charles had also been hoping for a son because he had hardly known his own father, who had died when he was just four. He was determined to create a warm father-son relationship of his own.

The proud parents gave the child two names – 'Charles' after his father and grandfather; and 'Latimer' after the Protestant martyr Hugh Latimer, who was burned at the stake in Oxford in 1555 for resisting the catholic comeback of Queen Mary. Ann Marson had been brought up as a strict evangelical Christian and wanted to provide her son with a suitable role model. Consciously or not, this name of Latimer would influence the child for the rest of his life in terms of courage, self-sacrifice and reforming zeal.

14

Baby Charles Latimer was a healthy infant and thrived in his settled surroundings. He had no special attributes, save only his very blue eyes and his father's prominent nose. His father only had a modest income to raise his growing family, but the three children were fussed over and Ann had two servants to help her run the new vicarage. It was five years since his father, whom we shall now call Charles Senior, had become curate in charge of St John's, a new church, built soon after the railway had come to Woking Common and changed Old Woking village and its ancient parish of St Peter's beyond recognition.

In 1861 the family moved house when Charles Senior took up a post as Assistant Secretary of the Church Missionary Society, basing himself in Lewisham. From there the new North Kent railway and South East railway gave him easy access into his offices in Salisbury Square in the city of London. His job was to support and correspond with missionaries abroad, sympathising with their difficulties or illnesses and reading of their successes, so as to spread their stories and promote fundraising at home. One such missionary was Revd John Gritton, with whom Charles Senior toured England when Gritton was home on leave from the Madras Mission in Southern India. No doubt these mission stories of courage in the face of adversity were retold in the Marson household, planting seeds in the mind of young Charles Latimer.

Meanwhile two more daughters were born, Edith (1861) and Grace (1864), and the five children were much spoiled in their new home in Granville Park by their neighbours, the Guest family. The Revd Benjamin Guest was in his 70s and enjoying retirement but his two unmarried daughters (Mary) Jane and Emily doted on the children, particularly Charles, with whom they would correspond intimately over the next thirty years. Jane was 32 and Emily 24. They had been pupils of John Ruskin and were cultured people with many interesting stories of their visits to Italy and Greece.

In 1864 Charles Senior was promoted and became vicar of Christ Church, Birmingham. This was another relatively new church, built in 1805 to accommodate the expanding population of the city. Once settled, the family grew again with the arrival of two sons Henry (Harry) in 1866 and Francis (Frank) in 1869. Charles Latimer was much older than his brothers and felt quite responsible for them in later life, especially Frank who was perhaps spoiled as youngest child and needed support later.

Charles Latimer was sent first to a local Dame school to start his education. He was a dark-haired boy, tall for his age but somewhat lacking in confidence. Looking back on his life later, he wrote a secret autobiographical piece called *The Life of Amos Peterson* in which he describes his early childhood: 'Three times a week in church and twice a day at family prayers, did Uncle Vensby (*code for his father*) pour out his exhortations . . . against corruptions and the subtle poisons of "Rome" . . . Mrs Vensby was anti-worldly, a fierce unswerving puritan with no weakness, no laughter, no delight in any thing but the Gospel'. Sadly there were no relatives in the area to relieve this oppression – no cousins to play with, no grandparents to supply alternative adult contact.

The Marson Family

Charles Latimer was puzzled that he had no living grandparents at all, so one day his father took down the precious family Bible and explained his side of the family. The Marsons came originally from the village of Old Swinford near Stourbridge, just 10 miles west of where they now lived in Birmingham. That had been an ironworking area, the most famous ironmasters there being the Foley family. John Marson (born 1751) made the move to London and from a wharf at Southwark shipped in iron products for retail in south London. The business passed to his son Charles (Charles Latimer's grandfather) but it faced great competition and dwindled over time. Fortunately 'Grandfather' Charles had married into a wealthy Italian family – his wife Harriet Milway Gattie was the daughter of a well-known Bond Street perfumer (William Gattie) and the granddaughter of an Italian Doctor Gatti(e). They had two children Charles (i.e. Charles Latimer's father, born 1822) and Harriet (born 1824). However, 'Grandfather' Charles unexpectedly died in 1826, aged only 39. In his will he left his widow over £1,000 (roughly equivalent to £75,000 today) to be spent, at least in part, on the education of his two children.

'Grandma' Harriet Marson brought up her two young children in Acre Lane, Clapham, where she became good friends with the Revd Charles Bradley, a member of the Clapham Sect. This group of evangelical philanthropists had set up the Church Missionary Society in 1799. Led by William Wilberforce, one of its aims was to secure the abolition of the slave trade (achieved in 1807). Harriet sent her son to be taught first at Clapham Grammar School by a brilliant young tutor Charles Pritchard, astronomer and fellow of St John's College Cambridge. 'Charles Senior' then went to school at Worcester and thence, aged 19, to Christ Church College Oxford in May 1841.

Unfortunately 'Grandma' Harriet died only a month later and though Charles Senior continued his studies, he and his sister, aged just 17, had to relocate and were looked after by their uncle Clement Peirce. He was executor of Harriet's will and a partner in the perfume business known as 'Gattie & Peirce (approved tradesmen to HRH the Prince of Wales)', which was based at 116 New Bond Street. Charles and Harriet spent many a night with the family, sleeping above the shop, overwhelmed by the aromas from below. The shop's two most advertised products were Treble Distilled Lavender Water and Atkinson's 'Bear Grease' for regeneration of hair! The business was still doing well, employing 14 men and allowing Clement to invest in other property. He himself had a son and two daughters roughly the same age as their cousin Charles and they stayed in touch all their lives.

Charles (Senior)

Born 1822

Photo courtesy

of St Andrews

Clevedon

However, Charles Senior was not interested in the perfume business and resolved to take holy orders. At Oxford he flirted with the new Oxford Movement led by (Cardinal) John Newman, which advocated a return to High Church ceremony but he eventually reverted to his evangelical roots, upholding the supremacy of the sermon and Bible over the eucharist and ritual. For two years he served a curacy at Biddenden, 10 miles west of Ashford in Kent, then went as curate to the village of Kimbolton, 10 miles north of Bedford, in 1847. It was there that he met Ann Jane Woolley (born 1827), who was a governess to a family there. They became engaged and were married at St Leonard's Chapel, Hastings on April 4th 1854.

The Woolley family

Ann Marson, Charles Latimer's mother, was, it seems, rather a cold person and a disciplinarian as opposed to her husband, who was warm, witty and generous, despite his fulminations from the pulpit. Ann had neither time nor inclination to argue. She had come from a tough background, had progressed by will and determination and her solemn task now was to raise seven children on a limited budget.

Her father Joseph Woolley had made his own way in life, leaving his village of Bilston nr Wolverhampton (another centre of iron-making) to enrol in the Royal Marines at Chatham, Kent in April 1805 aged just 18. No doubt the country-wide panic at the possibility of an imminent invasion by Napoleon's forces in the south-east corner of England prompted him to make his move. The Royal Military Canal was already under construction between Hythe and Rye, as Romney Marsh was considered the most likely invasion point; but all ports were on alert and Chatham would have been exceptionally busy. Within three months Joseph was quickly promoted to Sergeant and was assigned to serve under Lieutenant-General Barclay, although there is no record of his participation in the Battle of Trafalgar in October that year. In the end, Joseph served in the Marines for 34 years before his discharge in 1839. He certainly expected his own children to get a trade or training – for example, son Henry became a schoolmaster then a grocer, while son Edwin became a bootmaker.

Unfortunately, Joseph died in 1845 when Ann was just 18. She must have had some education because a few years later, aged 23, she was working as a governess for a widow and her family in Kimbolton. She had much in common with the village curate Charles Marson, therefore – their families both came from the industrial Midlands (just 10 miles apart) and their fathers had both died early, after inculcating 'Bible infallibility' in their offspring.

Charles Latimer's character

So how would Charles Latimer cope with this double dose of strict evangelicalism? Not well, initially. He wrote later: 'My mind turned in upon itself. I took to dreaming and to poetry. I had no friends except two guinea pigs and a magpie.' At school he 'held his own . . . by a certain power of tongue' (he did impressions of the teachers and other pupils). He took to keeping mice, not ordinary mice but coloured mice, which he introduced into the schoolmaster's pantry 'to try whether the domestic brown mouse could not be superseded by fancy mice. His efforts were so successful that later generations of scholars enriched themselves by trapping the piebald mice and selling them in Wolverhampton market!'

Charles Latimer

Age 7 in

Birmingham

His inability to bond with his mother may have handicapped him emotionally, for he would cultivate one or two maternal substitutes in his life – particularly the Guest sisters in Lewisham and then Miss Sophy Pedder at Clevedon. It is certainly interesting that not one of his four sisters had the luck or good management to make a marriage. Charles described his mother as 'a strong woman with a small frail body, of the stuff of which martyrs are made and not mothers usually'. She divided mankind, he said, into 'The Lord's own' and 'the World which was to be left to perish in frivolity. She knew the Truth and the Truth had made her free from all human sympathy and from all human weakness. She despised art and symbols, hated letters and any form of poetry.' Charles's reaction later, of course, was to treasure those very things, creating beauty out of church ritual and writing prose and poetry with great zest and imagination. He tried to please her in his studies and in his work but eventually she took little interest in him and particularly disapproved of the mistakes he made. It is not surprising that he became in some respects a *méchant garçon*.

When Charles Latimer was 12, the family upped sticks again, this time to Clevedon in Somerset, where his father became vicar of the main church St Andrews (population approx 3,000). At last he had some status and recognition at age 49, with a comfortable vicarage in a pleasant seaside town and a living of £460 pa (£25,000 today). Charles Latimer was delighted with the move. The new house had an empty plot at the back and a big garden on the other side leading down to the shops on Old Church Road – plenty of space for play. Most mornings he could smell the coffee aromas drifting up from Mr Radcliffe's Coffee House on the corner, and nearby William Maynard, the baker, competed for his attention too. Less than a mile away lay the sea with the town's new pier and attractions. Right opposite his road (*which is now called Marson Road*) was Clevedon Railway Station with the bustle of daytrippers arriving and the release of pent-up steam from the engines.

Charles quickly made new friends, because he started school at Mr Eustace Button's house *Lewesfell* in nearby Elton Road as a day boy – there were also 19 boarders ages 10-16. Mr Button was 41, an amiable and musical fellow – centre stage in the life of the school with his wife and large family in the wings. Charles enjoyed his schooldays there and frequently visited Mr Button in later life at

Christmas and other occasions. On his way back from school, Charles might call in at Tickton Lodge in Bellevue Road, to Miss Sophy Pedder's for tea. Sophy was the daughter of Revd William Pedder, former incumbent of St Andrews. She was in her late 30s, a warm and wise person, who took a great liking to the young boy.

After a few years, however, Charles was sent to Clifton College, Bristol as a boarder in Daykin's House. Clifton was then a new public school under the headmastership of the Revd Dr John Percival, preparing boys for the Army and the Indian Civil Service. Charles didn't like it much and didn't excel in any area. He was called 'the atheist', and earnestly and angrily dissuaded the boys in his dormitory from saying their prayers.

He left after the summer term in 1878 and proceeded to University College Oxford, whose new and invigorating Master was George Bradley, son of Revd Charles Bradley of Clapham who had been known to the Marson family so many years before. After an initial period of unease at his relative poverty and gaucheness, he found lasting friendships with several people – Robert Chalmers and the brothers Ronald and Charles Bayne.

These friends were all of a sceptical mind and were pronounced 'infidels' by their peers: 'If we attended any religious services, it was to disagree with them and to exalt ourselves above and sever ourselves from ignorant, ancient and canting religionists.' And yet they did all seem anxious to believe in something. Charles said he 'went to every church and chapel in or near Oxford vaguely feeling belief to be the natural attitude of the mind.' The one church that intrigued him was the Roman Catholic church of St Aloysius in Woodstock Road. Although his sceptical mind thought the worship was 'pretty mummery – the lights, incense, wafers and dresses were toys', his visual sense was actually relieved at last and he wrote, 'here and here only, rich and poor meet together . . . all are equal, all are knit together, the sceptic with his doubts, the harlot with her sins, the moral man with his virtues, the believer with his creeds and confusions – for once merely human.'

Although Charles discovered another pleasure at Oxford – fishing for chub near Godstowe, a hobby he would enjoy for the rest of his life – he had serious quarrels with his parents back home. His brush with Catholicism would, of course, have infuriated his parents. 'Terrific arguments ended in abuse on the one side and impudence

21

on the other. Home ties were snapt for ever. Life was so harsh and black for me, that I was often meditating suicide.' But his friends gave him support and counsel which he later acknowledged: 'Whatever I have done well or thought truly, is thanks to them and their help. Where I was illogical, they did not spare me. Where I was bitter, hasty or querulous, they were patient and good humoured. They could share poetical feelings and yet knew where fine sentiment becomes false or unreal. Above all they believed in me and to be believed in by folk we respect is an education in itself.'

With this newfound confidence Charles joined the Oxford Union and in November 1880 mischievously proposed the motion "That in the opinion of this House, the British Monarchy should cease with the present reign". The motion was lost by 33 votes to 4 but it was an indicator of Queen Victoria's loss of popularity, following her withdrawal from public life in grief at the loss of her husband Prince Albert. It would not recover until her Golden Jubilee in 1887.

Charles began to study philosophy as well as the classics Greek and Latin, all of which he continued to use throughout his life; but he was not perhaps best suited to an academic future and so, without the customary extra coaching, proceeded to take his degree in haste, leaving Oxford with only a Third in History in December 1881. Relations with family must have been somewhat restored, because his father wrote him a warm letter of congratulation upon his degree, with hopes that wherever Charles now found work, he would have no health problems – for Charles had become a chronic asthmatic. Little did his father know that Charles, Ronald Bayne and Robert Chalmers had just signed up to go to work as parish volunteers in the East End of London amid its smog and deprivation. This decision would transform all their lives.

2

'Oatmeal and Grapes'

Charles, Ronald and Robert arrived in Whitechapel in time for Christmas 1881 and moved into a block of 53 flats at 29, Morrison's Buildings ('Improved Industrial Dwellings') on Commercial Road. Their idea of economical housekeeping was to buy a sack of oatmeal and a barrel of grapes packed in sawdust to live on for the first month. But a diet of porridge and fruit did not ward off illness (possibly the unsafe water supply in the area affected them), so after ten days a doctor had to intervene and they had to rethink the simple life!

Pure idealism had brought them here, enticed by an appeal for helpers by Revd Samuel Barnett, vicar of St Jude's, at an open meeting of 100 students held on December 1st at Merton College, Oxford. As Charles left the safe and ordered confines of his Oxford college, what did he imagine his new life would be like? What briefing did Barnett give to the young graduates? How successful had he himself been in his first years in the parish?

Barnett had been offered his Whitechapel parish back in 1872 at the age of 28, after serving as curate with the innovative Revd William Fremantle at St Mary's Bryanston Square, a socially mixed parish just off the Edgware Road. There he had worked with the stern and formidable Miss Octavia Hill, who instituted a new system of rent-collecting. A team of female visitors went round the various tenements, discussing problems and dispensing advice on good housekeeping but efficiently collecting rents at the same time – a precursor perhaps to the social worker visits of today. Landlords were happy and within a few years the Ecclesiastical Commissioners had handed over all their properties to her and she led an army of visitors, managing 5,000 properties all over London.

The other major innovation at St Mary's was the formation of the Charity Organisation Society, which would also be replicated across London. By 1850 there were an estimated 500 charities in London, doling out relief in a random and confused way to a multitude of claimants. Statutorily, the Poor Laws dating from Elizabethan times charged local parishes (and thus ratepayers) with the delivery of poor relief to the elderly and the sick, to the widows, the disabled and the unemployed. Many parishes bonded together into Poor Law Unions to manage 'outrelief' (cash payments or 'doles') as well as the (last resort) workhouses, such as those described by Dickens in his book 'Oliver Twist' in 1838. But this whole system was becoming outdated and what was needed was a new social policy coupled with a more efficient system of delivery.

The new Charity Organisation Society required claimants to complete a form to explain their condition – the beginnings of a benefit bureaucracy. Charles Marson was impatient of this administrative side to his volunteering. He once mischievously filled out a fictional form as if completed by Jesus of Nazareth to test if he (Jesus) would have been one of the 'deserving poor' and had it published in a newspaper. He was, of course, objecting to the control of resources by one class over another. Charles Ashbee, another St Jude's volunteer, who left to found the Guild and School of Handicraft at nearby Mile End, spoke disparagingly of 'tophatty philanthropy'.

So Samuel Barnett brought this expertise in housing and 'efficient' charity relief to St Jude's, when he moved into the tiny vicarage with his new wife Henrietta in May 1873. According to her memoirs, the first act of welcome for Samuel from one of his parishioners was 'to be knocked down by him in Commercial Street and have his watch stolen'. Petty crime abounded in this neighbourhood, as people scrabbled to make a living. There were pick-pockets, burglars, forgers, rent-dodgers, beggars. When the convict ships ceased transporting criminals to Australia in 1868, the London prisons came under strain and the City and Metropolitan Police forces were unable and unwilling to conduct patrols in all areas.

Prostitution also was rife. For centuries sailors, on leave and paid up, would have their money relieved from them by the pubs and brothels along the notorious Ratcliffe Highway (*renamed St George Street, now The Highway, Shadwell*) one mile to the south but it was estimated that there were 1,200 prostitutes in Whitechapel and 80,000 in the whole of London. Charles later quoted these statistics in a sermon that shocked his congregation but he would have seen evidence of this all around him at this time.

24

So Charles and his two companions probably left their flat rather anxiously for their first morning's work, crossing over the splendidly broad thoroughfare of Whitechapel High Street into the packed network of mean streets to its north. Barnett quickly introduced them to other members of his team:-

- Miss Kate Potter, rent collector and visitor, age 34, daughter of a businessman and barrister. Kate had already worked at St Jude's for five years and currently was managing houses according to the 'Octavian' principle of visiting and befriending the tenants. She had the help of a team of 8 ladies, all working two days a week. Her sister Beatrice joined her in the work in 1884 and then assisted their cousin Charles Booth in his statistical survey of London's Poor (first 2 vols 1889-91). Eventually Beatrice married Sidney Webb and together they took over leadership of the Fabian Society.

- Miss Pauline Douglas Townsend, also 34, a solicitor's daughter from Paddington who had joined in 1875, was secretary of the Metropolitan Association for Befriending Young Servants (MABYS). This organisation had been started by Jane Senior, who was appointed the Government Inspector of Workhouses in 1873. St Jude's took up the idea when it was realised that many of the young girls from the Ragged Schools could be made fit for domestic service (then a major industry) instead of working in sweated workshops. The girls were deloused, dressed and given basic training, as well as receiving ongoing support in their placement. For some at least it was an escape from their degrading surroundings. About 200 girls were placed each year.

- Henrietta Barnett herself ran the Children's Country Holiday Fund (a St Jude's initiative), which started in 1877 when 9 sickly children were placed with host families in the countryside for a refreshing break from London's harsh environment. By 1880 over 400 children a year enjoyed a rural holiday and the charity is still very active today.

- Revd Thory Gage Gardiner, age 24, was born and raised in the Hornsey area, the son of a stationer. He was a graduate of Brasenose College Oxford and had recently been appointed curate of St Jude's. He stayed with the Barnetts until 1889.

- Edward Leonard, age 31, long-term volunteer who delivered the special Sunday school programme for the parish children. Attendance was good and he was obviously a popular leader.

- Revd Samuel Thompson Yates, age 38, who had left an 'easy' parish in Scarborough and had private means anyway but 'wanted to do hard work'. He lived at 396 Commercial Street and had been at St Jude's for 4 years.

- Last, but not least, came Marion Paterson, who was nineteen when she joined the Barnetts in 1877 and was to be Henrietta's secretary and close companion for nearly 60 years.

Charles as volunteer

at St Jude's 1881

aged 22

There were doubtless other helpers and possibly other Oxford students too. Charles, Ronald and Robert were soon set to work in the parish, paying house visits to the sick and to any charity applicants, liaising with Charity Organisation Society officers. They split up and an experienced guide took each of them on a tour of the area. The parish was bounded by Middlesex Street (originally called Petticoat Lane) in the west to Osborn Street (bottom of Brick Lane) in the east; and by Wentworth Street in the north to Whitechapel High Street in the south – a perimeter of less than a mile.

Map of the East End, St Jude's Parish highlighted

The 1871 census showed a population of 6,270 crammed into this tiny space, inhabiting 675 houses in a network of alleys and tight courtyards. These very streets became the focus of national notoriety a few years later, when in 1888-9 Jack the Ripper attacked and murdered his victims so brutally. At the time it was thought that he was responsible for three deaths in St Jude's parish – namely, Emma Smith in Osborn St; Martha Tabram in George's Yard (now Gunthorpe St); and Alice McKenzie in Castle Alley. Experts today particularly dispute the latter.

27

So Charles and his guide first of all visited the Industrial School (next door to St Jude's) which was registered in 1867 to take 'vagrant, destitute and disorderly' boys, to house them and to give them a trade. In 1881 Mr Langford the Superintendent had 131 boarding boys aged 12-15 in his care with his wife as matron and three live-in teaching staff. When it was closed two years later and the boys transferred to a new school at Leytonstone, the building was demolished and the land acquired by St Jude's to expand its work.

After this visit Charles headed up Commercial Street and turned left into Wentworth Street. This was where the overcrowded housing really started. There were frequently five families – 20 people – living in one property. Porters for the local markets like Spitalfields Vegetable Market lived here, along with second-hand clothes dealers from the Petticoat Lane stalls, dockers, hawkers, errand boys, packers, costermongers, laundresses: a teeming mass of people chasing employment which was often casual or 'sweated labour'. The clearance of parts of London for the new railway stations and docks was one cause of the overcrowding, compounded by immigration from rural England and Eastern Europe. These pressures came up against a medieval system of copyhold whereby investors were reluctant to develop and build on land held only on short leases. The result was too many people living in rotten, insanitary houses that, although condemned years ago by the medical officer under the Artisan's and Labourer's Dwellings Act of 1875, had not been cleared and continued to be a money-spinner for greedy landlords. Octavia Hill summed up the housing situation: 'The deeds were non-existent, the structure rotten, the reputation infamous.' It would take Barnett fifteen years of lobbying and legal work to make any significant progress with slum clearance.

Of course, Charles and his guide would not have been welcomed everywhere on their walking tour, being suspected as agents of the state or of the landlord. In Wentworth Street they did view four houses, which previously had a bad reputation as brothels but had recently been bought up by the church with funds from West End philanthropists and put into good repair for 'respectable tenants'. They might have been offered the ubiquitous cup of hot sweet tea in one of these cleaned up houses. Otherwise the common lodging-houses, or doss-houses, in Wentworth Street and particularly in the parallel Dorset Street and Flower and Dean Streets (technically in Christ Church Spitalfields parish) could let you have a bed for 8d a night or 4d if you shared it. Rooms were packed with iron bedsteads covered with grey blankets. Wallpaper was peeling off the walls and bugs and vermin were rife. Defective water supplies meant there was poor sanitation and little in the way of washing facilities.

Charles next turned south into Old Castle Street. In the four streets of this enclave (Old Castle St, Old Castle Court, New Castle Place and New Castle St) lived 729 people (138 families) in 98 properties. This was not in fact a greatly different situation from 1851 (712 people, 146 families in 103 properties) but the area was still overcrowded and definitely transient. Only 5 families from the 1851 census were living in the same houses in 1881. This was the bottom rung of the housing ladder and the aim was to move up and out as quickly as you could. For example, the 30 Irish families of 1851 had all moved out of the enclave into George's Yard and Castle Alley and been replaced by 38 Polish families, who had all arrived within the last ten years. These were Ashkenazi Jews, economic migrants whose livelihoods were increasingly restricted back home either by failed harvests or by political upheavals and discriminatory laws. They would be followed by a further wave of Russian Jews in the 1880s and 1890s, fleeing the murderous pogroms that came after the assassination in March 1881 of Tsar Alexander II (for which they were the scapegoats). It's estimated that approximately 150,000 Jews settled in the East End between 1881 and 1914. So Charles would see these poor Jews arriving, some on their way through to Liverpool and thus by boat to the USA, others being sucked into an East End that often exploited them straight off the boat. People trafficking is not so new.

So Charles wandered about, listening to the Yiddish and foreign languages on the street (17 Dutch families, 59 Polish, 10 German and 1 Russian) and looking at the tailoring workshops – 44 Polish tailors are listed in the census. He must have wondered what on earth the Church of England was supposed to be doing for these new parishioners, who might be keen to 'get on' and to integrate to some extent but would be wary of attempts to 'convert' them? But there was pressure on vicars to fill their churches – 'footfall' in modern parlance. The 1851 Religious Census had surprised and alarmed the Church with its findings that regular church attendance was very poor and falling, especially in the cities. For years afterwards a clergyman's 'success' was measured on his ability to attract communicants. Barnett set up a Communicants' Club in 1878 in an attempt to consolidate and deepen the faith and understanding of some parishioners but by 1885 he regarded it as a failure and gave up 'the numbers game'. St Mark's Whitechapel, a block south of St Jude's, did persevere with a 'conversion' policy towards the Jews, enrolling four former Jews as curates, one of whom even had a dispensation to preach in Hebrew.

However, Charles also saw around him lots of children. Exactly half the population of the enclave was under 20 years of age – 57 of them of Primary School age. So he went next to have a chat with Isaac Owen, the school-keeper at the Board School in Old Castle Street. Isaac had been a Scripture Reader in the East End for many years and by coincidence he was a Somerset man like Charles, so the two men had something in common. Isaac talked about his job and explained that he now opened the school on Sundays too, because the Jewish children had Hebrew instruction on that day. They talked about the teachers and how the children were getting on, so Charles could judge for himself whether or not education might act as a stepladder out of these difficult surroundings.

Next port of call was the Whitechapel Wash House in Goulston Street, built thirty years before – Queen Victoria herself had been moved to contribute £200. An ugly brown brick building with an iron roof, it at least offered bathing and laundry facilities. The usual rates were for bathers and washers to pay one penny, ironers a farthing. The wash house also provided whitewash and lent buckets and pails.

Adjacent to this Wash House was Castle Alley, which was later assumed by many to be the site of the Jack the Ripper murder in July 1889 of Alice McKenzie. Its description in the *East London Observer* then would be much as Charles would have seen it on his walk: 'The scene of the murder is probably one of the lowest quarters in the whole of East London . . . it is composed of workshops and is about 180 yards in length. The thoroughfare is blocked up, both day and night, with tradesmen's carts and wagons and costermongers' barrows . . . The murderer, on account of the narrowness and intricacy of the surrounding thoroughfares, would have no difficulty in getting away unobserved.'

Castle Alley led Charles back into Whitechapel High Street and there he came face to face with the Aldgate Butchers – over 500 employees – as they plied their trade. Carts were being pulled along, laden with fresh skins for the tanning trade to process. Henrietta Barnett recalled the typical scene: 'It was market day and the main street was filled with haycarts, entangled among which were droves of frightened cattle being driven to the slaughter-houses, sights to shock the sensitive and encourage vegetarianism.'

It was at least a reprieve to leave the dark and dingy back streets and be back on the main highway. A report at the time described the contrast: 'In Wentworth Street how black and unutterably gloomy all the houses look! It is a relief to get out of this vile little slum and to work one's way back into the life and light of the great highway, with its flaunting shops, its piles of glowing fruit, its glittering jewellery, its steaming cook-shops, its flaring gin-palaces and noisy shows, and clubs and assembly rooms, and churches and mission halls, its cheap jacks and shooting-galleries, its streaming naphtha lights and roar and rattle, and hurrying throngs and noisy groups.' Charles hurried along past two shopping parades – coffee houses, a couple of pubs, two chemists, drapers, one hatter and even a pastry cook before he reached the corner of Osborn Street. But then his eye was caught by a bookshop further along Whitechapel Road – 'Number 76 Robert Gladdings, Bookseller'. Mr Gladdings had been selling books for over 40 years and Charles was such an avid reader that he couldn't resist a look round. He was not disappointed and would order books from that shop from wherever he was living until Mr Gladdings retired in 1893.

Happy with this discovery, Charles turned back into Osborn Street to be shown the lodging-house at numbers 3-5. Such lodging-houses were of concern to social reformers. This one was run by Benjamin Buckey with his wife and 8 female servants. There were 55 male lodgers, of whom 41 were unmarried and 24 of these were in their 20s. These were mostly London men (33) or from the North and Scotland (12) with just 10 foreigners. The temptations to young unattached males were considerable – pubs and prostitutes and dark alleys, to state the obvious. The men did have trades – e.g. 9 carmen, 8 carpenters, 7 dockers, 7 tailors, 6 (each) labourers, porters, dealers – but some of these jobs were casual, so you celebrated a good payday when you could.

It was to provide alternative recreation that Barnett had started a young working men's club a few evenings per week in Commercial Street, and Charles really enjoyed this work. Wherever he went after his time with Barnett, he set up men's clubs – a few games like draughts or dominoes but no drink and no gambling; maybe some newspapers, a topic for discussion, some advice on the area for newcomers and support over any personal problems.

To complete his tour, Charles turned left into Wentworth Street again but the housing was still very poor here. In these desperate surroundings women, forced onto the streets and numbed by alcohol, might use this casual accommodation to entertain clients, so any children would be ejected to find shelter where they could. Dr Thomas Barnardo records a visit to the area in the early 1880s where he counted over 70 boys aged about 14 sleeping under tarpaulins. His first home for destitute children was already established in nearby Stepney Causeway.

By the time he had returned to St Jude's vicarage in Commercial Street therefore, Charles had had quite an education and would have been quite shocked by some of what he had seen – not that his family were wealthy but they had an ordered life, as opposed to some of the chaos and disorder he had just seen. The demoralising situation was that if you sought honest employment, it was usually either for casual work in the markets and more particularly at the Docks, where hundreds of men queued each morning outside the gates in the hope of being taken on for the day; or else you worked for low wages and long hours in the 'sweating' system, where you might be assembling items on a piecework basis – clothing (caps, waistcoats) or hardware objects like brushes, umbrellas and waterproofs – or you might be gluing matchboxes at 2d a gross, rolling cigars, or cutting out leather for boots ('boot-clicking').

There were also the traditional 'stink' industries that had grown up outside the city walls from times gone by – the tanneries, breweries, slaughterhouses and sugar bakeries. There was a sugar bakery in Back Church Lane just round the corner from Charles's flat and he could smell the sickly sweet fumes every day, as the men boiled the raw sugar cane, delivered from the West India Docks, in great vats to extract and process the sugar. One particularly dirty industry was the great rubbish tip in Wentworth Street, where the uncovered carts deposited their unpleasant loads from all over London to be crushed by heavy machinery. The noise and polluted air must have been appalling.

The alternative to honest work was petty thieving or cadging handouts from churches and charities. Before he began his ministry, Barnett was warned of this dependence on doles and determined to wean his parishioners off such charity, which he felt undermined their self-respect. He rejected what he called 'careless' relief and substituted instead 'thorough' relief, by which he meant proper assessment of needs and follow-up support. It sounded good but as soon as he put it into practice, he found his vicarage besieged by angry parishioners who demanded their rights in money and meal tickets. In the end Samuel Barnett had a door cut from their house through into the church to allow him to escape and summon the police. The Barnetts felt pained that they should be hated thus and were often despondent at their inadequacies in the face of such need.

To bolster their funds and to reassure themselves of the rightness of their course, the Barnetts began to invite philanthropists and politicians to visit them and examine their surroundings. They also used the Press. Henrietta's older sister Alice was married to Ernest Abraham Hart, ophthalmic surgeon and editor of the *British Medical Journal* and *The Sanitary Record*, and she persuaded him to write articles on the health aspects of living in the East End – it wasn't difficult to win him over because he was a City boy, son of a Jewish dentist from Shoreditch. He had, moreover, plenty of statistics to hand. By this time infant mortality figures as a guide to health standards were being assiduously recorded and figures showed that a Whitechapel baby was twice as likely to die from infant diarrhoea or respiratory infection as a Hampstead baby and three times more likely from measles. Among the adult population tuberculosis was still a threat but the cholera epidemic of 1866 was well behind the community and typhoid was likewise reducing, as water supplies and sanitation had somewhat improved. Life expectancy was about 43 years for an East Ender at the time.

Ernest Hart had considerable clout, being Chairman of the British Medical Association's Parliamentary Bill Committee. He had already prompted the enquiry into the state of London's workhouse infirmaries and he had a hand in various Public Health Acts, factory bills and so on. He was also on the staff of the *Pall Mall Gazette*, an evening newspaper, now of Liberal political bent (after several mergers it eventually became *The Evening Standard*).

Charles learned a great deal from watching this communications business and seeing the influence of newspapers. Whether through Hart or through Alfred Milner, a previous St Jude's volunteer from Oxford who had joined the *Pall Mall Gazette* staff in 1881, Charles began to write articles for that newspaper and found he was good at journalism. That left him with the dilemma of what career path to take next.

3

'Pen or Pulpit'

As Charles and his two companions, Ronald Bayne and Robert Chalmers, settled into their new way of life, they began to appreciate the resilience and good humour of many people in the parish despite or probably because of their harsh surroundings. As three young men without commitments, they no doubt found a good local pub and may even have tried a music hall such as the Royal Cambridge in Commercial Street or groaned at the melodramas at the Pavilion Theatre on Whitechapel Road. Charles revelled in literature and the classics but was neither a snob nor a puritan and had a ready wit and outgoing personality.

Robert Chalmers was a Londoner and he certainly would have been stimulated by his new surroundings. His father John Chalmers was a Scot, who had married a girl from Stoke Newington and settled in Hornsey as a bookseller's clerk. Robert was lucky enough to go to the City of London School before Oriel College Oxford but his modest background would have helped him to relate to the people he was now meeting. He would naturally have been interested in the life chances of the local children as well as the charitable system for the adults. Samuel Barnett had, for example, instituted as early as 1873 a 'Pensions Committee' to target the needs of the elderly in the parish. They may not have been numerous – the Castle Street district had just 2 people aged over 80 and only 10 over 70 out of a total population of 729 – but these elderly people were often widows or widowers and in danger of isolation in the community.

Barnett's support for this elderly group was significant and it is interesting that when Lloyd George's controversial Budget legislated for the first old-age pensions in 1908, the civil servant who drafted the bill was none other than Robert Chalmers. Robert joined the Treasury as a junior civil servant some time in 1882 and went on to become a Knight of the Realm. Though Robert left St Jude's early, Charles Marson was to be godfather to his second son and they stayed friends for many years.

Although Robert had left, Charles and Ronald continued enthusiastically with their new work – parish visiting, helping at the various clubs including the Mothers' Meetings which Henrietta Barnett had started in 1874: 'they simply meet, save pence for clothing, enjoy a chat and hear some reading.' Henrietta's sister Alice, wife of Dr Ernest Hart and herself a medical student at the University of Paris, once gave a series of lectures to the women on 'Bodies and Babies'. Ten years later, when three such Mothers' clubs existed with 120 on the books of the largest group, Henrietta concluded: '. . . the advantage consists not so much in the actual teaching which is given as in the sense of fellowship which is fostered.'

Charles always enjoyed Women's Groups throughout his clerical career and had a high respect for female education. In 1883 he wrote a letter to his friends Emily and Jane Guest, who lived just south of the river in Lewisham: 'You know my conviction that the energy for the next step upwards must be supplied by women. Nothing can be so important as female education, therefore. Perhaps the next Christ will be a woman.'

By 1882 Henrietta Barnett was a Manager of the District Schools and was trying to improve the conditions for the girls. In time there would be various initiatives in the parish — a girls' club after school with volunteer ladies running fun activities and guidance (no Girl Guides, of course, until 1909); a gymnasium to which girls could go and do physical exercise away from their crowded homes and street-play; and the St Jude's Guild whose aim was to keep the older girls together after leaving school. In 1880 with the help of Miss Townsend, Henrietta opened a Cottage Home where girls spent three months in training before going into service. All these ideas were developing while Charles was at St Jude's.

On one occasion when the Barnetts were away and Charles was holding the fort, a lady volunteer contacted him, offering to host a party for some of the Whitechapel children at her home. 'Will you have them tame or wild?' was Charles's mischievous reply. 'I will have them wild,' she courteously replied. For, not surprisingly, many families were brutalised by this harsh environment and it is for this reason that the Barnetts launched a 'cultural uplift' programme – lectures, musical concerts, art exhibitions, and 'at homes'. Although it was middle class in tone and values, the campaign was sincerely conceived and many fine musicians, artists and academics gave generously of their time to 'bring the best' to put before the community. The Whitechapel Art Exhibition, for example, first mounted by the Barnetts in April 1881 with 10,000 visitors, grew into an annual event with over 50,000 visitors and was eventually housed in 1901 in a new building – the Whitechapel Art Gallery, as it is today. Charles would certainly have helped at the next three exhibitions (1882-4) and copied the idea later in his life.

ART IN WHITECHAPEL—LOAN EXHIBITION OF PICTURES IN ST. JUDE'S SCHOOL HOUSE, COMMERCIAL STREET, E.

The Barnetts were keen supporters of adult education and introduced University Extension classes to the parish in 1877. Charles loved such 'second chance' educational work, compensating for the inadequacies of the existing school system. He introduced many such classes wherever he went afterwards, loaning his own books or setting up small libraries. The Whitechapel Public Library, funded by the philanthropist John Passmore Edwards, unfortunately would not materialise for another ten years.

So Charles and Ronald were both being exposed to a fantastic number of fresh ideas and new people. As they returned home every night during that first winter through the coalsmokey atmosphere, which was relieved only by short bursts of gaslight, they could at least share their experiences and in the evening read up and discuss possible solutions. They had now seen other operations in action like General William Booth's Salvation Army, which was well set with its Headquarters – The People's Mission Hall – just round the corner in Whitechapel Road; and the Methodist Mission in Whitechapel which had started in 1876; and, of course, St Jude's was part of the wider Whitechapel Poor Law Union – 9 parishes with a total population of 64,000 being represented by a Board of 25 Poor Law Guardians, of whom Samuel Barnett was but one.

Ⴍ—⚷

The two young men gradually absorbed this bigger picture and wondered if their 'good works' would ever really transform their beleaguered community or whether it required a more radical solution. Could the Church do this massive job and lead the nation once more or was a political party going to lead the way? The Liberal Government of the day, whose instinct was against State intervention in individual lives, was beginning to grapple with the possibility that poverty might not be a crime and the result of fecklessness, but might actually be 'involuntary' and beyond the control of individuals. John Morley, Liberal MP, had written in the Pall Mall Gazette when he was its editor in 1880: 'I am no partisan of incessant meddling with individual freedom but I do strongly believe that in so populous a society as ours now is, you may well have a certain protection thrown over classes of men and women who are unable to protect themselves.'

But what if benevolence and the quiet appeal for 'social justice' were not enough? Karl Marx in *Das Kapital* (1867) had affirmed that just as capitalism had replaced feudalism, so socialism would inevitably replace capitalism. Exploitation of one class by another had an inbuilt and fatal flaw. Would socialism be the future instead? Would the upheavals in Europe that followed the French surrender in 1871 to the new German Empire under Wilhelm I lead to a revolution in England? Could the masses arise and challenge Victorian order? Or would 'market forces' and enlightened philanthropy float the boat of poverty in time?

These were daily topics of debate among Barnett's team. Barnett was no revolutionary but came himself to the conclusion towards the end of his time that it was best, for example, just to give out free breakfasts to all hungry children, so that they could at least study properly and have a chance of self-improvement. For him, actions were better than endless debate. On the other hand, if clergymen and social reformers did not think through their actions and come to a philosophy and a clear vision, then they would be liable to the depressions and weariness that overcame Barnett at times and that sometimes led to suicides elsewhere. Charles himself would have spells of illness in his own career and the Church of England almost accepted that young clerics would do only five years or so in a tough urban parish before earning the reward of an easier rural situation. Barnett's twenty years at St Jude's were the absolute exception to the rule.

Amid all this exciting debate, Ronald Bayne's thoughts were interrupted in July 1882 by the sudden death of his stepmother Anna, aged only 37, who had raised her five stepchildren in such a loving and vivacious way, after their real mother had died in childbirth with the last child Clotilda. Anna's death was a bitter blow to the Bayne family and focused Ronald's mind quickly as to his future and his career.

Both he and Charles decided to go forward for ordination. Charles had already passed an examination in 'Rudimentis Religionis' as an undergraduate in 1880 but required further study and so enrolled at Wycliffe Hall Oxford, a new theological college founded by evangelical churchmen. He completed the course in the autumn of 1882 and became a deacon (probationary priest) attached to St Jude's once again. By now Charles's head was spinning again with ideas – Ronald wrote an amusing letter to his sister Clotilda (aged 15) 'I am glad Aunt Mary has made Marson's acquaintance. As to his theories, I don't believe he understands them himself and think that he makes them up as he goes along, being distracted by the multitude of teachers nowadays.'

Charles was indeed sharpening his wits and some of his outpourings were finding their way into print. Alfred Milner, an Oxford student volunteer at St Jude's from Barnett's first recruitment drive back in 1875 but now a qualified barrister and a working journalist on the *Pall Mall Gazette*, wrote to Charles in July 1883:

> 'I hope Saturday's paper has reached you with your article. As nature has gifted you with that oddly rare quality, the power of description, please don't "cultivate it" but use it as often as you can, of course for the benefit of the Pall Mall Gazette'.

Charles was soon asked to attend theatre performances and submit book reviews too. Two years later Milner wrote to offer Charles a proper job on the paper because he himself wanted to go into politics. He was successful, rising to be High Commissioner to South Africa during the Boer War and an important member of Lloyd George's war cabinet.

So for the next couple of years Charles had two parallel careers – the church and journalism. In the end he chose the church but he never stopped supplementing his meagre stipend with books and articles. Meanwhile there was parish work to be done and later in 1883 when Charles was officially appointed as curate to St Jude's, he had to learn to prepare and preach sermons and to conduct services on his own. He regularly visited the Whitechapel workhouse in South(ern) Grove, built in 1872 near Mile End tube station, as well as the workhouse infirmary at Charles Street, where he read prayers for the sick and comforted lost souls when he could. For that workhouse, colloquially known as The Bastille, was the last resort, when all other offers of food and shelter had failed. Margaret Harkness, whose pen name was John Law, wrote in her book *Captain Lobe* (1889):

> 'The Whitechapel Workhouse is a model workhouse: that is to say, it is the Poor Law incarnate in stone and brick . . . a little gruel morning and night, meat twice a week, that is the food of the grown-up people, seasoned with hard work and prison discipline . . . what shall we say of the woman, or man, maimed by misfortune, who must come there or die in the street?'

Charles also visited the casual ward at 35 Thomas Street, which opened every day at 4pm and received vagrants for overnight accommodation in return for a fixed amount of work the following day – crushing bones or stones; 'picking oakum' which meant untwisting lengths of old rope to extract the hemp fibres that were then rolled and covered with pine tar to caulk or seal the insides of ships. The American author Jack London had first-hand experience of this casual ward, albeit twenty years later, which he describes in his book *The People of the Abyss*.

> 'I stumbled on to a still darker room, where were benches and tables and men. The place smelled vilely. My pannikin contained skilly, a mixture of Indian corn and hot water. The skilly was coarse of texture, unseasoned, gross and bitter . . . (the ward was) a long, narrow room, traversed by two low iron rails. Between these rails were stretched, not hammocks, but pieces of canvas, six feet long and less than two feet wide. These were the beds, and they were six inches apart and about eight inches off the floor . . . being slung to the same rails, when one man moved, no matter how slightly, the rest were set rocking.'

While Charles was working away at his new responsibilities as curate, Ronald Bayne achieved his own first curacy and left Whitechapel in September 1883 to serve as curate to Revd Brooke Lambert at Greenwich. Lambert had been vicar of St Mark's church Whitechapel (1866-71) and had done remarkable and progressive work there until ill health forced him to withdraw, but he returned to help the Barnetts as a locum many times and must have met Charles and Ronald then. He was an impressive man, a good speaker and writer, from whom Ronald would learn much in the next few years. He even named his first son after him.

Lambert was a member of the Guild of St Matthew, founded in 1877 by a group of High Church socialist clergymen under the leadership of Revd Stewart Headlam. The latter had also worked in the East End at St Matthew's Bethnal Green until sacked by the Bishop of London for his socialist views. The Guild was one of the earliest socialist groups and at its peak had perhaps 400 members. Headlam was editor of its magazine *The Church Reformer*, in which Jesus was portrayed as a revolutionary figure, ushering in a new co-operative and egalitarian order. Headlam warned the working classes to be wary of middle-class reformers – quite strange talk from a man educated at Eton and Cambridge – but he had seen charity imposed on people without any consultation of their needs nor any ownership of new schemes. Much influenced by the writings of the American Henry George, Headlam advocated a tax on land and the redistribution of wealth.

41

These two men – Lambert and Headlam – exercised a powerful influence over Charles and Ronald. Headlam asked Charles to join him and co-write an article 'Christianity and Capitalism' for the new monthly journal called *To-Day*. Ronald wrote to his sister in September 1883: 'I have made Aunt Anna to her great horror order a socialist book for me.' Two months later he wrote again:

'I have just returned from a dinner of liberal clergy who discussed the special mission which the Bishop of London wants to get up. We were all pretty unanimous that missions usually do no good at all: one man insisted that they generally only increase the number of suicides but we thought that if we preached socialism, pointing out that Christianity denounces the possession of wealth, then a mission might do good.'

Charles by this time had moved house to 48 Great Prescot Street off Leman Street. Just a few properties along at number 30 was the new English Martyr's catholic church, one of Edward Pugin's last designs in 1875, which was much used by the Irish population in particular. It is very likely that Charles, after his contact with Lambert and High Church socialism, would have visited this church. Its splendid interior was a marked contrast to the St Jude's church, which Henrietta Barnett described as 'not only dark and dirty but unwarmed; it was a cheap structure, built by cheap thought and in cheap material'.

Letters from Headlam to Charles in December 1883 suggest that Charles had been growing frustrated at St Jude's and may even have fallen out with the Barnetts. Certainly Charles had already applied to the Bishop of Bath and Wells, Lord Arthur Hervey, to see if there were a post in Somerset nearer to his father at Clevedon. The Bishop had perhaps taken time to research Charles's form and refused him bluntly in a letter dated December 20th 1883: 'Dear Mr Marson, I am sorry that by some accident your letter has been left unanswered so many days. It appears to me that the views which you express and the special subjects which you have made your study are hardly suitable for a country parish.'

For Christmas 1883 the Barnetts had new and different plans, for this was the first Christmas when they invited some old people and children into their own home. Henrietta recorded: 'Following advice to give to the poor of your best, we made the tables beautiful with white linen and flowers. The old people behaved like true gentle people and I think only one child put out a grimy hand and took a cake before tea was quite ready'. Of course, it was a middle class set up; of course, it was a stilted affair initially but it was an attempt to reach across a divide of suspicion and it was done in all sincerity. Henrietta wrote: 'Our Lord did not think it beneath Him to make it a special command that His followers should entertain the poor. It is a religious service to visit and also to entertain the poor'. Cynics wrote that it was Mr Barnett's method 'to save starving souls by pictures, parties and pianos' but Charles was impressed by these parties, which happened more and more frequently and which he attended. In later life he would think nothing of opening up his vicarage for social gatherings or to anyone who was sick or in need.

Barnett with children of the Country Holiday Fund

Just before that Christmas 1883, Samuel Barnett went off on another recruiting drive to Oxford. He presented a paper in which he proposed a 'University Settlement' in Whitechapel, whereby undergraduates could become the neighbours of the poor, sharing their life, thinking about their problems and offering their own time, energy and skills to 'alleviate the sorrow and misery born of class

43

division and indifference.' This opportunity of community service – what today we might call a good GAP year – could change your life he explained: 'He who has even for a month shared the life of the poor can never rest again in his old thoughts.' Barnett's timing was perfect, coming just after the publication in October of Revd Andrew Mearns' 44-page penny pamphlet 'The Bitter Cry of Outcast London', which exposed the shocking housing conditions of the poor and caused a sensation when serialised by WT Stead in the *Pall Mall Gazette* and the *Daily News*. Middle-class consciences were galvanised into a determination to do better for the poor, so the response in terms of money and offers of help was considerable.

In fact at this time Samuel and his wife Henrietta had been toiling away for ten years and were seriously thinking of quitting. He was now 40 and had suffered spells of illness and depression when he thought of his failures and the amount of work still to do. He once received a letter that upset him terribly: 'You awful fraud. I wonder you are not struck down dead taking part in the service. The poor hate you like the bitterest poison. You are no good at all and not fit to be a clergyman. I hate you. I hope you will drop dead before long. Curse you.' But now with this uplifting response from a new wave of Oxford volunteers, he had the chance to expand his buildings and his workforce. It was a turning point. Raising £6,250 they purchased the disused boys' Industrial School next door, demolished it and, one year later, on Christmas Eve 1884, the first settlers slept in the new building – Toynbee Hall, named after Arnold Toynbee, the political economist who had worked at St Jude's in the early days but whose recent death in March 1883 at age 30 was widely mourned. It was Toynbee who had said in a lecture: 'We – the middle classes, not merely the very rich – we have neglected you; instead of justice we have offered you charity, and instead of sympathy we have offered you hard and unreal advice. We have sinned against you grievously. If you will forgive us, we are willing to give up the life we care for, the life with books and with those we love'. Charles would take this sentiment to heart and much of his subsequent life demonstrated such self-sacrifice.

Toynbee Hall was the first of several 'University Settlements' and its early 'settlers' include people like William Beveridge (the architect of the welfare state 1945) and Clement Attlee (Labour Party Leader 1935-55). Its motto was 'Fear not to sow because of the birds' and indeed a number of bodies started life there – the Workers' Educational Association (1903); one of the first Citizens' Advice Bureaux (1949); and the Child Poverty Action Group (1965). All developed from the foundations laid by the Barnetts.

Toynbee Hall today is easy to miss, as you walk up Commercial Street from Aldgate East tube station in the East End of London. Set back from the road, it looks incongruously like an Oxford College. Charles must have seen the plans of the new building in early 1884 – lecture halls, meeting rooms, a library – but he was not to be a part of it. He'd enjoyed his two and half years' apprenticeship under Barnett but was ready to start his own work. Who knows what would have happened if he had stayed on, as the Barnetts did for another ten years? What might he have achieved?

The Barnetts had taught him so much – the vital role of education; a variety of clubs and schemes to reach out into the community; a sincere sympathy and even friendship with the poor; their own 'creed' to guide them if times were tough. But the two things that Charles did not appreciate about them were, first, their ability to build teams of colleagues and sponsors to help them in their huge task; and, secondly, their personal bond – two people with a single aim. They were indeed a formidable pair, and Charles would find it very difficult to reproduce their force on his own. The Barnetts had no children and so drove themselves and others hard. Charles Ashbee, a later settler at Toynbee Hall, criticised Samuel Barnett for what he called his 'cold-blooded saintliness. He plays fast and loose with the moral enthusiasm of young men'.

So probably Samuel had no fatherly advice to give to Charles, although he did later write to him and urge him to be part of a 'system' that could better draw out his talents. But it was time to move on. Charles was not an 'admin man', not one for 'social machinery'. He was young (25) and confident and keen to win his spurs. He had hoped to gain a curacy at nearby St Botolph's Bishopsgate but that fell through and he went instead to St Peter's, Petersham, Surrey in April 1884. The next six months would nearly break him.

4

The Lady and the Bishop

Revd Percy Wemyss Nott had been curate and then vicar of Kew with Petersham since 1863. He was 45, an only child, unmarried and living at home with his widowed father Major-General Francis Nott – not exactly an inspiring figure perhaps for a new young curate to follow. St Anne's Kew was a Crown living of £450 per annum, a very comfortable income with a population of 2,696 spread lightly over 346 acres. By comparison, back in Whitechapel Samuel Barnett's living was £275 with a population of over 6,000, so Charles's new posting was utterly different in character and purpose. It would seem that Mr Nott took little interest in his other church, St Peter's Petersham – a smaller church (capacity only 362) serving a population of just 589 souls. He had engaged one curate after another recently to take charge of St Peter's but had fallen out with all of them, so much so that its parishioners were clamouring to be split off from Kew into their own parish. This would not happen until 1891, several years after Mr Nott's death.

So why it was that Charles agreed to take up Nott's offer of a three month trial curacy remains a mystery. He had misgivings about it from the start but received an encouraging letter from William Walsham How, Bishop of Bedford, who had responsibility from the Bishop of London for supervision of the church's work in the East End and thus knew much about Charles's work at St Jude's. He wrote to Charles on April 29th 1884:

'I trust sincerely you may be happy in your new work. If you can be peacemaker and smooth over the petty squabbles you mention, you will do good and if you can make the Church felt as a power and a reality, and more still as a friend and sympathizer of the working classes, you will also do good.'

But he went on to warn Charles about some of his recent writings and interpretations of theology, particularly the nature of the Divinity and of the Incarnation (Christ's human life on earth). He wrote: 'It would surely be far wiser to wait and read and think and pray more before laying down views so startling on such tremendous subjects. Now you must not think, my dear Marson, that I do not sympathise very greatly with your generous love of the people and fearless truthfulness. But do be patient and rather more reticent. May God help you in all things'.

Of course, Charles was not patient and wouldn't wait and these words of advice were unfortunately not heeded. However, other encouragement came from an unlikely source – the resident gentry in the form of Countess Frances Russell and her daughter Lady Agatha Russell. Frances Russell was the widow of Lord John Russell, former Liberal Prime Minister (1846-52 and 1865-6) who had only recently died in 1878. She now headed the household at Pembroke Lodge, the Georgian mansion in Richmond Park which was given to the Russells by Queen Victoria in 1847. She and her unmarried daughter Agatha aged 31 were bowled over by their charismatic new curate and Charles was quickly invited to the Sunday dinners where the conversation of the various guests was so stimulating. Justin MacCarthy, a young journalist at that time, recalled those meetings:

'Lady Russell loved to draw forth from the artist something about his art, from the scholar something about his books, to compare the ideas of the politician with her own, to lead the traveller into accounts of his travels, to get from the scientific student some of his experiences in this or that domain of science, and from those who visited the poor some suggestions which might serve her during her constant work in the same direction.'

Lady Frances had a busy household to run including responsibility for her two orphaned grandchildren Frank and Bertrand Russell, the latter being 12 and under education at home before his departure to Cambridge University to commence his outstanding career in mathematics and philosophy. In his autobiography Bertrand obviously did not share the enjoyment of adult conversation and later recalled the atmosphere at Pembroke Lodge as one of frequent prayer, emotional repression and formality.

His aunt Agatha, however, always thought of Pembroke Lodge as a happy place and she seems to have been a warm and sincere person, who helped her mother in good works, sponsoring the village school and responding to Charles's visits to the parish poor and to Richmond Union workhouse. The Union workhouse served the following towns – Barnes, Kew, Mortlake, Petersham and Richmond, so no doubt other clergymen visited there too.

Charles very soon asked Lady Agatha to accompany him to the workhouse to see the daily conditions for herself. It was not far from Pembroke Lodge, out of Richmond Gate into Queen's Road and right again at Grove Road. The 1881 census gives us a rough pattern that was probably still true for their visits in 1884 – there were 18 vagrants listed in the casual wards (15 men, 3 women); there were 94 infirmary patients and 63 workhouse inmates, a total of 157 people of whom 34 were widowers and 33 widows (i.e. 43% unattached). The bias was towards the elderly with 81 people over the age of 60 and only 26 under 40 (excluding 5 infants). All these people were looked after by the Master and his staff of 9 female and 5 male nurses.

Agatha, in common with many educated women of the time, was keen to make an impact and to do something with her brains. She held fast to her mother's motto from the Bible: 'Thou shalt not follow a multitude to do evil' (Exodus 23:2) and so was quite prepared to set her own course; and here was this young man, six years younger than her, tall, broad-shouldered, well-educated with confident opinions about literature and the arts, leading the way in her parish and boldly calling himself a socialist. That word 'socialist' was a dirty word to the bourgeoisie. Could she face her friends and relatives to admit her secret admiration for Charles? Agatha was a modest and sensitive soul. Was this her best chance not only to do good works but also to have a soul mate?

On his side, Charles was greatly attracted to Lady Agatha but also had a dilemma. His mindset now was hostile to the landed gentry, no matter how liberal and enlightened they might be. Stewart Headlam, his new mentor, had denounced wealth as robbery and was currently without a parish as a result. Luckily (and ironically) Headlam had private means to fall back on but Charles did not. This new relationship was his chance perhaps to gain influence and to make a real impact. Charles paused to consider that the one other factor behind the Barnetts' success was the fact that Henrietta had inherited a sizeable fortune (£7,400) upon the death of her merchant father, so that not only had they the resources to enhance their work but also they could employ three servants to do daily chores and they could travel abroad, away from their stressful work at any time.

Charles was genuinely not attracted by money but he did like *kudos*. Could he face his friends and admit his secret admiration for a 'bloated aristocrat' (as he jokingly wrote to his friend Miss Guest)?

So the two of them wrestled with their inner doubts in those first few weeks of encounter and then they ventured upon their engagement. Charles was very happy – perhaps he and Agatha might even be a double act to rival the Barnetts – but he knew he would expect a great deal from her in the short term, dragging her round the parish to help with his duties. He wondered how she would cope.

Lady Agatha Russell, to whom Charles was engaged, with her nephew Arthur

Meanwhile Charles was just enjoying his new environment, so different from the grubby East End. It was springtime and he waxed lyrical in a letter to Miss Guest on May 20th: 'This place is a most glorious one. I daresay you know the park at Richmond and its outlook upon the wooded valley with the silver river just visible here and there through the trees. If you do, you will appreciate what a scoundrel I am to have slid into such a berth as Petersham, while London seethes and sloughs in foulness.' Although he never complained about his asthma problems during his time at St Jude's, this new pure air would no doubt have given him a lift too, let alone the fact that he was in love.

On Wednesday June 11th 1884 he scurried over to St Mary's Church Balham to witness his friend Ronald Bayne's ordination. Ronald's sister Clotilda, aged 18, was there too, having taken special leave from Clapham High School for Girls to attend. She later recalled that 'Charles was there in his flappy surplice and somehow I remember him then best of all'.

⊝━ᴃ

Two days later, however, out of the blue Charles received a letter from the Bishop of Rochester Anthony Thorold, who had dominion over the diocese of Southwark in which Petersham lay. The Bishop had received an official complaint from another clergyman that Charles had preached a heretical sermon on the subject of Christ's Ascension. The Bishop went on that he had sent a telegram to Charles to request a personal interview to hear his side of the argument but that the telegram was misdelivered, by which time letters had crossed instead. This was unfortunate because the Bishop now took the drastic action of 'inhibiting' or suspending Charles:

> 'Now I quite see that you are unable to accept the fact of our Lord's actual Ascension and glorified body. As your view seems to me entirely inconsistent with the Fourth Article, I cannot give you permission to officiate in my diocese.'

This action by Bishop Thorold, without allowing Charles the opportunity of a personal interview or legal advisor, wouldn't satisfy an Industrial Tribunal today and badly damaged Charles's career prospects. In truth it was not really Thorold's style at all. Since his appointment seven years previously, he had dealt well with several tricky situations in his diocese, usually by personal interview and conciliation.

The problem went back to a sermon that Charles was invited to give at Christchurch, Hampstead on Ascension Day (May 22nd 1884). Revd Edward Henry Bickersteth was the host vicar and he had also invited representatives from the other two Hampstead parishes (Revd Hinkman from St John's and Revd Hill from St Stephen's). The church was packed and Charles delivered his sermon, extemporising a little on a draft which he had prepared and sent in advance to the *Church Reformer* magazine (Stewart Headlam's paper for the Guild of St Matthew membership).

The thrust of his sermon was that the Biblical references to Christ's physical Ascension to Heaven following his resurrection were neither numerous nor convincing – St Matthew's and St John's Gospels make no reference to it at all; Mark 16:9-20 is a passage disputed by scholars and simply says '. . . he was received up into heaven'; St Luke 24:51 is another disputed passage and reads '. . . he was parted from them and carried up into heaven'. Charles went on that it was not sensible for the church to argue for a provable physical Ascension, for that would be proposing a 'wrong or mythical view of Heaven, which is not by any means a place but a state of being.' With his usual humour he said that 'his hearers should not therefore believe that they would be any nearer heaven by climbing Richmond Hill or ascending the steeple of Petersham church'. He repeated his view that 'the bodily ascension was a myth'. Modern theologians might not blanch at such a 'symbolic' interpretation of the miracles of Jesus but Charles's notion was a bombshell to that audience. To compound his situation, he went on to talk about social questions: 'You know, or should know, that in and about London are 80,000 prostitutes, some mere children (1 in 14 of all the young girls between 14 and 20).'

This sort of candid talk on top of his liberal theology upset many of the congregation and the next week Revd MG Tracy preached at Hampstead, condemning Marson as 'dishonest and disloyal as a Christian.' The *Hampstead & Highgate Express* newspaper on June 7th continued the debate. However, some felt that Tracy's orthodox stance was not correct and that Marson had been wrongly condemned. One lady, however, wrote a wild letter to Charles that began: 'Blasphemous, dishonest and bigamous Sir . . .' Revd Bickersteth went ahead and formally complained about the sermon to Bishop Thorold.

Charles would undoubtedly have known that Edward Bickersteth was a devout evangelical, who was bound to be offended by any criticism of Biblical truths, particularly if delivered in a humorous and provocative way. Edward was brought up in a quiet country vicarage and was educated at home in a regulated, deeply religious regime, prior to diligent but not outstanding study at Cambridge University. His father's contacts had eased his way through two undemanding rural posts in Norfolk and Dorset, before he had settled with his large family at Christchurch Hampstead thirty years ago. Now, at the age of 59, Edward was keen on foreign missions (sending his own son out to India for four years) and on missions to the Jews and to the Irish. He was a member of the British and Foreign Bible Society and of the Evangelical Alliance. In recent years he had produced religious poetry and written 30 hymns (none memorable today). He spoke always of the 'higher life' and had set up a programme of 'Quiet Days' or Retreat Days for fellow clergymen in London. Charles, however, wanted action, not contemplation.

Edward was not unsympathetic to the poor, however, and had instituted a good team of district visitors in Hampstead. He was clearly liked and respected in his parish but Hampstead was not like the East End, so Charles probably thought him dull and complacent and couldn't resist the urge to stir him up. This would have embarrassed Edward, surrounded in his pew by his six sons and six daughters as well as friends like Revd Charles Carus-Wilson, a Cambridge contemporary and longstanding evangelical friend. The Bickersteth family was still in mourning for the recent death of Edward's cousin Robert Bickersteth, Bishop of Ripon and evangelical champion. Charles's attack must have seemed almost personal.

So why had Edward invited Charles to give the sermon in the first place? Was it an ambush, to put a young liberal priest in his place? Possibly. The fact that the *Church Reformer* magazine was geared up to print Charles's sermon, adding a provocative preface to it, suggests that the 'liberals' were spoiling for a fight too. Edward Bickersteth had written once that he would 'not turn aside from the green pastures and still waters of Holy Writ to wander on the bleak and barren mountains of controversy'. So when Charles made his play that Ascension morning, Edward Bickersteth retaliated with a formal complaint to his old friend and occasional visitor to his Hampstead home, Bishop Thorold.

Thorold had been a prep school (and lifelong) friend of Charles Carus-Wilson, with whom the Bickersteth family would often stay.

Indeed Thorold's first curacy was with Revd William Carus-Wilson at Whittington, Preston. Furthermore Thorold took over from Robert Bickersteth as Rector of St Giles in 1857, so the Bickersteths and Thorolds knew each other well. Charles Marson had, therefore, probably picked the wrong fight!

Countess Russell backed Charles in dispute with Bishop Thorold

THE DOWAGER COUNTESS RUSSELL, 1884

Anthony Thorold was a confirmed evangelical and had been appointed by Disraeli, with Queen Victoria's approval, to squash or at least dampen down the growing ritualist movement among London's parish priests. It was reported, for example, that in 1882 out of 903 churches in London, 37 had vestments, 10 used incense and 45 had candles on the altar. Basically, the Establishment was worried that Protestantism would be eroded by these Roman Catholic practices, which, for some people, introduced colour, imagery and inspiration to the drabness of their church building and lives in general. Many working-class people were simply not prepared to listen to the usual hour-long sermons of an evangelical preacher, no matter how sincerely delivered. So Thorold had the task of curbing some of his clergy in their drift towards ritualism. In the end after his 14 years in the diocese, he moved to a more moderate position, especially after his own son Algar embraced Catholicism at Oxford University in November 1884, plunging his father into deep embarrassment and depression.

But this was not the issue with Charles right now. It was a doctrinal issue and Thorold sided instinctively with his friend Bickersteth. Charles immediately took up the cudgels and replied to Thorold's letter of inhibition, supplying a philosophical justification for his belief that Heaven was not a place but a state of being but concluded his letter arrogantly:

> 'your lordship in brief asserts that a belief in a local heaven somewhere in space is necessary before your lordship will allow a curate to officiate. I most strongly protest against your lordship's action and I refuse to believe that the Church of England is represented in this instance by your lordship. Most obediently, Charles Latimer Marson.

Thorold replied on 17th June:

> 'It is not 'liberal Christianity', whatever that may mean, that I am taking a side against but teaching which seems to me to reduce the objective facts of our supernatural religion into mere ideas. The tone of your letter was so roughly contemptuous of those from whom you differ (you have been in priest's orders for only one year) that I felt it quite useless to argue the matter with you or to affording you an opportunity for what might but open the way to more undeserved rudeness. Believe me when I say that if any advice or fatherly words of mine could be in the least likely to keep you, they would be cheerfully at your service but your mind seems absolutely made up. I must do my duty as I see it in protecting my diocese from teaching which I feel to be fraught with peculiar danger. Yours in the much honest and not unkindly regret, Roffen.' (*Thorold's third forename*).

Charles then upped the stakes by appealing over the head of his bishop directly to the Archbishop of Canterbury Edward Benson in a letter dated 23rd June:

> 'To His Grace the Archbishop of Canterbury, Right Revd Father in God, in accordance with the custom prevalent in Rochester I have resided for nearly two months and officiated as a curate for Petersham without a licence. The Bishop of Rochester has now refused to allow me to officiate in his diocese on the ground that I do not believe Heaven to be a 'place' but only a state of being. No complaint has been made against me from

this place – but a strongly worded memorial in my favour has been signed by a great majority of the adult parishioners.

I have not contradicted any formulae of the Church nor said anything which will not bear the light of philosophic enquiry. I cannot allow myself to be severed from the Church which I love and for which I have given up other pursuits and more remunerative professions without appealing against this decision which is at once unjust, irrational and impolite . . . I have but two appeals possible, an appeal to your Grace publicly or an appeal to public opinion, as my poverty prevents the legal appeal – an action for libel. Several prominent liberal churchmen have written to me expressing their sympathy. I fear that this matter which is already public will bring discredit and ridicule upon a Church which has many enemies and will moreover frighten away many young liberal and earnest men from offering themselves for ordination. Is it possible for your Grace to avert this scandal either by advising me upon a less harmful way or by using otherwise your healing virtue as chief pastor? If not, under what form must I appeal to your Grace? Most obediently yours, Charles Latimer Marson.

This was a high risk strategy indeed. Charles had fed his story to the Press and must have surprised the Archbishop with his veiled threats to cause further trouble. Benson, who had been Archbishop for only 15 months and had more weighty matters to handle, was no doubt irritated by this 'little local difficulty' but replied personally to Charles with a holding letter on 28th June, requesting a copy of the original sermon: 'In the meantime you will, I think, have felt that there is something to be sorry about in the tone of your letter which you enclosed to me as your correspondence with the bishop'.

Benson had been a schoolmaster for 19 years, first at Rugby school then as headmaster at Wellington College. He must have felt like he was addressing an upstart prefect. Charles at least responded on 30th June:

'If I have said anything unkind to the Bishop of Rochester, I am quite willing to retract it and to do what I possibly can to make it easy for him to alter his verdict. The papers are anxious for further particulars and I have promised to take no further steps until Tuesday July 8th.'

Nothing like giving your adjudicator a deadline! Benson then instructed his chaplain to send a postcard and letter to Charles, requesting to see all correspondence to date. He also informed Charles that he had called in Revd Brooke Foss Westcott, Canon of Westminster and Regius Professor of Divinity at Cambridge to advise him on the doctrinal issues.

Revd Brooke Foss Westcott, future Bishop of Durham, supported Charles at crucial times in his life

This was a smart move. Benson went to the same school as Westcott, King Edward's Birmingham and then the same college Trinity Cambridge. They knew and trusted each other. Westcott had been the star undergraduate and had in fact been a tutor to Benson in his ordination preparations. Westcott was an acknowledged expert on the New Testament texts, having published numerous books and commentaries on the subject. In addition he had for many years taken a special interest in the training of young ordinands, culminating in his instituting the Cambridge Clergy Training School in 1881 (now called Westcott House). Furthermore Westcott also knew Edward Bickersteth personally because he was at Trinity College with him too.

Whether Charles appreciated all these incestuous relationships is unclear but he was very fortunate to have Westcott as an intermediary. For he was a very fair judge and had already replied to Benson that he was on his way from Cambridge to interview Marson personally:

> 'It is very desirable to see what the Bishop of Rochester did object to. I cannot for a moment suppose that he required anyone to localise Heaven. The reckless impatience of the Church Reformer school is, however, most sad and even

alarming. I don't think that Mr Marson has considered to what his reasoning leads . . . How weak and wilful we are.'

Westcott met Charles to quiz him on his theology and must have given him a clean bill of health, because Charles promptly wrote to his friend Robert Chalmers with the news that 'the Episcopal gaiters twinkle in flight'. Westcott, however, insisted that Charles should send an apology to Thorold, which was copied on to the Archbishop as follows:

'I most heartily and unfeignedly regret having written certain letters to your lordship and fully acknowledge their tone was not such as became a curate to his ecclesiastical superior . . . Should your lordship kindly think fit to withdraw your prohibition, I will endeavour in the future to avoid any such misunderstandings.'

Thorold was not wholly satisfied with this apology: 'Had he withdrawn the sermon, it would have been easier for me to license him.' But he asked for the Archbishop's guidance and Charles was reinstated.

This whole sorry episode is important to report in full, because it reveals not only Charles's courage but also his arrogance and, needless to say, this was not the end of the matter. The Establishment would have its way. Charles wrote to the Archbishop just two weeks later on 28th July 1884:

'My Lord, I must write a note of thanks for your Grace's kindness. The Bishop of Rochester has, upon my making of what apologies I could, withdrawn his prohibition. The vicar of Kew, however, does not see his way towards accepting my services further as curate in Petersham . . . I have therefore agreed to go in September to Holy Trinity, St Giles-in-the-Fields.'

So how did Charles feel at the end of his ordeal? He doesn't seem to have corresponded at all with his father during this time and perhaps missed the latter's diplomacy. His patron, the Countess Russell had tried by means of several rambling letters to intercede for him with the Archbishop. She wrote on the 5th of July:

'(he is) a young man of the greatest ability, of most noble and interesting character. He loves the Church to which he has devoted all his energies . . . (please to) deal gently with a man whom we might later be proud to have in the diocese.'

She wrote again on 22nd July regarding the vicar of Kew, Mr Nott, that he was 'irritated by the hold Mr Marson has on the affections of the people. This has happened with two former curates, of quite different theological views . . . so that deep resentment is felt against Mr Nott and a public meeting is planned.'

Finally she wrote on 24th July about Marson that

'his deep worship of Christ and earnest endeavours to live the life of a minister of Christ are beyond what I have ever seen in any young clergyman . . . deep resentment if we are deprived of so able and powerful a man.' She wrote also of 'a disposition of the Bishop to shift his ground and try to convict Mr Marson on other dogmatical points . . . there is a lamentable falling off in church attendance since he has been forbidden to preach and almost a rebellion in the choir.'

Lady Frances' influence, however, was failing and Archbishop Benson just stonewalled in his reply that everything should go through the Bishop of Rochester and he trusted that Mr Marson's friends would give him good counselling.

Revd Percy Nott died two years later and his parish was subdivided in 1891. So nobody came out of this ecclesiastical spat very well, except perhaps Bickersteth who was promoted within a year to become Bishop of Exeter, being presented at his inauguration by Bishop Thorold, no less. Charles's rather immature disdain for bishops as timeservers would not have been improved by that move; but Bickersteth had some success in that episcopate and Thorold was a good organiser at Rochester. In fact Charles could have contributed much to the diocese in the coming years, because Thorold followed the Toynbee Hall example and went to Cambridge University to recruit volunteers to fill new settlement links that sprang up – St John's College with Walworth parish; Trinity College with St George's Camberwell; and several others. But Charles was not involved and was on his way again.

5

Without a Cure

Although under notice to leave, Charles was busy in Petersham all July 1884. He wrote to his friend Miss Guest: 'I am working the parish and writing shoals of letters and a few articles.' But he was quite stoical about his predicament: 'I have played my stake and perhaps lost it, and have no right to grumble. One thing I have learned and that is how kind and real my friends are.' He still had Lady Agatha's love and support as well as that of the Countess. In the previous summer of 1883 Lady Agatha's older brother Rollo Russell had built a country house near Haslemere in Surrey which he called Dunrozel and Lady Frances Russell planned for them all to spend some time there again this year. No doubt through their influence, Charles was able to work as a locum at the nearby church of St Stephen's, Shotter Mill over the rest of that summer.

In the autumn Charles provided temporary cover for Revd RA Watson, the Rector of St Mary's Slaugham (5 miles south of Crawley). He took lodgings at Oak Cottage, Handcross whence he wrote again to Miss Guest on 30th October that her letter had at last found him 'kicked out (of Petersham) by a drove of Tories as a seditious heretic'. On the same day he wrote a rather pathetic letter to Archbishop Benson:

'My Lord, since I last wrote to your Grace from Petersham, I have had an unfortunate strain which the doctor considered sufficient to prevent me for a time from undertaking such work as that of Holy Trinity St Giles. I find much difficulty in getting a curacy as the men of my own ways of thinking are easily supplied with curates, a supply of young men of that way being greater than the demand. If I may presume upon your Grace's kindness any further, I should be glad to have your advice in the matter.'

Benson replied through his chaplain on 12th November that

'His Grace is sorry to hear of the accident which has interfered with your work. The Archbishop does not know of any curacy to which he could recommend you but will bear in mind what you have said in case any suitable opening should present itself.' Not much help there then.

In fact three months later an opening did come up via the Earl Granville, Secretary of State for Foreign Affairs, who wrote to the Archbishop on 23rd February 1885: 'The chaplaincy of the Embassy at Vienna is vacant. The value is £300 a year. Do you think that Mr Marson, of whom Lady Russell speaks highly, could be well suited to it?' The Archbishop effectively blackballs Marson in his reply:

> 'My dear Lord, my only knowledge of Mr Marson is due to my having intervened in a difficulty which arose between him and his Diocese, The Bishop of Rochester. Mr Marson professes to belong to a very advanced school of theology in the liberal direction . . . and was not very respectful to his Bishop . . . leads me to doubt him a very cultivated person . . . (but) it is to be said that he is an energetic person . . . I would refer you to the Bishop of Rochester for further information.'

It's unlikely that Charles would have wanted to go to Vienna anyway but he was certainly blocked of the opportunity. He had clearly been under stress and probably his chronic asthma had strained his whole system. But his next step would hardly improve matters because he moved back to London, to St Anne's in Stamford Hill and wrote to Miss Guest on 6th December 1884: 'Agatha was ill with neuralgia in the morning . . . here am I, amid a sort of East End people, smallpox, landlords, diphtheria, starvation, the devil all vigorous on their side, and I aghast can only look on.' On the 18th he wrote again: 'We are in a bad way here, the poor living like rats and Christianity represented by a do-nothing vicar, a few brimstone tracts and general bosh.' Clearly Agatha was still seeing Charles and presumably helping him occasionally. For Christmas she gave him a beautiful volume of sacred lyrics which he treasured.

It was probably in the autumn of 1884 that Charles became Editor of *The Christian Socialist* (monthly) newspaper. The fact that the names of contributors were not usually revealed (possibly to preserve their careers) means that we cannot tell exactly when Charles took over responsibility for this 16 page periodical – 'A Journal for thoughtful men', price 1 penny, obtainable from Mr

William Reeves of 185 Fleet Street. The paper acted as a networking tool for socialists – with notices and reports of meetings and lectures by the different socialist groups; reviews of books and pamphlets as well as political comment.

The Christian Socialist paper had begun in 1883 as the organ of the Land Reform Union. This group followed the American economist Henry George in advocating a single tax on large landowners – a windfall tax, so to speak, as land values rose with expanding populations and housing pressures. This would be the main way of raising money to tackle poverty but also served as a symbol that 'philosophically' land belongs equally to all humanity. The newspaper was initially edited by Harry Champion and James Joynes, and was so named in honour of the first wave of Christian Socialists under FD Maurice.

The guiding hand of Charles Marson is suspected from September 1884 with broader content and a much braver, wittier style of journalism. Lead articles began to appear: 'The Christ Life', 'The Christian standard of wages', but also 'The Factory Acts' and 'Bloodstained Coal' (about mining explosions and loss of life underground). The style was more personal and more committed, not so sociological and restrained. He preserved the section of the paper called 'Unconsidered Trifles', which was always filled with political gossip, snippets from letters or speeches or reports. But in Charles's hands the columns were funny and provocative and each month the list of London and provincial newsagents handling the paper lengthened.

He published letters from overseas and was happy to stir up debate, giving space to critics as well as supporters. He handled bad argument with a deflecting wit. Here's his amusing comment (March issue 1886) about one correspondent: 'Mr Arnold White has contributed an article How to help the unemployed: They must keep their families small, spend less in drink and tobacco . . . while we must provide public works, state-aided emigration, a protective tariff, abolition of short service in the army and the flagellation of venal vestrymen.' Charles replies deftly: 'Some of these remedies are ridiculous; some are reasonable, especially the last. Mr White knows nothing about the unemployed but, as he expresses a wish to help them, his suggestions deserve a passing consideration.' He was to sharpen and strengthen the paper over the next two and a half years.

All the while, he continued with his parish work in Stamford Hill, writing in January 1885: 'I have been today to a great number of most gruesome dens – man after man and woman after woman sick and out of work! Pale and gaunt faces and starvation ulcers!' When this temporary post ran out in February, Charles went for three months as a locum to Christchurch Cinderhill, Old Basford in the north west of the city of Nottingham. This new church was built in 1856 in the fashionable 'Decorated Gothic' style specifically for the miners of Babbington Colliery. It was a setting that he might ordinarily have enjoyed but the move was proving quite a wrench away from Lady Agatha and other friends. However, it was Charles's first experience of a community centred round a single industry – that of coalmining. Mr Fowler, the colliery manager, was churchwarden and an important figure, as the current vicar Revd George East was about to leave the parish. But Charles couldn't do much again here in such a short time.

He continued to learn more about socialism and had an extraordinary ability to read very quickly and extract maximum nourishment from any book. This facility was of great help to him, as he picked up other journalistic work in the form of reviews and articles as well as offers to lecture. For example, in March he was approached to give a talk in Oxford to the embryonic Socialist League group, which interestingly had more working-class members than students. They approached him because of an article he had just written for the *Pall Mall Gazette* about Christian Socialism.

However, for some of his time in Nottingham he was not functioning well. He was physically weak with more respiratory problems and was losing a lot of energy and self-confidence. He was pining to get back to London to sort out his relationship with Lady Agatha, who was finding their separation very enervating, particularly as some of her relations were becoming hostile to Charles's socialist outpourings against the rich. He wrote anxiously to Canon Barnett about his emotional and professional dilemmas. Barnett wrote back on March 15th 1885 advising patience and inviting Charles to come to see him at the Whitechapel Exhibition in April. They could converse more easily then and perhaps Charles could give a lecture on Art at the same visit.

He wrote also to Canon Westcott, who had grilled him over the Ascension affair and given him some much needed support. Westcott sent an encouraging reply at the end of April but by then the emotional storm had broken and Charles's engagement was over. Both parties were so stressed and unsure of their future that they fell back into a kind of brother-sister relationship, a friendship that in fact continued for many years. There are unfortunately no letters on either side to portray the hurt involved.

Agatha never married and, after her mother's death in 1898, made moves to leave Pembroke Lodge which she did in 1902. She edited her family letters in 1910, carried out sundry good works as patroness of charities and, although a heavy smoker like Charles, she died at the good age of 80 in 1933. She is buried at Grayshott, just a mile or so from Haslemere where perhaps she had spent a happy summer with Charles so many years before.

Lady Frances was greatly upset by the break-up of the engagement and sought solace in an even deeper religious fervour. Charles for his part never confided in his own mother or father at all in this unhappy period of his life. He only wrote to Miss Guest on 30th April: 'I feel as weak as a kitten and shall probably be enmeshed by the first pair of bright eyes that smile upon me in spite of resolutions to the contrary.' But he goes on that he is 'fully settled to come to Shoreditch, to St Agatha's Mission.' He ends morbidly that he is troubled 'by the suicide of one of us, Geldart, who was hounded out of the Church for his free thought, out of the Unitarians for his Socialism and out of the world for his manhood'.

To secure this new curacy, Charles needed a reference and was reassured to receive another encouraging letter from Westcott on May 12th:

'. . . you do not need scruple to ask your friends for the testimony . . . (I) should gladly welcome you as a fellow worker. I should be very glad to hear that you are at work in London. You will find this, I think, some pathetic counsel and help . . . I want very much to get to know some of the younger clergy. Yours most sincerely BF Westcott.'

The news of the move back to London was not welcomed, however, in Clevedon whence Charles's father wrote on May 15th 1885 (for Charles's 26th birthday):

'It is a source of grief to both of us that you are going again to London. The life there is unsuited altogether to one of your constitution: fresh air and exercise along with work among the poor is healthier alike for your body and mind than a half-clerical and half-literary life, which only wearies and fags without corresponding benefits. As to what you say about its being the only place for one of your views – your views must be extraordinary indeed not to admit of being set forth in any diocese but one. But as I know nothing about them, of course it is not for me to pronounce any opinion and if I were to do so, possibly it would be received as of no account, so I say nothing.'

This sounds like a low point in the father-son relationship but he encloses a cheque to encourage Charles to have a week by the sea between jobs to rebuild his health – 'to see you lean, gaunt, pale and hollow-eyed is not a very inspiring sight, my dear old man.'

Finally he gives Charles news from home – his three spinster sisters Annie, now 30, Edith, 24, and Grace, 21, were all well at home at Clevedon vicarage – their other sister Harriet (Hattie) had sadly died in March 1884 just before Charles's Petersham troubles, which is perhaps why Charles did not burden his father with more sadness. Of Charles's younger brothers, there was news from Henry (Harry), aged 19, that he was enjoying Sandhurst (apart from the drill) and that Frank, 15, had gone back to Bath College despite misgivings about his strength and health.

𝄞——𝄪

So in May 1885 Charles moved his belongings again – his sixth move in a year – to 7, H Block, Broad Street Station Dwellings, Wilson Street (a model dwelling mainly for railway employees). He was to work in this little pocket of London for nine months and it was to be another formative experience for him. St Agatha's Shoreditch (ironic name for Charles after his break up with Lady Agatha) was a new parish, carved out of the larger parish of St James to its north in 1872. It was then immediately gutted by the construction of Liverpool Street Station in 1874 on the site of the disused Bethlem Royal Hospital, the ancient mental hospital for London. The Great Eastern Railway needed a new terminus to serve the routes to Cambridge and Norwich and many people lost their homes on its arrival. The parish population in 1885 was about 4,000 people, for the most part unsettled and poor, continuing to dwindle to 1,600 by the time of its re-absorption into St James' in 1915.

Charles Booth in his 1898 survey and map of St Agatha's shows two black/dark blue blocks indicating 'Lowest class, vicious, semi-criminal, very poor'. The rest of the parish is shown in the next class, light blue (Poor: 18s to 21s per week for a moderate family). Booth's report comments that the Police described the district as 'frequented by young thieves'; that the four public houses and two beershops are 'well-supported'; that 'disorderly houses from time to time break out and some prostitutes live in the Model Dwellings'; that 'even the Model Dwellings are badly constructed with rooms that are small and dark with little circulation of air.' In summary, 'the population consists largely of people who will not be taken elsewhere'. Ironically, the land (the Broadgate Estate) is worth billions of pounds today.

There was the small mission church building itself, with rooms under it as well as offices in Finsbury Square and Sun Street. The smallness of the church was matched by a miserably small congregation of about 60 in number most Sundays. There were no facilities or resources for the sick and the Metropolitan Visiting & Relief Association gave a meagre £15 per year for relief. There was 'no co-operation' with the small Wesleyan Chapel nearby. The vicar of St Agatha's throughout the 1880s and 1890s was Revd Freeman Wills, born in Dublin around 1842.

Educated at Trinity College Dublin, Revd Wills was both a clergyman and a Lieutenant-Colonel in the Army. He supervised a Girls' Club, a Mothers' Meeting and a Penny Bank but put most of his energies into a cadet corps (nearly 600 strong) to give local lads some discipline. Yet he was not an archetypal army officer. His own father, also a clergyman, had not been a wealthy man but had written biographies of illustrious Irish men and passed his literary interests on to his sons. The oldest son William Wills moved to London and led a bohemian lifestyle – first as a fashionable portrait artist then as a popular playwright, writing for Henry Irving in his heyday as an actor. In 1885 Wills' adaptation of *Faust* began a two-year run at the Lyceum. His brother Freeman Wills never married nor experienced domesticity either but also enjoyed the theatre and literature. No doubt he took Charles along to view his brother's plays. So on his arrival at St Agatha's, Charles had to work with a personality quite different from any he'd ever met before.

Throughout the summer of 1885 Charles was busy with his parish work – clubs, poor relief and visiting, but whereas at St Jude's there was a big team working energetically in a systematic way – observing, collecting information and analysing problems – at St Agatha's there was no team and no strategy. Left to his own devices, Charles spent long hours getting to know and understand many of his parishioners. The 1891 census (Shoreditch South district 8) gives a helpful snapshot of one part of the parish demography – working people like railway porters, printers, warehousemen, furriers, office cleaners, boot makers, grooms, saddlers, umbrella makers – pretty similar to St Jude's but without the dockers. There were 83 lodgers out of a population of 814, and average occupancy was 7 people per property. There were no professional people, not even many shops – three pubs, a baker's, a general store and a Post Office. There was a German club in Wilson Street – roughly one eighth of the population came from Germany and one tenth from Ireland, but there was neither the Jewish presence nor the Polish influx that Whitechapel showed.

Now it had been agreed with Revd Wills from the start that Charles could engage in part-time journalism and so he continued editing the *Christian Socialist* but also renewed his contacts with the *Pall Mall Gazette* in the Strand. The editor now was William (WT) Stead who from July 6-10th 1885 wrote a series of controversial articles on child prostitution called 'The Maiden Tribute of Modern Babylon'. To prove a point, Stead set up the 'purchase' of the thirteen-year-old daughter of a chimney sweep, Eliza Armstrong and staged her abduction. This was done it must be said, with the co-operation of the Salvation Army. Sensational headlines followed ('The Violation of Virgins') and moral panic set in. As a result, the Criminal Law Amendment Act, which raised the age of consent for girls from 13 to 16, was passed on 14th August. Charles contributed in a small way to this campaign by sending Stead a briefing note about prostitution in Whitechapel. This was acknowledged in a letter dated July 6th:

> 'Dear Marson, Thanks for your note which Stead was very glad to see. He is sending a copy of today's paper together with a private letter to every Bishop. They shall certainly be cursed if they won't curse the evildoers, yrs ever ET Cook.'

Unfortunately for Stead, his new style of (investigative) journalism was not universally welcomed and he was actually convicted over the Eliza Armstrong case on the grounds that he had not obtained permission for the 'purchase' of the girl from her father! He was sent to prison for three months and eventually resigned from his newspaper. In the interim Charles wrote more reviews and articles for the *Pall Mall Gazette*. On September 10th 1885, Alfred Milner (Deputy Editor) wrote to Charles:

'Many thanks for your article the other day. All contributions gratefully received just now, for it is a dull time and we are very short-handed. Would you entertain the idea of coming here for a bit, to work regularly . . . every morning for an hour or two so that Cook may take my place and I may get away?'

This tentative job offer must have been tempting for Charles. Milner was about to leave the newspaper to stand for the first time as an MP in the forthcoming October elections and Stead's future as editor was still uncertain. Edward (ET) Cook did eventually take over as editor and became one of the leading journalists of the age.

Charles had plenty of work at that time as an editor in his own right. He wrote on September 1st 1885 to Edith Nesbit (who at that time was writing poetry and trying to get it published, fifteen years before the success of her children's stories):

'Dear Madam, I am sorry for my mistake but the signature, of course, puzzled me. I will send you the magazine in a day or two. I gladly try to clap in any real poetry I can lay my fingers upon, and if you can get any socialist poetry, I shall do my best to insert it.'

The mistaken signature may be due to the fact that Edith Nesbit's married name was Bland by this time. She was living then in Elswick Road, Blackheath and Charles ends his letter by asking if Edith knows his old friends Emily and Jane Guest, who lived just three streets away from her in Granville Park. As a result of this exchange of letters, Edith invited Charles for dinner at her house to meet her husband Hubert Bland, fellow Fabian Sidney Webb and the South African novelist Olive Schreiner. This in turn led to an invitation to Charles to attend and address the recently formed Fabian Society.

It was soon after this meeting, probably in the month of November 1885 that Charles changed his lifestyle and took up abstemious fasting. Christianity, in common with other religions, has encouraged fasting as a form of self-discipline (e.g. during Lent) or as a symbolic cleansing before taking communion. But Charles took this further, perhaps out of sympathy for the poor people he was now meeting, perhaps to test his own emotional strengths after his romantic disappointments or even as a kind of self-harming. Possibly also, living alone in lodgings, he lacked the personal organisation to look after himself properly. The poor nutrition was combined with his chronic asthma to bring on a period of serious illness, when he was looked after by some of the poorest and least reputable women in the parish. Their nursing touched his heart and changed his whole approach. Their warmth contrasted starkly with the coldness shown by his own mother when Charles eventually limped back to Clevedon for a break.

On recovery he managed to keep going on the journalistic front, publishing an eye-witness account of the Trafalgar Square riots of February 1886 but his parish work was proving frustrating. He wrote to Canon Barnett to ask his advice on the next possible step. Barnett replied on December 11th 1885: 'I believe you would do better if you were more part of a system, you were so much taken by the Catholic system. I don't know the Ritualist centres but I have always thought them to exist in provincial towns rather than in London – in provincial towns there is not quite the same temptation to play to the gallery. My own opinion still is in favour of the colonies. I think you would get health and foemen worthy of your steel.' Charles would indeed try the colonies but not for another three and a half years.

6

Fabians and all the rest

Charles was a bit nervous, as he hurried up Gower Street, clutching his battered briefcase, which contained the paper on 'Christian Socialism' that he would present that evening at his first Fabian Society meeting. This select little group, which had started in January 1884, met formally on the first Friday of each month and it was October 2nd 1885 when Charles made his first appearance. He already knew one or two members and had, of course, published reports on Fabian meetings for *The Christian Socialist* newspaper but meeting other members in the flesh, so to speak, would be novel.

The venue was Dr Williams' Library – Dr Williams was a Welsh Nonconformist minister who bequeathed in his will not only his book collection but also money to found a theological library, which opened in 1729. So Charles's Christian theme that evening must have won them the right to meet amidst the great tomes of theological wisdom that surrounded them. Although the Fabian Society had 40 members in London by this time, not many were regular attenders and tonight's meeting was no different.

The Chairman was William Kinnimond Burton, a young and outstanding engineer, trained in Edinburgh and now secretary of the London Sanitary Protection Association. Inspired by his aunt Mary Burton, a social reformer and fighter for women's education, Burton had a passionate belief in safe water systems to improve the health of the poor. He left London in 1887 for Japan where he spent over 20 years leading the design of sanitation systems for Tokyo and other cities.

Secretary for the evening was Frank Podmore, aged 29, one of several capable, unattached civil servants to join the Society. Some were sons of clergymen; all were looking for a new faith of some kind. Frank's father, for example, was Revd Thompson Podmore, Headmaster of Eastbourne College. Frank was one of the original nine 'founders' of the Fabian Society and offered his home 14 Dean's Yard Westminster as the Society's headquarters and regular meeting place. He would become a senior civil servant in the Post Office.

Another important early member was Edward Pease, who had originally met Frank Podmore at a Spiritualist séance. It was at Edward's house 17 Osnaburgh Street (opposite Gt Portland Street tube) that the Fabian Society was first formed. He came from a large and wealthy Quaker family near Bristol but, though educated at home, he felt distant from his parents and was shy in company. Moving to London at 17, he was a commercial clerk and then became a stockbroker on £400 a year. The contrast between his new wealth and the squalor of the slums troubled his conscience greatly. When his father died in 1884, Edward used the legacy to give up his job in the City and spent some time learning carpentry and working in a furniture co-operative in Newcastle. He returned to London and became the Society's first paid secretary.

Two recently elected Fabian members were Sydney Olivier and Sidney Webb, both high-flyers in the Colonial Office and born in the same year as Charles. Olivier had recently spent some time as a volunteer at Toynbee Hall and may even have met Charles there. He was a very handsome and confident individual, who had rebelled against the orthodox views of his clergyman father. His friend Webb, on the other hand, was painstakingly shy and gauche with a Cockney accent. His father was an accountant and his mother a devout evangelical. Their mutual friend Graham Wallas was another clergyman's son. After a spell as a classics teacher, he became a lecturer at the new London School of Economics.

However, the two figures that caught Charles's eye that night were those of George Bernard Shaw and Annie Besant. Shaw had arrived in London, aged 23, from Dublin in 1876, abandoning his alcoholic father and following his mother and her new partner George Vandeleur Lee. The latter was an ambiguous figure, setting himself up as a singing teacher and an impresario of occasional operettas and oratorios, in which Shaw's mother would feature with her fine mezzosoprano voice. For several years Shaw had no real job and felt himself a social misfit. His schooling had been disrupted and humiliating but now he took the opportunity to improve his knowledge by frequenting the British Museum Reading Room. He developed his speaking skills by attending debating societies and began writing – five unsuccessful novels as well as articles and music reviews. From 1885 to 1888 he wrote for the Pall Mall Gazette and may possibly have run into Charles at their offices. At any rate he joined the Fabian Society in May 1884 and had just spent a fruitful 18 months studying Karl Marx and socio-economic theory as well as articulating Fabian policy to the outside world. His success as a playwright (e.g. *Pygmalion)* would not come for another fifteen years or more but he must have seemed quite a daunting figure to Charles that evening.

Annie Besant, at 38 the oldest person in the room, was probably also the only woman present that evening. She too had fallen out of love with the Church – in the person of her husband, a conservative clergyman from whom she had separated in 1873. She had then become a campaigner for the National Secular Society and was greatly influenced by its leader Charles Bradlaugh, best-known perhaps for his refusal to take the oath of loyalty as an MP. Annie undertook public speaking engagements on wider issues like the trades unions, birth control and women's right to vote. In May 1885 Shaw introduced her to the Fabian Society and straightaway she put all her energies into it.

So this was the small but sophisticated audience that Charles had to address. For good personal reasons, most were not exactly hostile but were certainly wary of Christianity as a possible engine to drive their socialist dreams. However, Charles had had agonies over his own religious upbringing and had come through these to a new faith, so he felt confident now in his own powers of thought and speech. Unlike some in the room, he had had real experience of poverty and of the working man, for whom and with whom the 'new society' must be created.

He began by saying that, like all socialists, he had pondered long and hard about the mechanisms that would bring about a new social order. He reviewed the options. The Fabians, he suggested, favoured a 'gradualist' approach – evolution rather than revolution – permeating existing political parties and the public at large with information about current iniquities and suggesting new policy options. The Social Democratic Federation, on the other hand, under the leadership of Henry Hyndman had, since 1881, advocated a revolutionary line, attracting trade union leaders and workers into a membership by then of over 700 people. But, as they all knew, there had been divisions over Hyndman's highhanded style of leadership and in December 1884 the influential artist and poet William Morris had split away to form the Socialist League along with important figures like Eleanor Marx, Ernest Belfort Bax and Edward Aveling.

The niggling question that ate away at all their theories, then as now, was what higher motives should be in force to curb human selfishness and safeguard a 'disinterested' form of government, so that one corruptible élite would not simply be replaced by another corruptible élite? Furthermore, how can individuals develop their talents and be rewarded for effort and enterprise, without necessarily producing a competitive and stratified society? These were Charles's themes that evening.

His own starting point was simply that Jesus had taught that all men are brothers, so that any exploitation of one class by another through landlordism, poor wages and conditions was contrary to God's Plan. Christianity says that all the woe of the world is caused by selfishnesss and deceit. Charles talked about his previous uplifting work in Whitechapel in the face of such chronic poverty but also about the individual apathy and indifference he had encountered elsewhere. A concerted national effort at renewal was required. A vague appeal to man's better nature, as the Secularists and Humanists proposed, would not be enough. The only sure template for a new society, he argued, would be a Christian plan.

The Church had made wrong choices and failed the people, he agreed, quoting John Ruskin: 'The clergy dine with the rich and preach to the poor.' It was wrong to suggest that the world was just a vale of tears to be passed through on the way to eternal bliss or damnation and that the material life was of no consequence compared to the spiritual life. The appeal to the poor to be patient was no longer appropriate. No, what was needed was a new gospel of 'honest work for all and honest pay.' It was important to fight for better wages and conditions in this life, because Jesus was a supporter of the downtrodden against the rich and powerful. He required social justice now, as in the Parable of the Sheep and the Goats:

> Before him all the nations will be gathered, and he will separate them one from another, as a shepherd separates the sheep from the goats. He will set the sheep on his right hand,

but the goats on the left. Then the King will tell those on his right hand, 'Come, blessed of my Father, inherit the Kingdom prepared for you from the foundation of the world; for I was hungry, and you gave me food to eat. I was thirsty, and you gave me drink. I was a stranger, and you took me in. I was naked, and you clothed me. I was sick, and you visited me. I was in prison, and you came to me.' (Matthew 25:32-36)

Charles did not need to produce more quotes, for his audience knew their Bibles only too well, but then he drove it home personally: 'I know for certain that the world can be redeemed by the mere application of Christian principle. I am surfeited with all the middle-class pattering, while the poor rot just because we are not brave enough to quarrel with usury, anarchy, competition, swindling, banking and the like.'

Some socialists might argue that the world was a place for 'systematic improvement through human effort and intelligence without recourse to God or Church'; but he countered that, realistically, we are simply not strong enough nor wise enough to progress without a Christian faith to guide us. Faith was not an optional extra but a necessity. Anyway that was his position and the Chairman threw the matter open for discussion.

As usual, everyone was polite and tolerant of differences of opinion. That's why the Fabians had not splintered into so many factions. Edith Nesbit (Bland) once wrote to a friend: 'I do think the Fabians are quite the nicest set of people I ever knew.' So the discussion was basically positive and Revd Stewart Headlam (a guest for the evening and not a Fabian member yet) spoke strongly in support. Annie Besant, however, felt she had to respond and (without wishing to give offence) considered this claim for Christianity '. . . an impertinence. To think that there was a God, who could, yet did not, remove the suffering and misery we see around us, would be enough to drive her to madness'. Charles gave a summing up speech and the meeting broke up.

As he walked back home to St Agatha's, he thought things had gone quite well – a pleasant social evening, a little intellectual stimulation. Nice middle-class people but with no real creed about them. At least he knew what he believed. Did he actually want to join them? Was this the right group for him? They were a choosy bunch – would they even want him as a member?

George Bernard Shaw and Annie Besant –
both present at Charles's Fabian Lecture 1885:
GBS photo courtesy of the London School of Economics

Well, they did want him and at the next meeting on November 6th 1885 they duly elected Charles as a new member and he would remain a Fabian until 1913 – not always a very active member because he was often physically distant and had other interests and preoccupations but he remained keen to learn what this small but influential group was publishing and proposing. When Beatrice Potter, whom Charles had known at St Jude's, was introduced to Sidney Webb in 1890 and married him in 1892, the future of the Fabian Society was assured. Heavyweight research and analysis were then combined with Shaw's humour and journalistic skills to pack a powerful punch at national level and then at local level via the London County Council that came into being in 1889.

Another reason for Charles's ambivalence over the Fabians was their recruitment the following year (March 1886) of the services of Charles's mentor Revd Stewart Headlam. He had been the founder in 1877 of the Guild of St Matthew, which was arguably the first socialist grouping of them all. It combined radical social views with the support of High Church principles and in 1885 had 126 members throughout the country (one third in Holy Orders). Its newspaper *The Church Reformer*, edited by Headlam, ran from 1884 to 1895, largely at a loss that Headlam himself made up.

The Guild's original objects were:

1. To get rid, by every possible means, of the existing prejudices, especially on the part of "Secularists", against the Church, her sacraments and doctrines; and to endeavour to justify God to the people.

2. To promote frequent and reverent worship in the Holy Communion, and a better observance of the teaching of the Church of England as set forth in the Book of Common Prayer.

3. To promote the study of social and political questions in the light of the Incarnation.

Headlam needed to update these aims, particularly the first of these, when the Secularist attacks diminished over time. In 1884 he had put forward the Single Land Tax idea as a main plank of policy, along with redistribution of wealth, universal suffrage and the breakdown of class barriers. However, once he joined the Fabians, Headlam helped them to redraft their 'Basis' in 1887. He wrote important Tracts for them, developing their policy at the expense of the Guild's and thereby running into trouble with his own supporters.

Charles probably felt rather outranked by Headlam, who was 39 and in his prime, though still without a parish – he had been sacked in 1878 by John Jackson, the Bishop of London from his Bethnal Green parish for preaching of Jesus as a revolutionary figure. Educated at Eton and Cambridge, he had private means and could thus devote his time to politics. Preaching occasionally when invited, he was able to spend time also on the theatre which he loved. He threw his weight behind the Fabian Society and Charles simultaneously withdrew somewhat, attending only a few meetings in 1886, which proved to be a significant year for the Society and the socialist cause generally.

As Editor of the *Christian Socialist* newspaper, Charles had to keep his eye on the wider socialist movement and report the important events that now ensued. The 1885/6 winter (during which he was unfortunately very ill at St Agatha's) was to be an exceptionally cold one. The Agricultural Depression, which followed some poor domestic harvests and new competition from foreign food producers, encouraged movement by the rural poor to the cities to find work. In London the influx of East European Jewry was also adding to the population growth, so that the population of Greater London expanded from 4.76 million in 1881 to 5.63 million in 1891 (18.2% growth). Unemployment was fast becoming an issue, as was poor housing stock.

In response, William Morris' Socialist League held open air meetings regularly on Sundays in the East End at Dod Street, Limehouse for dockers and workers to attend. The Police made arrests after one particular meeting on September 20th 1885 – William Morris was not present but Lewis Lyons, leader of the Jewish Tailors' Trade Union was – and a court case followed on the next Tuesday, when Lyons received a two months' prison sentence. The following Sunday at least 30,000 people turned out to demand the right to Free Speech and the Police backed off this time. Annie Besant and GBS reported as much to the Fabian Society on the same night as Charles' talk.

The Social Democratic Federation in particular then began to mobilise protest marches of the unemployed in the streets of central London. From February 1886 disgruntlement with the newly elected Liberal Government under Gladstone was growing. In his previous parliament (1880-85), Gladstone had expanded the electorate from 3 to 5 million by his Reform Act of 1884, thus giving half the adult male population the vote – Charles, for example, voted for the first time – but progress on land reform and housing reform, as proposed by Joseph Chamberlain, now seemed unlikely in a hung parliament with the Liberals on 335 seats, the Tories on 249 and Parnell's Irish MPs holding the balance of power with 86 seats. Gladstone tried hard to appease the different factions in his party and proposed an Irish Home Rule Bill to keep Parnell's support but those Liberals who could not countenance such a constitutional change separated under Lord Hartington and Joseph Chamberlain into the 'Liberal Unionist' position, and Gladstone's government collapsed after just six months. This 'Liberal split' was confirmed at the General Election in July 1886, when the Tories won a large majority and would stay in power for most of the next twenty years.

So, during the first half of 1886, the government was perceived as weak and this emboldened the protest marches of the poor and the unemployed. Charles was among 20,000 demonstrators assembled in Trafalgar Square on Monday 8th February 1886 to hear speeches by Burns, Hyndman and Champion. Sir Edmund Henderson, in charge of the Metropolitan Police, held most of his force back to cover a possible march on the Commons and put out just 66 men into the Square. Scuffling broke out and the crowd surged through police lines into Pall Mall, the centre of the various gentlemen's clubs. Faced with jeering from the smart clubs, the angry mob picked up stones and broke their windows, rampaging up Piccadilly. Queen Victoria wrote to Gladstone that this was 'a monstrous riot . . . a momentary triumph for socialism and a disgrace to the capital'.

Charles covered it, of course, in his paper (March issue) under the headline 'Salvo for the Sleek': 'We cannot but rejoice that the well-fed have had thrust before them so roughly a vision of the misery, which they so persistently ignore.' The wealthy classes, worried that a revolution was building, threw money into the Lord Mayor's Poor Relief Fund – '£42,000 and of this sum no less than £39,000 have been subscribed since last Wednesday' (*Times* 17 Feb). Henderson was replaced by the more aggressive Sir Charles Warren. The Fabians, however, distanced themselves from the riot, so that the Press portrayed them as idealists rather than agitators.

In the second half of the year, with the change of government and the Liberal Split over Irish Home Rule, many socialists could see a gap in the market, so to speak. Should they stick with the Liberals or combine and create a new party of their own, as in France and Germany? It was Annie Besant, with her stronger grasp of practical politics, who took the initiative. Newly elected to the Fabian Executive in April, she first proposed that the Fabians open up branches outside of London to build a national base. Then she proposed that a conference be held on September 17th at Anderton's Hotel in the Strand to bring together the various socialist and radical groups. An inconsequential meeting had previously been held in June before the election and this had attracted representatives from 53 different societies, including William Morris' Socialist Leaguers. They did not really believe in the parliamentary process at all (a bourgeois institution) and neither, of course, did the Anarchist groups but at the September conference, after a noisy debate, Annie Besant's motion that 'socialists should organise themselves as a political party' was carried by 49 votes to 19.

The next meeting of the Fabians, a fortnight later on October 1st 1886, was held at Annie Besant's own house at 19 Avenue Rd, St John's Wood, and Charles attended. There was a talk on 'Socialism and the Family' but surprisingly no follow-up to the conference vote – nothing in the minutes of this or the next meeting about it at all. This was because some of the Fabians were simply not in favour of any new parliamentary party – Shaw was against it and Webb was cautious.

Nevertheless Annie Besant proposed a motion at the November 5th Fabian meeting to form a separate body to be called the Fabian Parliamentary League. Charles was in support – he had always been impressed with the mass membership of the Social Democratic Federation and the way it had brought in the trade unions and ordinary workers as members. He would not forget this lesson and wrote in to the Fabians to give his apologies that he could not actually attend the 5th November meeting but strongly supported the idea that

> 'socialists move as quickly as possible into the arena of politics . . . a single parliamentary member, of honour and resolution, will teach the people more than all our other efforts put together. Logical necessity compels us to try to work with such tools as this society has got, and parliament is the best of such tools . . . we cannot sweep clean the state until we have got hold of it . . . We cannot with any safety bottle up socialist energies any longer in rooms and papers. We are already tearing one another to pieces because we do not get a fair chance at the enemy. '

This was fighting talk from Charles and he was never one to set his sights low but in the end the Fabians compromised. Besant's Fabian Parliamentary League began but never prospered through lack of support. Although Annie Besant left the Fabians in 1890 to pursue her final faith choice – the new religion of Theosophy which drew ideas from many religions (particularly Hinduism) – her political instincts were vindicated by the eventual formation and success of the Labour Representation Committee of 1900. This became the Labour Party we know today. The Fabians supplied one member to that committee of twelve.

Another key supporter of parliamentary action was Hubert Bland, the one important Fabian figure not yet discussed. He had been present at Charles's talk the previous October and probably had met him some time before that through journalism. He was a tall man, broad-shouldered and handsome with dark hair and a moustache. He gave airs of being a gentleman but his social background was less assured. He was born in Woolwich; his grandfathers had been a plumber and a publican respectively. His father had been a successful commercial clerk, who had acquired two or three small terraced properties but unfortunately had died young. However, Hubert did well at school and wanted to join the Army. Every day he passed the Royal Artillery Barracks and watched the cadets in their fine uniforms but he had not the money to buy a commission and he resented a system that stopped his ambitions. So he took a job as a bank clerk and lived with his widowed mother, attending political meetings in the evening where he met Henry Hyndman among others.

Hubert knew he had ability and also exerted a powerful charm over women. He had by now formed a relationship with Margaret Doran, his mother's paid companion. She later bore him a son but he didn't marry her – instead he married Edith Nesbit on April 22nd 1880 when she was 21, two months before she had his baby son Paul. Yet Hubert continued to live with his mother and see Margaret, while Edith lived with her mother in a house in Blackheath. Hubert and Edith were re-united before long, but their marriage was an open one and had moments of great tension.

Hubert helped Edith with the magazine stories that she had begun writing to boost their income. He had always enjoyed poetry and was a member of the Lewisham Literary Society. He took to writing immediately. Invited to attend the first Fabian Society meeting, he became a stalwart of the group. When Hubert first met Shaw at the offices of the *Christian Socialist* paper in May 1884 and was helped by him with contacts in journalism, he never looked back.

However it was that Charles met Hubert – probably through journalism – he was now drawn into the Blands' unusual bohemian circle.

O—⚷

7

The Matchless Orinda

After his illness at St Agatha's Shoreditch back in November 1885, Charles had a very busy year ahead of him in 1886 with journalism and politics to the fore, as described. That year would end on a high with a romantic relationship, an infatuation in fact with the enigmatic writer Edith Nesbit (Bland). They had met through journalism and the Fabian Society. It is very unlikely that it was a physical affair but the 33 surviving letters that he wrote to her contain endearments and charming little cartoons. They went to stay with each other and sent each other gifts of flowers regularly. She took an interest in his parish work and they swapped gossip and stories about events and characters. She took her children down to him and he told them faery stories. In particular they discussed poetry and sent each other ideas and draft material. Edith was submitting poetry to magazines like *The Argosy* and *The Weekly Dispatch* at a half-guinea or a guinea per poem – all much needed income for her family. In every detail, therefore, their relationship looks exactly like a warm and respectful friendship. Charles's rather gauche comments at times on feminine sentiments and psychology indicate that he was not ready to (nor likely to) attract a deeper relationship. Edith was probably content with that.

A sketch of her life to that point may be helpful. She was a few months older than Charles, being born in August 1858 in Kennington, South London where her father John Nesbit ran a small college, teaching agriculture and chemistry. After her father's death when she was only three, Edith, her two older brothers and one older sister had a rather nomadic existence, receiving education at various schools in France and Germany. Although not all her experiences were happy ones, Edith, or Daisy as she was called at home, absorbed the languages and culture around her and developed a rather sensitive and unconventional personality. Her mother Sarah brought the family back to England in 1871 and for several years rented a house Halstead Hall, near Sevenoaks in Kent. Edith's story of *The Railway Children*, published in 1906, has many autobiographical references – the absent father, the resourceful mother and the adventurous children.

After marrying Hubert Bland and giving birth to their first child Paul in 1880, Edith began to bring in valuable income through writing. Her second child Iris Mary was born in December 1881 and her third child Fabian in January 1885. Edith asked Charles to be godfather to Fabian and he did take a great interest in the child, who would sadly die from a botched tonsils operation in 1900.

However, the Bland household was much more complex than this. Edith had previously made good friends with Miss Alice Hoatson, who in 1882 was working at *Sylvia's Home Journal*, a magazine that took some of Edith's stories. Some time later, Alice met and fell in love with Hubert. Because she was a capable, cheerful person, Alice made herself indispensable to the Blands. First in June 1885 she became assistant secretary to the Fabian Society and later when Edith was pregnant in February 1886, Alice moved in to nurse her. Sadly Edith's child was stillborn and she was distraught for weeks. She little realised that during all this time her over-sexed husband was busy seducing Alice, who bore his child Rosamund in early November that year. Alice did not confess as to who was the child's father and, to save her friend's reputation, Edith took over the child as her own. When Edith eventually found out that Alice was Hubert's mistress, she was certainly upset but did not kick her out of the house. Indeed Alice remained with Hubert until his death in 1914, fulfilling certain wifely and motherly roles that Edith left to her.

After the upset of her stillborn child in February 1886, Edith had gone back to her writing, sending poetry and stories off to the publisher Robert Mack, among others. It was during that summer, however, that Edith fell passionately in love for the second time in her life, this time with George Bernard Shaw. He was then nearly thirty, two years older than her and heartened by his recent successes with women – Jenny Patterson, a wealthy widow, and Annie Besant in particular. But Shaw was sexually insecure and unable to offer commitment in relationships. He was flattered by Edith's attentions and met her regularly at the British Museum, escorting her home to Blackheath and happily making closer friendship with Hubert Bland too. This pattern of moving in like a cuckoo into a marital nest was a feature of Shaw's emotional life. It was as if he was repeating the *ménage à trois* of his own parents. As

Edith's passion grew over the summer months, so Shaw began to find excuses to put her off. She offered to leave her husband and run away with Shaw but by October Shaw had definitely decided against any such action. By the following spring (1887) they had reverted to an ordinary friendship.

This is all very pertinent to Edith's relationship with Charles in the autumn of 1886 and later on with other young male friends – e.g. Noel Griffith, Laurence Housman. After the disappointment with Shaw, Edith perhaps preferred to be the senior party in relationships - the more experienced person engaging in the sentimental education of younger impressionable men.

Just before his relationship with Edith commenced, Charles too had had upheavals and a complete change in his personal life. He had left London and moved in March 1886 to be Rector of Orlestone, a small village near Ashford in Kent. It was a two-stage train journey up to London via the Ashford to Rye line, though he could still get up for the occasional Fabian meeting in town or for a party at the Blands' new, if still modest, house at Dorville Road at Lee. At the same time Edith could leave London with her children and spend time in the country with Charles in his spacious Rectory.

Orlestone was a strange place for Charles after the urban poverty of Shoreditch – remote and rural with a population of 440 souls. Although he was still on the mend from his recent illness, the timing of the move was not good for him. Along with the Canadian WHP Campbell and the Fabian Alfred Howard (both laymen), Charles had used his position as editor of *The Christian Socialist* monthly newspaper to start a new society, the Christian Socialist Society (CSS), which intended to reach out both to lay people and to a non-denominational audience (not just C of E). The CSS published its manifesto in May 1886 as follows:-

1. The union of all men in a real universal brotherhood free from all artificial distinctions founded merely upon class.
2. Education, liberal, free, compulsory, industrial, for all.
3. Substitution of a system of production for use instead of the present system of production for profit.
4. The organization of society on a basis of industry and

manual worth, rather than of wealth, privilege and monopoly as at present; industry being understood to comprise both mental and manual work.

5. Public control of land, capital and all means of production, distribution and exchange, involving the abolition of all interest.

6. The ennobling of domestic, public and national life; the development of free and independent nationalities; the union of labour; and the promotion of peace and goodwill all over the world.

Quite a hippie charter really! Its Treasurer was to be Charles's old friend Miss Emily Guest and the CSS held its first meeting on 21 June 1886. Summer outdoor meetings were planned and the first branch of the society was already set up in Bristol under Hugh Holmes Gore – a solicitor, Fabian and lay member of the Guild of St Matthew. Branches were later formed at Leicester, Glasgow and Liverpool. For the first six months, Charles was delighted by the progress of the CSS and wrote in the October issue of his paper that it had become 'a greater success even than we dared to hope. The untiring energy of its officers . . . has produced an important society in a very few months.' Weekly meetings were now being held in London, issuing leaflets and raising funds. In January 1887 the Society took over the *Christian Socialist* newspaper as its own organ, anticipating greater sales, and Charles surrendered editorship to Campbell and Howard. He had done over two and a half years as editor – all through his troubled and nomadic years – and had attracted strong contributions from other writers.

The paper had certainly been provocative in his last year with recent sideswipes at the monarchy and at bishops in particular: 'The truth is that our present bishops with their "faithful laymen" must be got rid of, if the old Church is to be set in working order once again. Sweep them out, baubles, dignities, palaces, playthings, fawning chaplains and all.' In another issue he had a go at both the Temperance Movement and colonial attitudes:

'The Temperance Congress . . . thinks that rum should not be sold, and syphilis not given to the races, whose countries we steal and whose treasure houses we "open up". . . Our efforts to cheat, rob, murder and enslave them require as much denunciation as the fact that we dram, drug and syphilize them. It is something to get these watery worthies to admit

83

this much but they ought to demand about 10,000 times as much . . . These Temperance people are too modest.'

This was strong meat and bound to upset people like his father, a former Church Missionary Society secretary. In the June 1886 issue he had written an article 'The Right Reverend Creepy Crawleys', condemning the Church's weak proposals (hatched at a conference held in Crawley, Sussex) for reform of its pay structures and working practices. He exclaimed:

'The prelates do not think there is much amiss and do not want much done, except to the power and glory of bishops. Poor old gentlemen! There they sit, not seeing that their Church has alienated and disgusted the poor; that it is despised by the very land-owners and butter-men to whom it panders.'

Finally in August 1886 Charles republished in *The Christian Socialist* his jokey dole application to the Charity Organisation Committee, as if completed by Jesus – *Addresses*: Egypt in early life, Nazareth etc. *Occupation* Ex- carpenter, vagrant preacher and socialist; *Assistance sought*: Board & Lodging during Preaching Tour; *Statement:* Applicant stated that he lived almost entirely upon alms and tramped about with a number of low fellows, who sometimes did odd jobs, fishing and the like; *Report:* Rt Revd Caiaphas and the Revd Pharisees and the Church-workers . . . all begged the Society not to help him in any way.'

The Christian Socialist was never more lively than with such caustic contributions. It was no surprise, therefore, that circulation figures fell back when the new editors of the paper, lacking Charles's imagination and journalistic flair, went off in new directions, featuring long, earnest articles on economic socialism by the American Laurence Gronlund. In September 1887, after nine months of heavy losses, the CSS sent the paper back into independence. Over the next few years new editors did manage to keep the paper going with good reporting of labour disputes like the Dock Strike, regular features on the Fabian Society and on new groups like the Christian Social Union but it eventually ran out of money and support in December 1891.

Charles was even more disappointed when, as happened in various other socialist groups, divisions sprang up in the Christian Socialist Society between personalities and over policy issues. Once he had given up his newspaper role, Charles watched in frustration as the Society agonised over its political programme and toned down its Christian principles. His friend Revd Philip Peach put it quite well: 'I do not look upon Christianity as merely an additional shovelful of coals in the engine-furnace of socialism.' Charles wrote to another friend in April 1887:

> 'Can you possibly come up to town for the CSS (annual general) meeting in May? The Philistines are seizing upon it and must be smitten hip and thigh . . . the *Christian Socialist* is dolefully dull and shrivelling in circulation. Howard (the ass) and Campbell insult Miss Guest and play the Jackape generally . . . These silly and malpert cocks are so desirous of crowing alone upon the small dunghill that they declare that none with any 'pretence of learning' are welcome in the Society. They are wholly guiltless of learning themselves but they must not be allowed to pose as the sample of the CSS sack, still less to lead. (Stopford) Brooke and (Henry) Shuttleworth will write for us, if we ask them by a big majority. Do come and help. It will be both fun and duty to rescue the poor Society.'

Unfortunately for Charles, Stopford Brooke was taken ill and unable to edit the paper and the Society blundered on. Charles himself was very busy that spring, not only with parish affairs but also with concern for his old friend Ronald Bayne. In May of the previous year Ronald had married Miss Jessie Cassels in Greenwich but she now lay mortally ill with puerperal fever, after giving birth to their baby daughter. Ronald was devastated and his Christian faith was badly shaken. In despair he wrote to Charles, who replied with a most tender letter, rekindling both his Christian faith in the hereafter and his important work in the real and present world. It is never easy to give help and advice in bereavement and Charles was writing to a friend and fellow priest, frankly, confidently and without false sentiment. Ronald no doubt appreciated this support and would raise his daughter on his own until he married again nine years later.

Charles did withdraw gradually from the CSS, writing in September 1887 to Miss Guest: 'I think these societies are of little use.' He had not given up hope completely, however, as he was prepared to travel to the Bristol branch of the CSS in December that

85

year to lecture and preach over four days. The truth is that Charles was not a student of economics nor was he much interested in policy detail and argument, tending towards the idea that 'those who do the work shall know the doctrine.' Furthermore he had no interest in the administration and mechanics of building and maintaining any organisation. What he did possess, however, was good vision, coupled with abilities as a great speaker and an acerbic and witty writer. So he was vital at the birth of the CSS but saw no role for himself in its meanderings later. He certainly learned lessons from the experience, which he would try to use subsequently. As for the Society, it picked up speed again in 1889-90 but eventually wound itself up in June 1892.

O—u

However, to return to his emotional life, Charles was brimming with confidence in the autumn of 1886 when he took up with Edith Nesbit. His newspaper was doing well at that time and his new Socialist group was as yet undivided; his first initiatives in Orlestone parish were underway; and the political climate generally was conducive to new ideas and possibilities. Edith, on the other hand, was on the rebound after her failed affair with Shaw but must have been an attractive figure. Charles would be only the first of several young men with whom she would have relationships. She was by then 28 years of age – tall, with her hair cut short in the new style and often dressed in flowing Liberty gowns rather than corseted dresses, smoking cigarettes from a long holder. She must have presented as a sophisticated and fun personality.

There is certainly a hint of infatuation in Charles's letters from the start. For example, he writes to Miss Guest on Jan 8th 1887: 'I have had a glorious respite lately sitting at the feet of our dear Mrs Bland, whose graceful and brave life and light have been an unspeakable solace and pleasure to me.' Edith and her children had visited Orlestone Rectory over the Christmas period and obviously had a wonderful time. Perhaps because of his vivid imagination and lively personality, Charles was always very good with children and probably began his story-telling career with Edith's children. She may even have learned something from his style, which put children as the protagonists in the story, facing dangers on their own with little adult help (see Chapter 13 for his 1892 Australian Faery Stories). He did not find it difficult to see beyond the mere appearance of the material world. He wrote to Edith later that year: 'Tell Bunny from me that I have heard a lot of horrible stories about trolls lately and if she comes to stay with me at Xmas, I will tell them to her.'

Edith Nesbit, who wrote and discussed poetry with Charles in the 1880s

The Blands had pet names for each other – 'Bunny' was Iris's name (then aged 6); Alice Hoatson was 'Mouse'; Edith and Hubert were interchangeably 'Cat'. So it's no surprise that Charles devised his own pet name for Edith, which was 'Finch'. Because of their shared love of poetry, Charles was referring to Anne Finch, the Countess of Winchilsea (1661-1720), one of England's first published female poets. Because Edith was prone to 'perpetual colds', Charles would commence his letters to her with a little joke 'Dear coldfinch'. Another nickname he developed with her was that of 'The Matchless Orinda'. This was a reference to Katherine Philips, the so-called first Lesbian poet (1631-64), who wrote her coded poems under the pseudonym 'Orinda'. A new edition of her poems had been published in 1883 and was no doubt fresh in their minds.

For Edith was indeed a published poet herself now and growing in confidence. Between June 1885 and June 1889 she had a total of 13 poems published in the *'To-Day'* (monthly) periodical. Her book of poems *Lays and Legends* came out in the autumn of 1886. Charles wrote to Edith that he would review it in *Eastward Ho!* (a periodical to which he contributed occasionally). He also wrote a lengthy review of it in the December issue of *The Christian Socialist* – his last as editor. He forwarded a copy of the book to Lady Russell, whose favourable opinion he had sent on to Edith. She always craved good reviews.

Charles regularly inserted poems into *The Christian Socialist* and in the November 1886 issue he included another poem by Edith called The Socialist Marching Song, to be sung to the tune of The Red White and Blue. We must not underestimate the excitement of the period. They were times for anthems, as socialists felt that their time was coming – similar, in a way, to the folk songs of the CND marches or the hippy anthems of the 1960s. In her turn Edith encouraged Charles to write for other journals and between June 1886 and November 1888 he contributed one poem and five articles to the *'To-Day'* periodical.

Through several visits to Orlestone, Edith took a genuine interest in Charles's parish, learning about the various clubs and support for the poor. She used this experience to set up her own Christmas treats for the poor children of Deptford, which she instituted at Christmas 1888 in her own home, setting all her friends to work – making presents, cooking treats – for 20 children. Charles sent a tree up from Orlestone. Each year the numbers grew and the event had to be relocated to Deptford Board School for extra room.

In addition Edith was introduced to and came to love the Romney Marsh area of Kent that lay stretched out and visible from Orlestone. During one particular visit to Charles, they visited the nearby dilapidated church at Ruckinge. Edith wrote a poem about this church and it appeared in *Lays and Legends series 2* in 1889. After Hubert's death, Edith eventually settled at St Mary's Bay and is buried at St Mary-in-the-Marsh.

Charles regularly reminded her of the Orlestone woods that they often walked through together and of the flowers there in spring. In fact he often sent her snowdrops, daffodils and primroses up by train. These woods formed part of the ancient forest of the Kent Weald and are now Sites of Special Scientific Interest – altogether an amazing contrast for Charles after the oppression of the London slums. It was at this time in his life that he began to study botany seriously.

In return Charles talked poetry and journalism with Edith. They occasionally met in the Reading Room at the British Museum – an acceptable meeting place for men and women of culture to have assignations and where Edith and Shaw had often met the previous year. On January 11th 1887 Charles wrote to apologise for missing a rendez-vous: 'I thought today that I would seize an excuse and opportunity to have a day at the British Museum but I cannot – I find there is too much to be done.' He confessed that anyway his own poetry was of poor quality, though he could contribute better in prose.

One project in particular that they did work closely on together was the ghost story *Man-size in Marble*. Romney Marsh had been a centre for smuggling for centuries – wool from its sheep being sent abroad, while brandy and tobacco came in through Lydd and Rye, all avoiding government duty. The misty and mysterious marsh had fostered numerous legends and ghost stories, as told in the Ingoldsby Legends – books written in the 1840s by Revd Richard Barham, popular in Victorian times but not well-known today.

Man-size in Marble is set in the village of Brenzett, five miles south of Orlestone on the marsh. There today, in the chancel of the little church of St Eanswyth's, lie two marble statues – father and son, both named John Fagge, gentlemen of Rye, buried 1639 and 1646. Charles must have taken Edith to this church and they began to construct the story, imagining that these two figures were really smugglers of old, whose ill-gotten gains paid for their splendid resting place. Suffice to say, in the story these two ghosts rise up at Hallowe'en and cause trouble.

Certain elements of the story are definitely Charles's contributions – the narrator is a man who smokes a pipe (as he did); who confesses to never having had any money in his life (Charles was always broke); and has a housekeeper Mrs Dorman – there were three families of that name in Charles's parish and he was godfather to one boy Charles Dorman; and Mrs Dorman comes out with odd bits of folklore and clumsy phrases like 'Man-size in marble'. On January 14th 1887 Charles wrote to Edith: 'Such misty weather! I have been parishing steadily all the week and find mines of spiritual wealth and poetry in the sayings of old women.' Again a few days later he writes: 'If I can be of any use in stringing together homely sayings of the poor old women I visit or otherwise help in the work, you shall instruct me how.'

The description of the church in the story is one that could only have been given by an expert witness, someone who had a real feel for church interior decor and understood the meaning of a 'bier-balk' – the long path between church and cemetery. Further proof of Charles's mark lies in the phrase 'keep the pot simmering', to mean earning enough, and only enough, to provide for the next meal. He used it several times in letters to Edith that year. The Blands were also struggling to earn money at that time, before Shaw recommended them as editors for the *'To-Day'* newspaper and brought them into the wider world of journalism.

Charles's contribution to *Man-Size in Marble* was given freely and generously. On January 11th 1887 he wrote to Edith: 'No, you must not put my name to Man-Size in Marble, for I only contributed a little padding to it.' Much later on November 8th 1887 he wrote that he had received the proofs of the story in error: 'Here is Man-Size come to me, instead of thee. Very little misprint – but All Hallowe'en is the last day of October – All Hallows (or Saints) is Nov 1st and All Souls' Day Nov 2nd, a feast not kept in England since the Reformation. More is the pity.' These last distinctions were pertinent to the storyline.

It does not much matter that Charles's efforts were not acknowledged when the story was eventually published in *Grim Tales* (1893). It is not exactly a literary gem but it represented for him a very pleasant partnership with a lady whom he much admired, indeed revered. Their relationship may have faded as Edith acquired other admirers, but she kept in touch. When she eventually was converted to Catholicism and baptised, she asked Charles to stand as her godfather.

8

St Mary's Orlestone

Charles, aged nearly 27, left Shoreditch in April 1886 to take up the post of Rector of St Mary the Virgin, Orlestone in Kent. He replaced Revd Philip Peach, a man of similar age and background (born 1858 Bath). Philip had served for less than a year, during which time he had got married. His wife Rose preferred to deliver their first child back in Somerset, so he resigned and took a post at Pawlett near Bridgwater.

The previous incumbent to Philip had been Revd George Sarson, a fellow socialist in his 30's. Like Charles, Sarson had left a curacy in London because of ill health and he was at Orlestone for seven years, before moving on with his wife and six children to a better living at Holy Trinity Dover. The truth is that Orlestone was a poor living – just £151 per year, albeit with a large house thrown in. It was a backwater – a tiny medieval church (capacity just 100) serving a population of 443 people (1891 census). But at least Charles was now running his own show. He was no longer a curate working as a helper to the vicar in charge.

George Sarson was a hard act to follow. The son of a Leicester grocer, he had not followed his older brothers into the family business, but instead won a place at St Catharine's College, Cambridge. He was a curate, first at Holy Trinity Westminster and then at St Martin-in-the-Fields (1874-78). It was there that he joined the Junior Clergy Society and met Thomas Hancock and John Elliotson Symes. All three were radical young priests and members of the recently formed Guild of St Matthew under the leadership of Revd Stewart Headlam. Perhaps because of his modest background, Sarson was very much aware of the class prejudices within an Established Church and of the obstacles to advancement for certain men. For example, he called for an end to the system of patronage, whereby private individuals, trustees and even Oxbridge colleges owned the right (called an advowson) to make their own choice of clergyman to present to the relevant bishop for approval. It was argued that the patronage system at least kept many clergy appointments out of the centralising hands of bishops and made for a diverse constituency of interests, but the converse of this argument was that some patrons either exercised a certain nepotism ('the old school tie' syndrome) or were absentees and took little interest in their parishes; worse, a few patrons were interfering and even maverick in the exercise of their responsibilities. Relationships between Hall and Vicarage could sometimes be strained.

This was to be the case for Charles at Orlestone, where the patron was a Mr Roderic Oliver, of Oliver & Lyall Solicitors, 52 Cornhill EC3. He and his older brother Edmund had houses in the Regent's Park and Kensington areas respectively, as well as a farm and property in Orlestone itself. Their father had been a solicitor before them and they had both received a good education with an appreciation of arts and literature and a liberal philosophy to boot. George Sarson had rubbed along well enough with the Olivers, despite his tirades against patronage. He had married a doctor's daughter, Mary Symes, sister of his friend John Elliotson Symes, and she was always a gracious hostess, raising a happy brood of six children. George and Mary (always called Minnie by her friends) stayed friends with Charles for years afterwards but Charles himself was to have trouble with the Olivers, once he began to criticise their paternalistic rule in the village.

Another bone of contention was to be Charles's lurch towards Catholicism. George Sarson had made Baptism and Holy Communion the focal points of his ministry. These rituals are the great levellers, reminding us of the equal worth of every human being, at the font and at the altar rail. Charles was happy to continue this style of ministry and in fact increase the ritualism. His shift to a High Church style was apparently quite sudden. It is said that Charles left the village one day wearing his corduroy suit with red tie and sporting his usual brown beard but returned a few days later, clean-shaven with lawn (fine linen) collar in place and clutching a silver pyx containing the consecrated bread for the visited sick to receive at mass.

On 17th May 1886 he wrote to his family friend Miss Sophy Pedder back in Clevedon to thank her for her birthday wishes to him:

'I know you will not cease to love me, wherever the whirl of the time stream takes me, which I think may be to Rome, because Rome calls on men to give up all and follow her and when you

92

do follow her, she knows how to use your wits and strength whereas this wretched, superstitious proud bourgeois Church is all in confusion.'

A fortnight later he wrote for advice to Cardinal John Newman, who had converted to Catholicism 40 years previously and who, curiously enough, had known Charles when he was a boy back in Edgbaston. Newman wrote back with the careful advice that Charles should 'know more of the doctrines and usages of the Catholic Religion before taking the step of professing it'. Charles took this advice and stayed within the Church of England for the rest of his life, though he may have nudged others towards Rome – Hubert Bland, for example, became a Roman Catholic in 1900 and Edith not long afterwards.

For the rest of the year 1886, despite any misgivings the Olivers may have had over Charles's style, they could admire both his stimulating preaching and tremendous energy in the parish. His newspaper was doing well and he was often invited to lecture and speak outside the parish. However, he did sometimes feel depressed and isolated. By Christmas he'd begun his friendship with Edith Nesbit and the warmth of his letters to her, often decorated with little cartoons and sketches, suggest a lost soul searching for a kindred spirit. He was beset too with certain domestic problems, running a large rectory with a difficult housekeeper and no money. The editorship of *The Christian Socialist* was unpaid and his stipend inadequate.

Sometimes he was terribly busy, dividing his time between the two halves of his parish – Orlestone village (up the hill where the church was situated: population 191) and Ham Street village (down the hill where the new train station was built: population 252). He had to familiarise himself with a different workforce from his London parishes. Here the majority of the male workforce (84 out of a total of 130) worked directly on the land – 5 farmers employing 65 labourers, 4 shepherds and 10 others – while many other men were in related services (e.g. 3 blacksmiths, 5 each carpenters/wheelwrights, 3 saddlers, 3 grooms). Six men worked on the railways, however, and there were a few small tradesmen (2 bakers, 3 dealers, 2 grocers, 2 coalmen, 1 butcher, 1 publican and 1 confectioner) plus sundry others. The confectioner had a good trade because 46% of the population was under 20 years of age and you could buy a lot of sweets for a farthing!

What made life difficult for many families was that there was so little work for the women to do to supplement the meagre wages of the labourers. Perhaps in the summer there would be seasonal work – fruit-picking or hopping – but the regular female workforce was just 30 in number: 22 in domestic service of some kind, 3 at the Post Office, 2 governesses plus 3 teachers working with Mr Harold Bryen, headteacher at the primary school, which catered for 108 children. Charles visited the school regularly to give religious instruction. There was incidentally a Wesleyan minister in Ham Street but there was probably not much co-operation there. Charles wrote to Edith Nesbit in May 1887:

> 'The choir is doing grandly and the dissenters sadly – which is well. We are having a long discussion as to whether Mr Dawson Watson (Wesleyan) should be allowed to preach in the church. I would rather have Mrs Besant but if the parishioners wish it, I will have sultanas (*muslims*) to preach but especially agnostics and Jesuits. We are to have grand doings on Ascension Day – Church, Club, Dinner, Sports, Dances, Merry-go-rounds etc.'

Charles was never fearful of rival ministries and doctrines! He was now busy several evenings a week with the various parish clubs. In October 1887 he wrote again to Edith:

> 'Dear Lady, Miss Guest has just been staying with me. She talked a good deal about you: you are a favourite of hers but she does not read your poetry because it is too melancholy. The Maternity Society has had another row and the godly matrons are at scissors drawn with one another, and full of humbug too. All the club are draught-tournamenting for prizes and I am getting up a chrysanthemum show. Everything is in full swing. PS I will not send my love to the Mouse (i.e. Alice Hoatson) until it answers all the letters it owes me for.'

There were problems and moments of doubt too. In June 1887 he had written to Edith:

> 'Yesterday I went to the police courts to hear the issue of a headbreaking row in the parish. Three young men got mulct (*fined*) and to save them from prison I offered to pay the £5 fine and let them repay me by instalments. They jumped at the offer in court; went out and never said "thank you" and now

boast that they will never pay a *** penny of it. This not only hugely inconveniences me but it makes one feel all hopeless about these fellows . . . all the rest of the Orlestone news is sad and dispiriting.'

On October 4th, however, he joyfully wrote again to Edith:

'Dear Donna, Jack Harden has repaid me his fine (£4 and that will keep us for a week). Hurrah! He is much the better man for it and I the richer. If the others pay up, I shall go to Clevedon for a holiday. I have not been there since January.'

His mood swings were matched by the variable state of his physical health in 1887. His chronic asthma was still dogging him as well as occasional bouts of marsh fever. But he was determined to get out and about and it was during this summer that he took up gardening. Although he had actually loved London life, its bustle and energy, Charles was not immune to the fashionable 'back to the land' ideas of the time. Just as the recent collapse in agriculture had driven yet more labourers off the land into urban industry or emigration, so paradoxically a rural nostalgia set in among the middle class, hankering for a simpler, more honest lifestyle, where manual labour and old crafts were seen as a good alternative to machinery and the office desk. The working class, on the other hand, had little enthusiasm for a return to the land with its associations of poverty. But maybe Charles was just trying to learn new skills from his parishioners and better understand their lives.

Certainly the widespread and patronising image of 'Hodge', the countryman with mud on his boots and straw in his brain, needed improvement. Thomas Hardy's Wessex novels of the 1870s and 1880s at least peopled his imaginary landscape with characters of substance; and Charles would probably have just read Edward Carpenter's book *England's Ideal* (1887), which saw work on the land as a kind of salvation and even outlined a plan and budget for those wishing to drop out of society. Charles had first met Carpenter at a Fabian meeting in January 1886, when the latter read a paper entitled 'Private Property'. In this talk he made reference to how he had used an inheritance in 1882 to buy a small market garden at Millthorpe near Sheffield (three fields, a stream and a wood) and run it successfully with a few friends. The modern idea of self-sufficiency thus has deep roots, as does the notion of the rural retreat – the wealthy had no trouble then buying a second home in a depopulated countryside. Charles wrote of just such a visit to friends near Tunbridge Wells in a letter to Edith in October:

'My dear Lady Orinda,

Such a pleasant vegetarian time at Paddock Wood with walks and drives among the thick wooded hills, a rough and tumble life in a creeper-ed cottage near a lake! . . . PS Give a kiss to my bull pup Godson and kindly remembrances to all about you and accept the homage of   Yours ever Charles Marson.'

Whatever quaint ideas may or may not have been in his head, Charles set about planning a garden. Encouraged by Edith, he planted several mixed beds but made a feature of his roses that he would send to her from time to time. In return she sent him lots of sunflowers. He doesn't mention growing vegetables but he kept a wild garden and in later years lectured on the botany of wildflowers. In May he acquired a she-goat, a dog called Luke, some piglets and several rabbits.

As another year at Orlestone drew to a close in December 1887, he could look back on new friendships and new hobbies – as well as gardening he had taken up astronomy with Leonard Dorman, one of his young parishioners. He had sent stories and poems to the Blands for them to use (or not) in their takeover of the 'To-Day' periodical. He had muddled along with the Olivers and, although he had not visited his parents in Clevedon much during the year, relationships there were quite restored. In fact his father had confided in him back in March over a family scandal brought on by his son Harry forging a letter to obtain money under false pretences. Harry, still only 21, had joined the Army but, finding himself short of money, posed as his younger brother Frank in making application for a loan. The whole affair looked bad for a clergyman's son, but his father placed everything in the hands of the Olivers' firm of solicitors and all was eventually resolved. Harry was promptly posted abroad with the Army to India, chastened but forgiven by his father.

However, the following year (1888) would not go so well for Charles. First his younger sister Edith died in April in Bristol Hospital, aged only 26 and then his letters to his confidante Edith Nesbit become less regular. There's no sign of a 'break', and they kept in touch for several years, but the ardour clearly faded. As regards his parish, the seeds of division had been there for some time. Charles had previously written to his friend Ernest Beach, lay worker at St Agatha's:

> 'My heart aches and burns here at the degradation of village life. These poor folk of mine are swinking (*toiling*) and sweating to produce £1,500 a year for one person and similar sums for others, and their own children go short and are half-clad, and they none of them have time to read, think, dance, play music or games. They are mere mill horses; and all they do – can do – to amuse themselves is sotting and fornication. Yet these are men and women made in the image of God, and co-heirs with all of his children of the earth and the fullness thereof . . . they are so tied down that they do not even know what Liberty is. How can we help them?'

Charles's writings and sermons had also reached the ears of his bishop, Edward Parry, the Bishop of Dover. Parry was then aged 57 and clearly a conservative, who disliked Charles's socialistic views. He wrote to Charles in March 1887: 'The natural fruit of "socialistic tendencies" is clearly visible on the Continent . . . I earnestly pray that our Church, in our own schools and elsewhere, may use both hands to stem this mischievous current.'

However, the real stumbling block was to be the relationship with the farm bailiff, Mr Albert Weller, a man twenty years older than Charles. As the landowner's agent, the farm bailiff's job was to ensure that the tenant farmers were running their farms properly and paying their rent on time. In a small village he would get to hear of any complaints of bad management and could see the quality of husbandry exercised by the farmer and his labourers. He would also know about the various tied cottages belonging to the landowner and the families living in them. The usual practice was that the vicar, who visited families and learned of their needs, could intercede on their behalf to request that the landowner might authorise improvements in pay or conditions on his farms. The bailiff would then carry out any instructions. This system had gone on for years with the Olivers showing kindly but paternalistic interest in their little empire but it is likely that Charles shared his objections with the 'downtrodden tenants' and the flustered bailiff communicated this to the Olivers. The friction between Charles and bailiff Weller increased over the summer. Weller was born in nearby Tenterden, the son of a basketmaker, and had moved to Orlestone twenty years previously, working his way up as a carpenter and farmworker till promotion beckoned. He wasn't going to be dislodged by an incomer and his loyalty to the Olivers over many years was not in question. By October 10th 1888 Charles was writing to his father:

'The Olivers are seldom down here and chiefly see local matters through the eyes of their steward. This man leads them by the nose and I fear is a self-seeking and even swindling fellow. They will not hear a word breathed against him . . . this steward takes alternate fits of licking my shoes hard and backbiting me with equal vigour and he may have worked upon the Olivers not to ask me to stay on – I know not.'

His three-year contract would need renewing in March 1889 and yet again Charles was thinking of moving on. It had not been a great year for him and many of his plans had not worked out. Back in January he had written an unlikely letter to the Archbishop of Canterbury, requesting that dispensation be given for a fellow Fabian – Hugh Holmes Gore – then a 24-year-old solicitor in Bristol, to be ordained as a deacon to help Charles in his work at Orlestone. This sounds like team-building in the Barnett style, but the trouble was that Gore did not have a university degree and that was an absolute requirement for a clerk in holy orders. Even today the Church of England requires at least two years of training for most ordinands. Charles wrote impatiently to the Archbishop:

'it would be a great help to me in a rapidly enlarging circle of work in which I have no helper . . . the isolation and hopelessly inactive state of the church in this district make it impossible for me to stay here unless I get help . . . the Patrons pay £150 a year which I propose to share with a brother priest . . . we propose to start a monastic community here in Orlestone of strictly Anglican confession, a community to be gathered out of the Christian Socialist ranks.'

This was a pretty hippie idea that was never going to win friends in high places, although curiously the idea of a 'modern' monastic order had been first suggested by Westcott at Harrow in 1868 and was to be implemented by Charles Gore in Oxford in 1891 just three years after Charles's letter. Charles wanted and needed a bigger project, more suited to his considerable powers but this was neither

98

the time nor the place. Rather than arranging pastoral support for a fellow priest clearly under stress, the Archbishop replied through his chaplain to scotch any idea of ordination without a degree and simply enclosed a minimum standards pamphlet. Charles replied curtly to the chaplain: 'I need not trouble his Grace any further in the matter and only regret that I wrote at all.' In fact he did send off a parting shot to the Archbishop to the effect that he was sad that 'Mr Gore has not the hallmark of respectability. The English Church does not thrive in these parts as well as she did in the Middle Ages when not half her priests were University men.' He didn't mince his words, as usual, and would return to the theme of ordination training in a powerful and witty pamphlet called 'And Ard' in 1904, which caused quite a stir.

In mid-July 1888, perhaps to get away from the village for a change, Charles travelled up to Cambridge to stay with a family friend from Clevedon, Elfrida Visger, who had recently married Nigel Pearce, classics tutor at the University. Pearce certainly knew Clotilda Bayne (Ronald's younger sister) who was now aged 22 and in her third year at Newnham College studying classics. Elfrida lived at Grantchester and had two young babies to look after. Charles and Clotilda became good friends of the young family. Charles spent a splendid week there, visiting libraries and listening to services at King's College chapel. After that, he went back to London for a one week trial at Shoreditch to see if he might fit in there in the future. He visited the workhouse and infirmary next to St Columba's church and preached at various services but thought he would clash with 'these brutal Guardians'. He wrote to Edith Nesbit in August about what he saw:

> 'I cannot convey to you the vistas of misery and horrors it opened up to me. Incurable diseases: the sweepings of human wreckage . . . I did the place diligently and spent hours in ward after ward but it gave me a series of nightmares. Some of the diseases seemed to destroy all personality.'

He ended the letter on a more cheerful note, however: 'Some children have just come to hear fairy stories, so I must not keep them waiting.'

However, family matters took a serious turn for the worse that autumn, when in September 1888 his mother Ann died after a long illness, aged 61. His father was devastated and fell back on the care of his two remaining daughters Annie and Grace. Charles got back just in time to say goodbye to his mother and was somewhat surprised that she was most affectionate towards him. The funeral at Clevedon was on September 22nd and Charles wrote to his old friends the Guests:

> 'My mother's wish was to have no flowers at her funeral – but all unrelieved gloom. So it was, dreadful and sternly unchristian to my thinking, but at the last, we found kind folk had ringed the inside of the grave with asters so the kinder thoughts prevailed at the last minute of all. I was deeply touched at this. The human love and kindlier faith which would not be kept out.'

In October and November Charles was not well at all with congestion on the lungs – his smoking would not have helped his asthma. So he referred his future to the Bishop of Dover and, not surprisingly, he released him to look for another clerical post early in the New Year. Charles wrote to his old friend Robert Chalmers: 'My embarrassed affairs are troubling me somewhat. You know I always live upon my income to the last shilling. My mother's death, my own illness and a few such leakages have made a mess of my accounts.' He goes on that he had placed an advert in The Church Times but if nothing came of it, he would try newspaper work. His father was naturally anxious about the future and wondered if Charles had quarrelled needlessly or resigned on a whim but Charles assured him that the move was what he wanted and apologised for worrying his father so soon after his mother's passing. The opportunity of going to Queensland had come up and he thought he might go out with his brother Frank who, like himself, suffered from asthma. Frank had just turned 19 and was enrolled at Emmanuel College Cambridge but could interrupt his studies without forfeit and even study for a time in Australia. Charles clarified the situation to his father:

> 'I am willing to go out next April and to take Frank with me, if you like to take a passage for him. I will board and lodge and clothe him for a year at least; and send him back at my own expense. When out there, if Frank's health improved, he could

100

become anything he wished. There are medical schools in the south . . . The thing that I most hate about the plan is to leave you, dearest of Fathers, in your trouble and new loneliness.'

Finally in February 1889 it was decided that Charles would go not to Queensland but to Adelaide in South Australia. He sold some of his books and furniture to his old friend Robert Chalmers and removed the rest of his goods to Clevedon. His replacement at Orlestone was to be his old college friend Ronald Bayne. When he reflected on his three years there, Charles felt he had enjoyed mixed success. He had wanted to make a bigger impact but in a letter to his friend Ernest Beach, he expressed not a tone of compromise but a more mature understanding: 'We (parsons) can rarely see any result for what we do but this seeming solid material world rests upon and is ruled by a thought world; and if we can get any right thought planted, it will grow and grow until it takes material shape perhaps years hence.'

Charles had three months to wait before departure and it was during this time that he visited and came to an understanding with Ronald Bayne's sister Clotilda. They became engaged on April 18th 1889 and this momentous twist of events took everyone by surprise. There are no letters of their courtship unfortunately but they had known each other for the best part of ten years. Was she the soulmate that he clearly needed?

9

The Bayne of My Life

Clotilda (or Chloe as she was called by family and friends) Bayne was twenty-three and a half years of age when she became engaged to Charles. He was nearly thirty. He wrote to his family friend Miss Sophy Pedder on April 26th 1889: 'I am mated to the holiest and sweetest of women – just my contrary in every way is Chloe B.A.' Chloe was near to completing her studies at Newnham College, Cambridge, although that University was to hold out against awarding degrees to women until 1948. She was a very intelligent and promising young woman – and her friends were slightly surprised at her choice of fiancé. She had started at Newnham as a Winkworth Scholar in 1885, studying classics – Latin and Greek were to be a shared pleasure for the young couple, as Charles also loved the language and literature of the classical world. But whereas he was tall, of striking (rather than handsome) appearance and with a charismatic outgoing personality, utterly confident of his own opinions, she was diminutive and pretty, introspective and somewhat highly strung. She could be feisty at times, for she was of proud Scottish stock and had grown up holding her own against three older brothers, the oldest of whom was Ronald. Her older sister Isabella 'Janie' was not academic and stayed clear of intellectual arguments with the boys!

Ronald in particular knew Charles well from their time together at Oxford and in Whitechapel and, although the Bayne family had all enjoyed his company over many years, Ronald was not altogether sure that Charles was the right choice of husband for his younger sister. Indeed Ronald was even now preparing to leave his curacy at Greenwich to take over from Charles at Orlestone and he wondered what sort of mess he might be inheriting there. But it was springtime in Cambridge and the young couple had obviously hit it off in the time they had spent together. Chloe had thoroughly enjoyed her time at Newnham and stayed in touch with several friends for years to come. There were 47 students in her year and she was particular friends with Philippa Garrett Fawcett, the outstanding mathematics student of her day.

Girton College was the first women's college in Cambridge (1869) but Newnham was close behind, having been started by Anne Clough in 1871 with just five students. With the support of Henry Sidgwick, Professor of Philosophy at Trinity College, accommodation buildings had been quickly designed and built (Old Hall with 67 rooms 1875; Sidgwick Hall 63 rooms 1880; and Clough Hall 70 rooms 1887). So Chloe could feel the excitement of her college growing around her – for example, she was there to see the Princess of Wales officially open Clough Hall during her second year. That kind of bonding with both your peers and your seniors, as you grow together, would have been a deep one.

Newnham was known, in its early years at least, as a place that encouraged and developed political awareness among its students. There were debates on the social issues of the day – the Irish question, unemployment, House of Lords reform, free education – and even a mock Parliament with voting on 'bills'. Perhaps it was this exposure to 'social questions' that drew Chloe towards Charles's greater experience in these areas. Perhaps she was also impressed with Charles's more robust faith. It is interesting that, in large part because of Henry Sidgwick's own agnosticism, no chapel was ever built at Newnham. From an early age Chloe had had doubts about her faith, though brother Ronald had written many letters to her to encourage her away from 'backsliding'.

Newnham friends in 1889: Left to Right: Philippa Fawcett, Chloe, Constance Crommelin and Dora Pease

103

For his part, Charles found he had much in common with Chloe's father Peter Bayne (1830-96). Peter was born in Fodderty near Dingwall in the Scottish Highlands, son of a minister Charles Bayne and his wife Isabella Jane Duguid. He graduated from Marischal College Aberdeen and initially worked as a classics master at Merchiston Castle Academy in Edinburgh. He intended to take holy orders but had to abandon his theological classes when his asthma and respiratory illnesses made this idea impractical. So he turned instead to journalism and literary work as a profession. He became friends with Hugh Miller (born 1802), who was at the peak of his powers as a geologist, writer and church reformer. Miller was a native of Cromarty, only 17 miles from Fodderty, but had moved to Edinburgh to edit *The Witness* newspaper, an evangelical Christian periodical. Peter Bayne took over the editorship of the paper upon Miller's tragic death by suicide in 1856 and went on to produce *The Life and Letters of Hugh Miller* in 1871 in his memory.

During a visit to Germany in 1858 Peter Bayne met and married Klothilde Dorothy Gerwien, a General's daughter from Fürstenwalde near Berlin. Their first son Ronald was born in Edinburgh in 1859 but the following year Peter was persuaded to move to London as editor of a new weekly newspaper called *The Dial*. The paper was a financial failure and Peter lost all his own property in the venture. Burdened with debts, he became editor of the *Weekly Review*, the paper of the English Presbyterian church, from 1862-5 and then leader writer for the *Christian World*. He contributed articles and reviews to a wide range of other periodicals. It is no surprise that Peter should see Charles in a good light – as another journalist, earnest churchman and reformer, and a fellow asthmatic into the bargain.

After their initial years in Brixton, the Bayne family moved to Harlington (then a very rural area, now squashed between the M4 and Heathrow Airport). However, Peter Bayne's financial difficulties were then compounded by the death of his wife Klothilde in childbirth, following Chloe's birth in December 1865. Any child, upon learning that at their birth they lived but their mother died, must be affected. Klothilde's death certificate (Dec 12 1865) records the cause of death as 'Exhaustion after confinement'.

Chloe was quickly bonded with a new mother, however, when Peter married Anna Katherine Mayo just a few years later in 1869.

104

Anna, only 25, was considerably younger than her husband but took on the care of his five children with an energy and warmth that overwhelmed them all. She was financially provided for, which must have eased Peter's money worries. Her father, Herbert Mayo, was a wealthy colonial broker, born in the City of London but resident for many years in Hampstead. As a child, Chloe visited her step-grandfather often and was thoroughly spoiled by his other three daughters Aunts Mary, Agnes and Constance. Chloe's brothers Ronald and Charles may have benefited from easier family funds, as they both attended private school before matriculating at the same time in 1878 at University College Oxford.

In the 1881 census the Baynes are in Willesden but must then have moved to South London where in July 1882, unexpectedly, Anna died, aged only 37. Chloe was sixteen at the time and just settling into her new school Clapham High School for Girls. It was there that she met Philippa Fawcett, two and a half years her junior. Philippa was a talented girl but also a very modest, quiet and unassuming person. Perhaps she took it upon herself to befriend Chloe, a new arrival at the school.

The Bayne family 1887: L to R (Standing) Peter, Chloe, William, Charles Marson; (L to R Seated) Marie, Ronald with Jessie, Janie

Philippa's parents were the formidable Henry and Millicent Fawcett, who divided their time between their Cambridge house and their London home at 51 The Lawn, Lambeth. Probably Philippa acquired her sensitive outlook through her support for her father, who had been blinded in a shooting accident when he was 25, not long after he graduated from Cambridge. She would talk with him and read to him at the end of a busy day, because he was in no way daunted by his handicap. He became a Professor of Economics at Cambridge and was also elected as an MP. In 1880 he was appointed Postmaster General by Gladstone. With his wife Millicent, he had also put his weight behind the development of Newnham College. Furthermore the Fawcetts' drawing room in Cambridge was the meeting place for the supporters of women's vote in Cambridge – the National Society for Women's Suffrage had been recently founded in 1872. In years to come Millicent would lead the Women's Suffragist movement.

Thus the young Philippa Fawcett had busy parents who were often away, so it was agreed in the end that she should stay as a paying guest with her new friend Chloe in a boarding house in Worcester Park run by the Miss Wilsons. Peter Bayne, newly widowed, obviously thought this was the best arrangement for Chloe, even though his two oldest boys, Ronald and Charles, were both away at Oxford and the next boy William had gone to be an engineering apprentice in Govan, Glasgow. Chloe's older sister Isabella Jane remained at home, however, to look after her father.

This practical arrangement continued even when Peter was married for the third time in October 1883 to Marie Meuret, the daughter of a French tailor. Marie was 28 and had for a time been a governess to a family in Wiltshire. Chloe now had the opportunity to develop her French with her new step-mother. She then spent much of 1884 with her Berlin relatives, polishing her German, before switching to classics at Newnham. Philippa's strength, on the other hand, was not so much in languages as in mathematics. She showed such potential that her parents paid for a private tutor for her and she proceeded to Newnham with a scholarship in 1887.

It is difficult to speculate as to what Chloe's plans were, before Charles swept her away that April in 1889. Her father Peter was 59 and nearing retirement, with a wife and one daughter already to support, so Chloe must have been considering an independent life –

106

teaching or some such paid work. Her options were limited – of the 720 students who attended Newnham between 1871 and 1893, 155 married (22%) and 374 (52%) went into teaching.

Another possibility was social work. At Easter 1887 Henrietta Barnett had read a paper at Newnham College on Toynbee Hall, and a Women's University Association was formed to carry out 'work in the poorer districts of London'. Links were made with the Children's Country Holiday Fund and other agencies that Charles knew so well. However, Chloe had made a different decision and was now engaged to a man who had taken a two-year curacy in far off Adelaide. Indeed Charles was to set sail on May 10th, with his brother Frank but without her, for it was agreed she should take her time to prepare for this next step.

$$\vphantom{x}$$

The last time Charles contracted an engagement (with Lady Agatha Russell), it had not stood the test of separation. So Charles must have been somewhat unsure of the future, as he stood on the second-class deck of the RMS Austral (a sail boat boosted with steam engines), pulling out of Southampton Dock on that Friday morning. He wrote at once to Chloe: 'Now I have a vision to carry over the seas and the hopes of a beautiful future.' He was content with his berth but upset that the purser had charged him over £7 (£400 in today's money) for the excess weight of books he had stowed in the hold. However, one friend Mrs Elfrida Pearce had given him a 'splendid box of games' and 'kind Miss Pedder has sent me a nosebag of books' to while away the time during his six-week trip.

Indeed in a letter to Chloe dated May 14th 1889, Charles mentions that he'd already begun to read a short story *The Merry Men* by Robert Louis Stevenson (ironically about shipwrecks) as well as Henry Morley's *The Cavalier Ballads and Songs of 1642-84*. This book, printed in 1863, reproduced the words of over 100 songs from the Stuart period, drawn from 75 sources and collections. These reference works included Thomas D'Urfey's *Pills to Purge Melancholy* (1720); Thomas Percy's *Reliques of Ancient English Poetry* (1765); Joseph Ritson's *Ancient Songs* (1792); and the *Roxburghe Ballads* (originally collected by Robert Harley, Earl of Oxford around 1710 but reprinted by John Collier in 1847); as well as works by Samuel Pepys and John Playford.

Nowadays a 'ballad' means a slow sentimental love-song but in previous centuries a 'ballad' was a particular form of verse, often a story, and sometimes set to music, for example, by wandering minstrels. There were ballads about Robin Hood from as early as the end of the fourteenth century. Later topics would include the supernatural (ghosts and goblins), tragic and comic themes, love stories, political events, even disasters at sea. From the mid-17th century onwards the printing on single sheets of cheap paper (called 'broadsides') spread these ballads (usually words only) in huge numbers throughout the country from city market stalls to country fairs.

By the mid-19th century ballads had acquired a poor reputation among the educated elite – even sympathetic authors like Professor Child or Revd Baring-Gould, who collected and studied the genre, felt that the ballad sheets had debased or corrupted older and finer verse forms. The fact that Charles was already steeping himself in this area of poetry as early as 1889 – learning of its content, history and scholarship – is of great significance to his future partnership with Cecil Sharp, the folk collector, who was at this time solely focused on classical music. In fact Charles felt confident enough to lecture on 'Ballads' during his stay in Australia and later wrote articles for magazines like *The Commonwealth.*

Of course, some of these early ballads were of a racy, indeed bawdy nature. So what is equally important is Charles's next statement in that May 14th letter to Chloe (re Morley's Cavalier Ballads): 'They are stupidly bowdlerised. How editors do despise poor women! Your frail hold upon eternal verities would be relaxed at once, they think, if some coarse or lewd lines met your eyes.' This confirms that Charles was no prude and later accusations against him as a censorious editor of folk lyrics look ill-founded.

Charles continues his stream of long letters – not too gushing in tone but with regular terms of endearment as 'Goodbye my true love, a thousand kisses and oceans of love to thee and all the blessings of a man you make very happy . . . My dearest sweetheart, we have been having as delicious a day or two as I have ever expected, apart from the fact that my white mouse was not here . . .' He was, however, much disturbed to see the state of his brother up close.

Frank, now almost 20, had been admitted to Emmanuel College Cambridge over a year ago with the hopes of pursuing a medical training but ill-health had disrupted his studies. He was a fellow asthmatic like Charles but had been a sickly child for years, suffering especially with stomach ailments.

A lot of Victorian patent medicines – from pain relief (e.g. to treat menstrual cramps) to diarrhoea treatment, even childhood remedies like Godfrey's cordial for colic or anti-tussives for croup and whooping cough – contained opium tinctures like laudanum, which was 10% opium and 1% morphine. The side effects of these drugs were not well understood and controls were not put in place till the twentieth century. It is no surprise that Frank gradually became addicted to opium. Charles writes in that same letter of May 10th 1889: '(Frank) took some of his filthy drugs which upset him . . . he looks grisly and his dark hair stands out against his skin.' He was to worry about his brother for years to come but at least, after a short spell of seasickness in the next day or so, Frank's health seemed to improve with the sun and sea air doing him good.

On May 11th Charles wrote again to Chloe, this time commenting on her brother: 'I am sorry Ronald has so come to blows. It is sad to leave my old chum like that but if he tries to prevent you coming to Australia, I shall never forgive him the attempt.' Charles had lost Agatha Russell partly through the meddling of her relatives, now he had to worry that Ronald might work on Chloe over the next few months to break her pledge to him. On May 16th he counters more criticism levelled at him by Chloe's family:

> 'They think that I am a changeable man and that we are very new to one another, do they? Dear Lassie, do not be troubled at folks' talk. Folk have loved truelier than the cynics would have us believe, under all suns and throughout all almanacs, and why not? I wish, instead of writing to you in a crowded, buzzing, yellow lighted saloon, I could sit on the deck with your head on my shoulders in the dying light, and play with your soft golden hair!'

The first stop for Charles was to be Gibraltar on May 16th 1889, where he disembarked and was immediately thrilled with the colour and noise of the place:

> 'Having posted our letters and bought some long cigars and a drink, we took an open sort of fly, covered with a white awning,

and gallop and slash! Away we spun through cursing crowds to call on Colonel Lloyd. We found him and his handsome girl Madge in the verandah, the air thick with heliotrope smell and the orange blossoms out on the trees. Below lay the deep blue sea and the eye was dazzled with the masses of scarlet geraniums. The very wild flowers are glorious here . . . We plunged into the motley crowd of the market and quay. Such brown and bright-eyed girls with brilliant colours and Moorish ornaments. I lost my heart – such as I have left – at every street corner. We went into shops and said "Quanto?" and immediately "E troppo! E troppo!" so that the price fell immediately. Dr Merrilees joined us there and we bought 1/- worth of oranges and lemons, a huge basket full. With cigarettes and tobacco and our lemons we made for the pier and got away a few minutes before sailing time.'

Back on ship, 'we had a general election and I was made Secretary of the Amusements Committee. I have to do most of the work I find. A concert, a dance, cricket match, sweepstakes, private theatricals, Heaven knows what are to be set on foot, something every day . . . We are looking forward to a long day in Naples, a whole Sunday. High Mass and the opera. I fancy myself among my organ-grinding relatives, larking about (*reference to his Italian forebears, the Gattis*).'

Life on Board the RMS Austral, photo courtesy of the State Library of Victoria

110

He continues:

'By the way, it is my birthday and dear Frank has given me my new grand pipe, a most lordly one! The ring has never been off my finger since you put it there. Well, my chuck, how art thou, I wonder. Perhaps I shall hear at Naples how my little wench is getting on at Cambridge among the old trees and quiet river! With Philippina (*Fawcett*) and Maria (*Mary Bateson*) and all the other blue-legged ones (*reference to the 'blue-stocking' stereotype*). Give my love to the Principal – that dear old gal – your loving pal and I hope she's wal! . . . My concert is all snugly arranged and bills printed by passenger Perrott, a white-faced, type-writing man. Two kind girls, Meikle and Morris, are the only two I can get to sing. It is fun to be secretary and one gets to know, and therefore like, a lot of folk. We have organised a ball for tomorrow night. I stayed up very late last night watching the moon on the seas. I have a lively habit of taking salt baths whenever I feel warm and that makes one lively at night. We have shower baths as well as tubs. You turn a screw and the Mediterranean pours upon your head. An idea has come into my brain "The Austral Gazette" with original compositions in prose and verse and satire. I mean to tackle it tomorrow. The typewriter man will print and the first number will be ready by next Wednesday. Ever your very loving sweetheart, Charles.'

Next stop Naples:

'After a hasty breakfast we were rowed in a boat by a cut-throat to the quay. We picked up a man Giuseppe to guide us and got two tickets for Pompeii and the train furnished us with much laughter. It wound through the base of glorious hills wreathed in cloud and standing most eerily above deep blue waters and grey white houses. Fig trees and poppies and large yellow daisies and hawkweed the chiefest vegetation . . . At last we alighted and got to a flight of stone steps. In we stalked and under a heavy old Roman arch into a narrow flagged street, with grooved gutters and a path on each side. Lo, we were in that strange pickled Roman town. How modern is one's first thought. Shop fronts with back rooms, the paint on the plaster, the ovens, doorways, just as they were in Nero's time. The altars still standing in the temple and images, carvings, book

111

cupboards, all quite new looking . . . We trod their pavements and saw their very names . . . In the museum we saw men and women. The old rings on their fingers, their teeth grinning out of green-grey lips, just as they died.'

Charles's vivid, visual mind and great skill with words have again sketched these events so quickly for Chloe that she can easily share his new experiences. He concludes his letter: 'In the (*Sunday*) evening we played whist to the fury of Scotch people, who glowered at us. At last a female rushed up and told me it was the Lord's Day and asked if I were not ashamed of myself. I said "Madam, I belong to the Church of England" and played out a splendid hand of trumps, so that she fell back, routed by nonchalance.'

Three days later the ship reached Port Said at the northern end of the Suez Canal. The canal had been completed twenty years previously in 1869 and was over 100 miles long, linking the Mediterranean with the Red Sea, the Gulf of Aden and eventually the Indian Ocean. On May 26th Charles mused on the vast deserts that stretched away either side of the canal: 'Our little jerry civilization looks so flimsy against the desert's dusty face. If the Pharoahs fared so badly at the hands of time, what shall we do?'

Once through the canal, the ship steamed into the Indian Ocean, heading for Colombo, and the daytime temperatures rose ever higher. On June 1st (three weeks into the trip) Charles writes:

'Dearest Chloe, since I last wrote we have had a spell of fierce heat. And now the Typhoon is upon us and such rain as I have never seen in my life. We are having a roll, which makes writing difficult. I have passed my week in bathing, reading and playing draughts with the head steward. This man is a skilful hand at it and we have some exciting games. Several people are dead – sunstroke and dysentery were the cause. I fear we may be put in quarantine in Colombo. The thing they most fear is a cyclone which would sink us in ten minutes, the sailors say.

Mrs Kinnaird has become a pal of mine. She sings me Volkslieder such as my Chuck likes too. Aye me! While I am stuffed to death in this sweat and sickness, you are perhaps in sight of may and chestnut blossom – are the roses out there? I can picture Orlestone in the fragrant spring rains and Cambridge alive with flower-boxes and foliages. With tenderest love, C.'

On June 4th he wrote again:

'Dearest of girls, When I realise the huge stretches of oceans and climate that divide us, and the huger stretches of thought, it seems a miracle surpassing belief that we should ever have got so far together as we have. I have never taken off your posy ring from my finger or your memory from my brain since we parted in dear shade-blest England. (*Here*) not a breath of air stirs at night and one lies in a sticky miserable mass, sleeping heavy, lethargic slumbers, then all day one feels dull and out of spirits . . . but my great female friends are the Convent Sisters of Mercy and I read ballads to them and hear Faery Stories from Ireland of the O'Donoghue and the Banshee and the Moss folk. Do not forget to give me any Orlestone news you get. I spent Sunday in thinking of everyone in the parish and hoping and praying they may grow in gracefulness of thought and act and body. My lasting love to thee dear white mouse and a kiss.'

After a short stop at Colombo for fresh provisions, the ship steamed on till, on June 20th, it reached Port Adelaide. Charles and Frank bade farewell to the remaining passengers sailing on to Sydney and boarded the tender that would take them to the jetty. There they were met by Canon French, who greeted them warmly and was very kind. Away they rattled to Adelaide by train.

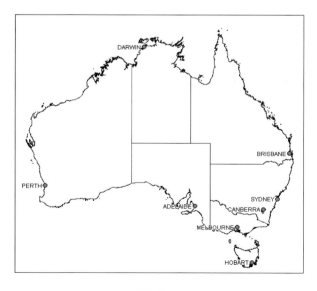

Meanwhile back in Cambridge, term was ending and Chloe was saying her goodbyes to her Newnham friends. She then spent some time in London with the Fawcetts at their new London home at 2 Gower Street. As soon as her brother Ronald was settled into his new house, the Rectory at Orlestone, Chloe moved her belongings there, so that she could help her sister Isabella Jane (always called Janie) look after Ronald's little girl Jessie, who was then aged two. With their support, Ronald would cope quite well as a single parent and he would not remarry for another seven years. He was really quite a different character to Charles and would not have ruffled any feathers in the new parish. At an interview conducted by one of Charles Booth's Poverty Survey team ten years later, Ronald is described as: 'of a delicate, gentle rather weak appearance . . . The impression that he gives is that he is smug, unpractical, un-businesslike, more a student and a recluse than a man of the world. Fit for no career but the church.' This sounds a bit harsh, but he at least kept his household together that autumn and winter, so that Chloe could pack and prepare for her trip to Australia.

In the meantime Charles's letters kept arriving . . .

10

Glenelg

Charles had written jokingly to his friend Robert Chalmers on February 19th 1889: 'I am off to Adelaide. My brother Frank is to come too and we start in May . . . Are there nightingales in Australia? Is there old China ware? Works of old poets in yellow vellum? A tear dilutes my ink and I can write no more, Yours under sentence of transportation, Charles.' Like many an emigrant, Charles had mixed feelings about his new venture. He had just turned thirty and had enjoyed some success in his career to date but also suffered some reverses. Perhaps Australia would be a fresh start for him, releasing him from the ties of a conservative church and a class-based society. Could this be the New Jerusalem? Yet he had heard that in some ways expatriates had not shed their English bad habits and mindset in the new country. Landgrabbing capitalists had moved in quickly to establish themselves and made it difficult and expensive for others to acquire land and property. The native aboriginal people had been supplanted, and his misgivings about missionaries were already in print and gone before him. So he was concerned that he might not be exactly welcomed with open arms on arrival.

However, his new boss Canon Samuel French, incumbent of St Peter's Glenelg since 1881, travelled up to Port Adelaide in the early morning of June 20th to meet the RMS Austral, as she discharged some passengers before steaming on to Melbourne. He greeted Charles and brother Frank warmly and escorted them by train into Adelaide itself and then on again by train for the seven miles journey south to Glenelg. The two men were installed in lodgings in Sussex Street:

> 'a house, one storey high with a zinc verandah four feet wide and doors of wire gauze. A grim Irish woman opened the door, shewed us into the room on the right and here we are. The room is 14ftx14x12 I should say. It is soon described. Two wicker chairs and a wicker sofa, a writing table, a round table and a wicker table, a fire, a hideous wallpaper . . . our bedroom

lies behind – two showy four poster beds. East of us lives L'Estrange who breeds cattle 1000 miles away and below him is our joint feeding room. But our lodgings are delightfully clean and we are fed three meals a day.'

It was, of course, winter-time there and cold at night. Charles wrote to Chloe that he felt homesick with warm summer memories of Orlestone, where she was now living with her brother Ronald. He jokingly nicknamed his lodgings the 'cold cowshed' by contrast. At least it was convenient for him, being very close to St Peter's Church in Torrens Square in the heart of the growing town. Charles took up his duties straightaway. He was given responsibility for occasional preaching and Sunday school work at St Peter's; for regular ministry at the Mission Church of St Jude's at Brighton two miles further south; and for developing work at the Sells Memorial Mission in Hastings Street in New Glenelg (new housing in the south of the town). In addition, as the only curate, he worked with a team of district visitors to make regular visits to parishioners. Of course, Charles was looking for action and went looking for problems in his usual zeal to help the 'Have-nots'. He would be curiously disappointed, for Glenelg was basically a prosperous town without a downtrodden poor and this initially threw him off balance in his early sermons and messages.

As a new arrival, Charles had a lot to learn and quickly. The town (population 3,000) had just celebrated its golden jubilee (50 years), and its second and third generation colonists were naturally proud of their achievements to date. It was at Glenelg that South Australia as a new colony was first proclaimed on December 28th 1836 and the city of Adelaide was surveyed and planned from that time. Whereas Sydney and Hobart had been started as penal colonies in 1788 and 1803, South Australia was a free settlement and showed determination from the start to be a place of religious equality, with no established church and no favoured parties. Indeed it was to be dubbed the 'Paradise of Dissent' and the first sermon ever preached in Glenelg was given by a Wesleyan Methodist preacher.

Many of the early settlers, given free passages, came from southern England, specifically Cornwall, Devon and Somerset where Methodism was strong. Neither church buildings nor paid clergy were necessary for the development of that sect, as local preachers would meet the people in their own houses. By the census of 1866 it

116

was reported that the various Methodist denominations (Wesleyans, Bible Christians and Primitive Methodists), if combined, formed 21.1% of the colony's population of 163,000 people. This pattern was true of Glenelg. Although the first Wesleyan chapel was constructed at a late date (1864), its newer chapel built in 1876 had a capacity for 350 people, with its Sunday school attracting 100 children. The Primitive Methodist chapel held a further 160 people.

Other significant competition as far as Charles was concerned were the Congregationalists who got their church up earlier in 1849, with a much grander building superseding it in 1880 under their longstanding pastor Revd Charles Manthorpe. In 1883 its capacity was put at 650. This church is now St Andrew's Uniting Church in Jetty Road. Finally with the influx of Irish immigrants in the 1850s, the Roman Catholic church was built to hold 100 people.

The Church of England, by comparison, was slow off the mark, erecting St Peter's Church in 1852 but then demolishing and rebuilding it (consecration1883) with a capacity of 600. It is substantially the same building today and it is of an impressively solid and pleasant design. It would have been full when Charles got up to deliver his first sermon. Parishioners came out of curiosity to hear the new man preach under the gaze of Canon French, who had been there for six years and would spend twelve years there in all.

And that was the problem. The parishioners were in their comfort zone and Charles delivered a series of challenging sermons that woke them up and caused a great stir. As early as August 29th 1889 (two months into his job) he wrote to Chloe: 'They say that my sermons are making a sensation . . . a fool named Munton proposes to prosecute me.' Again on September 13th 'I have had several clashings and letters of complaint to French about my sermons and sayings. Two have gone to the Bishop and cussing flows free. French is getting ruffled and alarmed. He jaws away in a nervous and even feminine manner. Some more are offended because of my speech in Adelaide about the Dock Labourers.' That speech was not about a local issue but about the London Dock Strike. The telegraph system (Morse code) linked Adelaide with Melbourne in 1858; with Sydney in 1867; and finally with London in 1872 via Darwin, Singapore and Bombay. This meant that news of the London Dock Strike, commenced on August 14th 1889, reached Charles within four days and this really excited him. He had seen for himself in Whitechapel

117

how dockers had suffered from casual, ill-paid work for many years, and their demand for 6d an hour ('the docker's tanner') was fully justified to his mind.

Furthermore he knew the strike leaders personally – he was actually present at the meeting that approved Tom Mann's Fabian membership in June 1886 and, as editor of the *Christian Socialist*, he had come across both John Burns and Ben Tillett. So Charles can be forgiven for sounding off on a subject dear to his heart. In fact Australian support for the London strike was absolutely crucial. By August 30th Tom Mann was running out of relief funds for the thousands of men now on strike and, despite a sympathetic press campaign and generous public support of nearly £12,000, the strike looked like collapsing until on that same day £250 was telegraphed by the Brisbane dockers. This was followed by £500 from the Sydney dockers and contributions from Adelaide and Hobart too. In total £30,000 was sent from Australia and after five weeks the employers caved in. By September 22nd the dockers' demands were largely met and, buoyed by their success, over 20,000 men immediately joined Tillett's 'Dock, Wharf, Riverside and General Labourers' Union'. This milestone in the British Labour Movement would have been welcomed by Charles miles away in Glenelg but possibly not by his parishioners, many of whom were businessmen unhappy with such developments.

'What a cocky individual! He only looks about 20', they must have thought, listening to his sermons. 'He's only been here a couple of months and he's telling us how to conduct our business.' They no doubt thought of themselves as responsible and respectable people. After all, their fathers had built this town and set its purpose. Although the long jetty erected in 1859 to receive the P&O liners bringing mail and light freight had not in the end made Glenelg into a working port – Port Adelaide won that battle – it had instead become a desirable seaside resort with eight well-furnished hotels by 1883. Men and women had separate bathing areas with a splendid array of bathing machines (wooden carts) that allowed you to change out of heavy Victorian clothes in due modesty. Then a horse would pull the cart and wheel you out into the sea, so you could tiptoe down steps and enjoy the Southern Ocean. Glenelg to this day is a seaside resort with high property prices and a weekend influx of thousands of city dwellers, who speed down the Anzac Highway or catch the electric tram from central Adelaide.

Glenelg beach on 'Founder's Day' holiday 1890s –
Photo courtesy of Holdfast Bay History Centre

What else had the City Fathers done for the town? By 1883 Glenelg boasted two public and nine private schools; of three miles of tarmac roads; of not one but two railway lines to Adelaide taking 1.2 million passengers per year (commuters as well as trippers); of a Gas Works in Osmond Terrace that supplied light; and of pipelines to the Adelaide Reservoir that had supplied clean water since 1875. There was a Literary Society, a Bank and Building Society, a post and telegraph office, a fire brigade, a yacht club, hot and cold seabaths. As regards crime, one commentator of the time stated that in early decades at least Glenelg had been a very secure and orderly place:

> 'Our immigrants were well-selected and many of them raised themselves to positions of comfort and not a few became wealthy and respected. Our laws against the admission of transportees were most firm. The working classes were industrious and provident and we had no poor amongst us. The people generally had plenty of work and good wages. The population as a whole was a religious one.'

However, this situation had somewhat changed, requiring the establishment of a permanent police station in 1864 under the

119

admirably named PC Badman. In December 1876 *The Register* newspaper reported one incident when 'Glenelg was visited by several cabloads of the most degraded of both sexes', proving that weekend drunkenness is not really a modern phenomenon!

But given the overall social benefits, what more could you ask for in a town? Well, of course, there always are some real problems. The typhoid outbreak of May 1884 that the local doctor, Dr Ferguson, reported and managed was a warning that the town's drainage system was inadequate. The Patawalonga Creek to the north remained a concern with its noxious smells. Ratepayers were reluctant to pay for the various schemes proposed and rather hoped health problems would just go away. Some drains were laid and a Dry Earth Closet system adopted by some householders, but a major deep drainage scheme was not undertaken till 1904.

The economic climate was changing also. The prosperous years of 1876 to 1884 had given way to a contraction in agriculture that was drawing the unemployed towards the city. The State of South Australia was now locked into a protectionist policy that imposed tariffs on incoming goods from Victoria and New South Wales. To a large extent Victoria had initiated this tariff war, when its Gold Rush petered out and it needed to rebuild its economy and redeploy its new workforce. But protectionism was stifling trade, so politicians and businessmen were already discussing dismantling this policy and even proposing the federation of Australia's six states, which eventually occurred in 1901.

This downturn in economic confidence was filtering through to the citizens of Glenelg in subtle ways. Their splendid new Institute, built in 1876, with a lecture hall, council chamber and library (membership 10/6d a year with 143 members in 1883) was by 1888 short of members and funds. The library stocked old literature, its clock was not lit at night in order to save gas and its debt stood at £3,000. It was actually closed for seven years between 1888 and 1895, while Charles was there.

All this background information perfectly explains the mindset of the parishioners, as they listened to Charles's sermons. They had 'made it' and were really resting on their laurels. He was saying how much more was to be done to achieve a fairer and more equal society in terms of free and better education, votes for all, tax and control of rampant capitalism and land ownership – in other words, Christian

120

Socialism. His parishioners wanted to be free to enjoy their hard-won gains, while he wanted them to go forward together towards a better community and to resist falling back into individual materialism. He was pricking their conscience as to how they treated their servants and even how they had usurped aboriginal land to get established in the first place. In short, Charles was way ahead of them in his vision for the future and many did not like his ideas. He was perceived as an outsider and his Anglo-Catholic inclinations also jarred with the dissenting history of the town.

So Charles definitely found life at St Peter's difficult. Records of the vestry meetings show that Charles attended the monthly meeting in July 1889, where he was perhaps dismayed that, instead of discussing the needs of the parish, the whole meeting was given over to Canon French's plans for his new parsonage. Alfred Bonnin, Adelaide solicitor and local resident, chaired the meeting and explained that the church was now free of debt and able to take on this new task as a reward for the Canon's hard work since 1881. Tenders had been submitted for the design and work had been agreed at a cost of £1,529. The stipend for Canon French for the next year was also voted on at £400 (approx £24,000 in today's prices). Charles's own stipend was £200, but he did not suffer from the 'politics of envy' and never cared too much for his own accommodation and remuneration anyway. However, he did not attend further vestry meetings, which laboured over the new parsonage until its completion in 1891, incurring a debt of £485.

So Charles just got on with his work and wrote regular reports of his new life to Chloe back home. On July 17th he sketched his week out as follows: 'Sunday: 8am Celebration, 10 Mattins, 11 preached and assisted, 3pm Sunday School then calls, tram to Brighton, Evensong and sermon; Every weekday morning 7.30 am Mattins plus Litany and confessions on Wed and Fri and two more evening services and one choir practice; Men's clubs to start and committees three times a week.' In the afternoons he did his parish (sick) visits and also taught twice a week at the Day School, run by the suitably severe Mrs Clinch. He had time to himself in the mornings for letters, sermons, reading and organ practice – Charles very much enjoyed his musical accomplishments.

Though he loved his parish work, he was already getting out and about. On July 7th 1889 he wrote: 'One thing I like about these folk, they are bold riders and reckless. Every Saturday there is a drag hunt and a wild scene. Fellows go over the wire fences (awfully risky jumps) and fling themselves headlong into the chase. Others gallop along the road in gigs with pairs of blood horses, perhaps only half broken.' Charles loved riding and later describes how he 'went for a gallop on the sands with young Bonnin on a shapely and skittish little pony. It went like the wind and I enjoyed it.' On August 17th he wrote of an expedition into the Adelaide Hills:

'A lovely ravine with huge careless showers of blue gum trees with their bunched leaves. They please me more and more. They have such variety of shape and are always standing at ease with their hands in their pockets. Down this ravine tumbled a stream and by its banks were orange trees and flowers. Lots of English flowers – rib wort plantains, thyme, marjoram, sweet and wild briars, primroses, oxlips, shepherd's purses, foxgloves. Then the Australian flowers were lovely also.'

Charles was a keen botanist and began beach-combing too, sending Chloe a sample of the seaweed and describing the cuttle sticks and sea rosaries he found on the seashore.

Socially he was out and about, attending a varsity dinner in Adelaide, which he described to Chloe on July 17th: 'It was very grand, wines, menu, music, flowers. There were 37 there. I met one man I greatly liked – Cecil Sharp, a Cantab, musical and instructive.' This was the beginning of a long friendship between the two men and they had a long list of things in common – born in the same year, with West Country schooling (Charles at Clevedon, Cecil at Mr Heppel's school in Weston-super-Mare); both were eldest sons in large families with heavy expectations laid upon them; both had had grandfathers in trade at Southwark wharves (the Sharps were in slates, the Marsons in ironmongery); neither of them had very warm relationships with their mothers (see Charles's comments on his mother's death the previous year, while Cecil would later confide to his fiancée Constance "I do not think I can recall a single soft episode between myself and my mother" – letter Feb 11th 1893); both men resorted to mother-figure confidantes (Charles to Miss Sophy Pedder and the Guest sisters, Cecil to Mrs Alice Howard and Mrs Heppel); they each had false starts in romance (Charles lost his engagement to Lady Agatha Russell and Cecil had broken 'an understanding' with a Miss Ida Canning), both eventually marrying childhood sweethearts.

Furthermore they each suffered from chronic asthma that sapped their energies at times and gave them a testy temperament; physically they were similar with pronounced aquiline noses; they had both anguished over their choice of professions – Charles vacillated between journalism and the Church, whereas Cecil, having studied mathematics at Cambridge, was now desperate to succeed as a professional musician but without formal qualifications; both were talented, driven men, who sometimes fell out with their colleagues or alternatively were spurned by the 'establishment' and thus found it difficult to build a career to gain the success they felt they deserved; both were charismatic figures, inspirational preacher and teacher respectively.

Two other small coincidences catch the eye. First it was Cecil Sharp who was asked in 1888 to design and commission the organ for St Peter's Glenelg at a cost of £700, the same organ on which Charles was now practising. Cecil was by then assistant organist at Adelaide Cathedral and no doubt had an occasional go on the Glenelg organ with Charles's blessing when he came to visit. Secondly, they had both been working on material that related to children, possibly to rediscover some of the warmth missing in their own upbringing. In 1887 Cecil had published in Adelaide his own arrangements of Nursery Rhymes (Three sets for Piano and Four Voices). He would later show great interest in children's games and songs in co-operation with Lady Alice Gomme. Meanwhile Charles was writing Fairy Stories, which he shared with Chloe and eventually had published in Adelaide in 1891. Henry Ford, an old Cambridge friend of Cecil Sharp, would later recall for Sharp's 1933 biography that Cecil as a student had been a freethinker but was brought back to Christianity by 'seeing a young parson in Australia sitting on a fence telling fairy stories to a lot of children'. That parson was, of course, Charles Marson.

Finally it is fair to say that the two men would not have been far apart in their politics, Cecil being more of a Liberal perhaps to Charles's socialist stance. Chloe records in her diary that the two men had intense discussions from time to time and it's doubtful whether either of them would have tolerated a wide gap between themselves on social issues. Sharp's biography records that Cecil eventually joined the Fabian Society in December 1900.

L: Charles in 1890

R: Cecil in 1893

Scott Barry 146 RUNDLE STREET ADELAIDE.

The other person that Charles met, but this time disliked, was the Bishop of Adelaide, George Wyndham Kennion (nicknamed 'Windy' by Charles). On July 12th 1889 Charles wrote to Chloe: 'I went to a clerical meeting and went to lunch with the Bishop. He himself is a pretty amiable man, no scholar or ruler . . . but we quarrelled and he defended the indefensible – the behaviour of whites against blacks. I thought him an ass and unworthy of his office and he thought me a beast, irreverent and doctrinaire.' They would clash together in the future on many occasions.

Despite these various distractions, Charles was back at his post in August:

> 'I have started a most successful Club for Men in Mrs Andrewes' Mission Hall on the Creek. They are such jolly fellows and we play whist, chess etc three nights a week together . . . The East Glenelg library is almost in order and is to be opened next week. I am getting the part of the parish apportioned to me into some sort of order, have got a meeting of my staff tomorrow and am making friends with the fellows.

They are all so shy of priests and no wonder! Folks have hectored them terribly and unsympathetically, I find.' *(letter to Chloe Aug 9th)*

Once settled into his various routines, Charles began to receive invitations to speak and one of the first of these was a lecture on ballads. He wrote to Chloe on August 29th 1889 *(italics are author's notes)*:

'A good big audience and a very appreciative one. They got quite excited over some of the ballads. The ancient one of 'The Hunting of the Cheviot' *(Child Ballad 162);* the Scotch 'Battle of Otterbourne' *(Child Ballad 161);* the 'Douglas Tragedy' *(Child Ballad 7);* 'King Estmere' *(Child Ballad 60);* Drayton's 'Agincourt' *(Michael Drayton, English poet, published this poem in 1605);* snips of 'Frithiof Saga' *(Icelandic Saga ca 1300, first translated 1737);* 'Sir Roland' *(from William Motherwell's Minstrelsy 1827);* and lastly Heine's 'Mein kind, wir waren Kinder' *(Heinrich Heine, German Romantic poet 1797-1856).* I meant to read them the 'Nut Brown Maid' *(written in 1502 and in Bishop Percy's Reliques of Ancient English Poetry 1765)* which I like hugely and Lockhart's 'Guarinos' *(John Lockhart translated a number of ancient Spanish Ballads about El Cid, the Moors etc)* but there was no time.'

Charles had clearly done a great deal of research into the subject with examples of English, Scottish and European material. Although he perhaps lacked the patience and analytical mind of an academic, he certainly had a passion for poetry and for years had been a serious student of English literature, deriving an almost physical pleasure in reciting poetry and stories. A voracious reader, he had great recall and could quote easily from writers of different eras. He had, of course, composed verse himself and discussed poets with Edith Nesbit in their collaboration two years ago, when he frequented the British Museum in search of literary gems. His letters to Chloe now, in their period of separation, refer to the books they are both reading and one can imagine that all Charles's pent up knowledge and enthusiasm were poured out into this 'Ballads' lecture.

One set of books that he probably did not have to hand at the time (though he had acquired them by 1904) was the five-volume set of *English and Scottish Popular Ballads* by the American academic Francis James Child (1825-1896). Child was a professor at Harvard University and corresponded with scholars throughout Europe before producing his canon of 305 ballads between 1882 and 1898. Child's index numbers are quoted in the notes above only as short-hand references for modern readers.

Charles was a lover of antiquarian bookshops and did have a huge collection of books shipped out with him. He certainly had a copy of Bishop Percy's *Reliques*, because Chloe records in her 1890 diary receiving a copy from him in the post on January 18th. His scholarship in this subject area at this early date (1889) is crucial proof that he was first in this field in advance of his new friend Cecil Sharp, who at this time was still concentrating on classical music with the Adelaide Philharmonic Society and in his role as a Director of the Adelaide College of Music. Sharp could certainly relax and have fun with his music – in a spell of sick leave he had learned to play the banjo and even the humble ocarina – but he was mainly known as a classical conductor, as a singing teacher and as an excellent piano accompanist. He could turn his hand to non-classical glees and comic songs at a party, but there is no evidence of his knowledge nor interest in traditional folk ballads at this time, so we must assume that it was Charles Marson who turned Cecil Sharp on to folk music and not vice versa.

11

The Year Apart

After graduation in the summer of 1889, Chloe went to stay with her brother Ronald Bayne at the Rectory at Orlestone in Kent. He had now taken over from Charles, and Chloe could happily write to Charles to keep him up to date with parish news and gossip. Although he had left under a cloud, Charles would have been a hard act to follow. One friend wrote of him: 'He let light in all around.' Another friend, Paul Stacy, commented: 'I cannot remember any conversation with him that would have been called ordinary; everything he said either informed, arrested, pleased or amused.' Ronald had not the same charisma and charm, and he would not have been human, if he had not felt some jealousy over comparisons made between the two men. No doubt he soon changed the style of church services, for he did not share Charles's Anglo-Catholic ways.

Perhaps he went into print over these theological differences, because there was now some sort of rupture between the two old friends, who had known each other at Oxford ten years ago and had worked together in the slums of Whitechapel. Charles wrote to Chloe on July 12th: 'Poor old Ronald, if he ever cares for me as I do for him, he must be grieved at having made a mess of things, but the friendship of me is an egg that, when broken, can never be cemented together. We have been growing apart for a long time, I now see. There was almost nothing I would not have done for him, since the first time we met. We now merely disagree and are miles apart.'

This was all a bit awkward for Chloe, as she would not wish to take sides between her brother and her fiancé. She was certainly grateful to her brother for the roof over her head, though her father gave her a monthly allowance of £2-10/- towards her upkeep. As a single parent and sole breadwinner, Ronald had still to focus on his parish work and was grateful that Chloe and sister Janie were there to help look after his two-year-old daughter Jessie. Chloe learned some useful nurturing skills that winter and also shared in the general running of the house. They had a cook and a servant, but it was a happy household and Chloe's diary records her helping out in various chores. She was not a very practical person, as she admits: 'Feb 3: I clean windows lugubriously after mending Baby's socks and my stockings. I am bad at cleaning windows, forgetting which done and creating no perceptible difference.' She also helped Ronald with some of his visiting and Sunday school commitments – all good preparation for her future life with Charles. Another way she showed her continuing love for Ronald was the hours they spent together studying the classics. They worked through hundreds of lines in the original Greek out of pleasure and to keep up their skills.

On the other hand, she naturally craved reassurance and continuing signs of love from her distant fiancé. Charles, busy in his new work, did not quite understand this and replied to her rebukes on July 7th: 'My dearest Chloe, we are very strange still to one another. I cannot yet read the ideas under your language nor you under mine with any ease.' And again on July 12th: 'I did not think my letters lacked tenderness . . . Here is my pierced and bleeding heart laid at your feet then . . . I am moribund without you.'

They continued to wrestle with each other – every exchange of letters taking six weeks each way. It was a strange correspondence, fraught with possibilities of misunderstanding and yet they were articulating deeply felt convictions and ideas. Charles was sometimes hard on his young fiancée, undercutting her expectations: 'Do not talk any nonsense about "being made better by me". You have a very average man and a most ordinary character to deal with, not a "prophet", pillar of strength, "noble", heroic or otherwise distinguished person. I do not know if you will make me better but it will be a hard job and for years of harder work. People do not get improved in character all of a sudden.' This was not false modesty on his part. As a priest – especially at the confessional – he was quite aware of human inadequacy but was determined to act in the world and enjoy life. Chloe was more given to introspection and Charles chided her:

> 'I hate all the introspection and self-examination of individualist pietists, and frankly plead guilty to all the vices. Look at Amiel *(Swiss philosopher)*. Do you know his *Journal Intime*? What an unhealthy hypochondriac! I do like objective people and not that everlasting exploration of one's own inside. The fellow could never do anything, he was so everlastingly employed in self-analysis, always picking his soul out of its

shell and weeping that it is shrivelled, lost, fat and was a bad colour. Our judgements on our own characters are so valueless. No wonder you protestants talk so much about sin. Can you find so much evil in such a lovely world? Look outwards, dearest Chloe.'

He also surprised Chloe by his attitude to prayer, though his comments may have been deliberatively provocative: 'I am not much given to prayer myself but not from theory so much as from reaction to the nauseous Evangelical upbringing which choked much of the good wheat in me.'

They disagreed too about politics, he being more radical than her. On December 11th he wrote:

'I advise you to ask Emily Guest for the Fabian Tracts before you undertake to reprove the Socialist spirit so dauntlessly. I have given up writing much upon these questions and many others upon which we greatly disagree, because your very idea of controversy seems to involve the use of wrathful words and (yet) you request non-controversial letters. When you reflect that I have met most of the Liberal chiefs and yet have come emphatically to the conclusion that they and their nostrums are unsatisfactory, then, my dear Clotilda, I think I may fairly suggest to you once more Clough's advice "Ah! Yet consider it again" *(Anne Clough, Chloe's Principal at Newnham College).'*

In her diary Chloe once or twice records that she was upset by some of Charles's comments but she had been brought up in a household of debate and controversy, so she fought back and accused him of hypocrisy. He replies: 'It always strikes me that to be consistent is a very poor kind of virtue. The consistent person is concise and mean.' He loved her feisty attitude and knew he had met the right mate. On December 20th he wrote: 'I am rather pleased to find we do not coincide in our admirations, for the joint company, thus walking apart, shoots more game.'

All these exchanges are important to our story because of later marital tensions and it is sensible to record the young couple's mindsets at this point in time. For example, it might be supposed that Charles, with his advantage in years and experience, was somewhat patronising and even chauvinistic in this considerable correspondence. His intentions were certainly nobler than this, however. As a bachelor by habit and a workaholic by temperament, he was uneasy about the domestic life ahead of him. On July 12th he wrote:

'Did not Byron mean that men have much more sense of work? I do not mean industry, for we are idler dogs, but the idea that home, wife and weans are pleasant, necessary perhaps, chiefly because one works better because of them. The woman, by virtue of her office, thinks largelier of the domestic life and also because in the past, sadly enough, she has not been allowed to think she has any work in the world, which idea is the oxygen of the soul.'

Neither did he mind showing vulnerability at times – December 11th: 'Dearest golden-haired Chloe, my poor and much bothered mate, I cling to thee as a drowning man clings to a spar – so madly and selfishly words cannot utter it.' And he felt he had clearly warned her of the hard and difficult life ahead of her as a clergy wife: 'You are being dedicated to God anew and to the strengthening of one of His faltering priests, a hard mission, an ascetic life with need of every muscle of the body, soul and spirit – and at the end of the day perhaps only tired limbs and tears. I shall strive to light up our bare home and hard work with all the enthusiasm of love and tenderness.' Not exactly an invitation to look through home furnishing catalogues or open the bubbly!

But that was Charles – dedicated to his work at the expense of himself and of Chloe too, if she decided to take up his challenge. She pondered this over her autumn months, but this was, of course, Charles's springtime. He and his brother Frank had both enjoyed a couple of months of good health without asthma attacks. By the end of August Frank, who had just turned 20, was going out to parties, staying up late, even smoking cigars 'until he is bilious but the result is only a bit of a wheeze'. But in September both men began to suffer with asthma again with the onset of spring.

Without modern-day inhalers, their chosen form of treatment was Himrod, an American preparation that they took out from England and subsequently ordered from Mr Hitchcox, the Glenelg pharmacist. Its powder was burned and inhaled. Most of these combustible powders contained stramonium and other alkaloids, some of which were hallucinogens – the product is a banned substance today. The unpleasant, anti-social fumes released were a concern to the two men and they decided to leave their small boarding house. So they left the 'cowshed' and moved into the 'elephant house', six rooms to themselves at 25/- a week plus an extra 10/- a week for the services of a maid Martha. Within a week they were beset by complaints about her. Charles writes on September 21st:

> 'We have had rather a shock by learning that our girl Martha had a baby last year, which died in April. Complaint is made to Canon French and the godly matrons are prepared to bless us backwards but after much thought I have decided to keep the lassie. I talked to her and told her how I would trust her and that we believe in the forgiveness of sins. As for the godly matrons, they may say their fill of evil things but the girl is under our protection and so long as she is faithful to her trust, they may do their worst. To tell you the truth, I am glad to run a little risk, for the supreme duty of protesting against the "morality" current in a dissenting colony. Poor child! She wept and was cast down when I talked to her but she is a good and modest woman and will, I am sure, act well.'

The move was good for Frank with no more reports of asthma or his old dyspepsia problems. Charles received an annual allowance of £100 from his father to look after Frank and kept him in touch with Frank's efforts to attend classes in preparation for his matriculation exams the following April. Although Frank had originally enrolled at Emmanuel College, Cambridge, his plan now was to study medicine at a London hospital. Working long days himself because French was currently 'off sick with boils', Charles had suggested that Frank should also get out and try to earn something but 'he is very apathetic and hard to stir up; he has no taste or capacity for business and no bodily health for manual labour.' Right now he seemed more keen on flirting with the girls and playing tennis, as the weather grew warmer.

On October 5th they both had time off to enjoy a 'glorious picnic on Mount Lofty with the Bonnin family and lots of girls and lads. It was such fun. We (all eighteen) drove in a brake with five frisky brown horses from Adelaide. Hampers of provision and holiday faces were the order of the day. The road wound up the cliffs almost like Cheddar but not so steep, 1500 ft up. The dusky gum woods were on either side, their trunks quite black by summer fires. The flowers were lovely – yellow scabious, red lilac, dark orchids and pretty creepers trailing down the scarps. Far beyond stretched the plains out to the sea and a little white patch was distant Adelaide. I did not see a single bird but Frank saw a cockatoo. While we were at the top, we had a grand lunch, turkey and jellies, bottled beer, claret, pastry, game and heaven knows what! After lunch we played rounders. We found some bulldog ants, brutes, who will be torn to pieces sooner than let go of your flesh when once they nip. There is also a purple kind of ant which smells like strong peppermint. These pursue you in thousands if you tap near their holes, until the ground is quite black with them.'

A couple of days later Charles gave a talk on education to a diocesan group of clergy. It was stunning in its vision and foresight, and could have been given a hundred and twenty years later to good effect. He contrasted the poverty of state provision compared with the private sector. The *Advertiser* newspaper of 15th October 1889 carried the report:

> The (State) teachers were in his view 'pitiable creatures whose minds have been banged into official dullness by blinding showers of rules, codes and regulations – utter badness palmed off on the poor . . . all subjects requiring most thought and nimbleness of wits come last, i.e. educationally the list is upside down.' The measures required to remedy the situation involved:
>
> – 'State education from top to bottom, such as would draw into State Schools all the more thoughtful parents, and would set such parents zealously struggling to better national education', so as to 'fuse classes and give the unity between men which it effects in Switzerland';
>
> – abolition of 'the mischievous system of payment by results' in favour of putting 'casual, constant and unexpected visits by examiners in the place of the formal fiasco now endured';
>
> – 'the introduction of gymnasia, music and gardening or swimming into every school.'

132

Charles had his own experience of the English 'public school' (which he had not enjoyed) and this was augmented by his working knowledge of the board schools in Whitechapel and in Glenelg, enabling him to make such comparisons. The Victorian system, introduced in 1861, whereby schools received 2/8d for each subject passed by each child in the annual examinations, was well-known to him. He realised that, in the early stages of education provision at least, churches had volunteered the building of many schools – e.g. Adelaide had St Peter's College (Anglican 1847) and Prince Alfred College (Methodist 1869) – but in future he wanted the poor to have equal access to good education without fees and this would help to break up the social class system. In a new country the State had the chance simply to take over responsibility, wipe the slate clean and put a wholly government-funded system in place. This never came about and those private schools flourish today. The paradox of how any centrally controlled education system can yet encourage great leadership in individual schools was not easily addressed then or now. Charles's rather maverick aversion to rules and regulations led him into interesting areas, when he actually took up teaching himself in later years!

His talk was met with some criticism, which he had anticipated in a letter to his father: 'I am going to have a brush with the dissenters in the newspapers, I expect. But I have Professor Kelly on my side and the best of the clergy, so that I think the attack will be well followed up.' Professor David Kelly was Hughes Professor of Classics and Literature at Adelaide University and a useful ally. On October 19th the *Quiz* newspaper, a 'weekly satirical, social and sporting journal 12 pages 3d' (akin to *Punch* magazine), did indeed attack Charles for dragging the Church back into any new social order. Its cynical writer had not come across Charles before and assumed him to be a self-publicist.

The paper jumped on him again a few months later (February 21st 1890) after Charles had sent off a slick but unflattering piece on South Australia to be published in *The Church Reformer* journal back in England: 'Our public life is corrupt, our buildings are shoddy, our youths are pale, slight and undisciplined, our birds are songless and our flowers are scentless', quotes the *Quiz*. Charles's article actually reported favourably on Adelaide's free library, museum and art gallery, and his own letters confirm that he didn't really think so badly of the flora and fauna, but the jokiness of the piece backfired and any nostalgic comparisons with the 'mother country' or suggestions that Australia was in any way second-rate were very unwelcome (cf. 'whingeing Poms' today). *Quiz* recommended a spell on a farm or sheep station to remedy his English prejudice.

Back at St Peter's Glenelg Charles hit his Christmas congregation with a (far-sighted) sermon about the treatment of the aboriginal people. On December 26th 1889 he wrote to Chloe:

> 'It is missionary Sunday and I have had three sermons to do. The last one was on the blacks and our treatment of them and I am very hot about that – and got wild and said just what came uppermost – reproach, jest, entreaty and appeal. The audience listened, breathed in time, stopped their fans, hung on the words, were impressed but angry . . . It is dreadful to know what they (the blacks) have suffered at our hands. We, the murderers, debauchees and callous aggressors, we go and subscribe to Melanesian missions to blacks a thousand miles away with smug pharisaism. I was to plead for this mission but I cursed it altogether and cried for justice and chivalry at home. Look at the facts. No knowledge procurable of any Australian language. No Bible or prayer-book. Not even a lexicon. Constant massacres and venality and contempt for these folk. Their tribal organisations broken up, their game all killed, their lands annexed, their wives and daughters taken to be harlots – then in exchange a few Government blankets, and a weekly allowance of tea and flour given them. Their sons are made slaves of and all by people who talk about the love of Christ and profess piety. Faugh. How sick it makes one.'

Charles had only been at Glenelg for six months but would have sought out information on this issue. It's most likely that he would already have bought and read a book by Mrs Christina Smith (1809-93), which was printed in Adelaide in 1880 and called *The Booandik Tribe* (modern name Bungandidj). Mrs Smith had settled in 1846 at Rivoli Bay, an isolated district near Mount Gambier (280 miles south of Adelaide), where her husband was the postmaster. The couple wanted to bring education and Christianity to the tribal people. They learned some of their language and tried to understand their customs. Her book is in effect an early anthropological project.

134

Later on Chloe's diary records that in July 1890 Charles invited an Aborigine 'Archie' to tea, and a friend Mr F Cairns wrote that Charles had said he 'found him as presentable as the ordinary Englishman'. Charles may also have researched the Kaurna tribe, whose land included the Adelaide plains and Glenelg itself. In 1836 it was estimated that there were between 300 and 500 Kaurna people in that area but by 1860 Dr William Wyatt, one of the first 'Protectors of Aborigines', gave evidence that the tribe 'had nearly died out.'

The 1988 book *Survival in our own land*, edited by Christobel Mattingley, describes how the 40 or so Aboriginal tribes of South Australia were stripped of their land and rights over the years of colonialism. The ongoing Aborigine Land Rights campaign, and recent formal apology to that people by the Australian Prime Minister, come a hundred years or more after isolated voices like Charles's were expressing disquiet and anger on the subject.

On a lesser note, Charles courted controversy again on May 27th 1890, when he replied to a letter in the *Express & Telegraph* newspaper from a temperance supporter, who was protesting against the use of barmaids to serve alcohol in hotels and bars and suggesting that their morals must be in doubt. Charles wrote:

> 'Allow me to protest against the dirty-minded and insolent people who would, under plea of advocating "gospel temperance", affix the brand of harlotry upon those engaged in one branch of the church's ministry – our barmaids. I indignantly deny that the vocation of barmaid is generally inconsistent with chastity. I have many friends among those so engaged . . . and can only recommend these unfortunate slanderers to go regularly to the bar and drink (temperately) of the excellent wines of the colony.'

There were letters against him and letters in support. *Quiz*, a newspaper which (according to Chloe's diary) Charles enjoyed reading – especially articles like the one on April 11th which lampooned his nemesis Bishop 'Windy' Kennion – quite swung round behind him, so that by October 1890 (a year after his education speech) *Quiz* wrote of Charles: 'I believe you to be eccentric, able and original . . . a man with his heart in the right place who, if he is permitted, may do a large amount of good for suffering humanity . . . It is my mission in life to expose shams. When I discover the real article, I hope I am sufficiently honest to express my admiration.'

So much for his variable relations with the local Press in his first year. Charles's own moods went up and down during this time. He had been upbeat in the spring, enjoying a school outing with 'a mob of boys, playing cricket and football' as well as socialising and playing tennis at the Duffields (friends of Cecil Sharp) – 'I worked my old bones at it with small effect, for I have never played since I was ordained'. He was open to new experiences – travelling to preach at Moonta, 100 miles north west of Adelaide in 'the land of ruthless mining', and at Meningie, 100 miles south east of Adelaide at the top of the Coorong Peninsula. Now a National Park, the Coorong is a long coastal strip of shallow, salty lagoons where birdlife is especially rich. Charles caught the steamer down the coast and wrote excitedly to Chloe on November 16th 1889:

'You ought to be here to play the bushranger with me. This is really great fun. Early this morning I took off my coat and put on leggings and mounted a steed named Jup. My host Ted Mann with his fawn-coloured puppy and I rode over a gentle hill until we came to an iron fence and through a gate entered the everlasting bush. Things start out and run or fly – great black birds or rabbits. If you do start a kangaroo, you have to go at full speed after him. We rode miles and I enjoyed the ride immensely.

'Sunday dawned and at 11, with wooden cup and supper-plate, I celebrated and preached. There were 75 at Evensong out of a population of 110. On Monday we drove out to the Coorong – such a wild, lovely drive by the blue lake. Every now and then we saw great birds on the water – white and black swans, ducks and crows of many colours. Now and then a large snake glided out of the path. At last we sailed on the Coorong. I had a rifle (borrowed) and shot at a huge bird way ahead. I am glad (on reflection) to say that I only knocked a feather out of its tail. He was a pelican by profession and I hope he will be none the worse for his fright.

'On Monday night we had a concert and dance in a zinc goods shed. I sang and was encored, being in good form for 'The Botany Bay', 'Tarpaulin Jacket' etc. We danced until 4am. Such queer quadrilles and the mazurka was galloped through and the accordion never ceased playing.

136

'Next day we went for another ride. It was over 100 degrees in the sun and I was baked a chocolate red. The people are so kind. They loaded me with presents – 4 emu eggs, some pink amaranths, cakes etc. Kind host would not take a farthing for all my board and lodging and explained kindly that he was not much for church-going but shewed his respect for religion by feeding the priest.'

As the summer heat built up, however, both Charles and Frank were beginning to suffer badly. Charles wrote to Chloe on November 29th 1889: 'My liver has gone wrong and given me one of those black fits of utter depression which lasts for days sometimes. There is only one thing to be done in such a case with a man and that is to let him alone very severely. If you come to him in the dark with well-meant cordials, they are rudely pushed away. It is a great art to know when to let folk be sulky.' And to his father a week later he wrote: 'I am sorry to tell you bad news. Frank has had a sharp asthma again and it is only now on the 6th day going slowly away. A week and four days of it not dressed – it's a sad anti-climax after three months of rude health. He must not live alone.' Adelaide has a dry climate and it may be that the north winds blowing down pollen from the pastoral lands were now affecting both men.

There was something of the manic-depressive about Charles – tremendously enthusiastic one minute and quite cast down the next: 'I often feel inclined to throw up my profession. It is too deep and subtle for me. Yet when I am out of harness – clerical harness – I am miserable and long for the galling collar again.' His mood had not been helped by the recent anniversary of his mother's death:

'Frank and I have been talking much about her. The curse of evangelical tenets centred her in herself until her sympathies were stunted and impoverished. But I admired her greatly and wished I had loved her more. A mother is so easy to love as a rule, and I love so many old ladies that I am ashamed to think how bitterly we always clashed. She has left a great gap and yet no gap. All idea of home goes when the Mother is dead. I have hardly a crumb of nourishing thought which I can say she gave me. If she had only taught me some little Nursery Rhymes, or the names of wild flowers, or "Matthew, Mark, Luke and John, Bless the bed that I lie on", it would sweeten my memory of her. She loved flowers in her last years and used to

137

potter about the garden and porch over them. How much I often longed to have her face bending tenderly over me, when I was ill – as it did when I was a child. But when I had the fever at Shoreditch and went to her to be nursed, she did not notice that I had been ill and quarrelled with me the first night. So I went up to the sea and sat on the rocks in the sun, and I fear I closed my heart with an impatient click. She never asked about my work and was always pained, shocked or indignant if she heard anything about it. She only heard, of course, the shocking things I said or did. Requiescat in pace!' *(letter to Chloe September 13th)*

The run-up to Christmas was, however, a very busy time and Charles just had to work through his problems. He had committed himself to a deal of parish work in Advent. He had also made arrangements to leave the 'elephant house' and move to Alma Street further south. This made sense, as he was now nearer the Mission Church and the horse-drawn trams that plied the Brighton Road to St Jude's. The former was a stone-built church (capacity 90) in Hastings Street and had only been commenced the year before, whereas St Jude's in Brighton was older (1854), though equally modest in size. The former is now called St Martin's, while the latter has been completely rebuilt in a modern design. Charles had sole charge of St Jude's, and one of his first acts was to instigate a surpliced choir to galvanise and involve the community in his services.

It's important to realise that his Anglo-Catholic ways were not a conservative position, not an attempt simply to reinstate the old order of things before the Reformation. It's true that he did not much care for Puritanism, which had taken so much colour and life out of communities, but his study of the old Prayer Book had shown him the meaning and beauty of rituals and of the Saints' calendar of feasts and fasting and so on. Furthermore he found that the writings of the Early Fathers (the Early Christian Church) denounced usury, the misuse of riches and the exploitation of labour. This Gospel of social justice was for him a modern message and one that looked forward to a new society. It has similarities with the Catholic Church's Liberation Theology in Latin America in the 1970s.

This respect and understanding of the past informed every action in his ministry. In particular he brought the Mass forward as his

138

main act of worship. Times have now changed, but in the late nineteenth century the Service of Holy Communion was regarded as something extra and special for the 'bettermost folk', the well-to-do and respectable, not for the labouring man. This was anathema to Charles who believed strongly that everyone is equal at the baptismal font and at the communion rail. By his powerful imagination and sense of theatre, his services were never dull. He had found that in the slums of London, poor illiterate people could learn the Christian message, not through study or Bible-bashing but through stained glass and music and ceremony, sometimes patronisingly called 'smells and bells'. To this visual process Charles now added good sermons. He didn't preach for too long and could speak plainly despite his erudition. Frank Etherington, who as a young man had only just met Charles the year before but became his lifelong friend, later described him thus:

> 'It must not be imagined that Marson's life was made up of squabbles with church officials and acrimonious controversial discussions. He had the power of effective detachment, and when he came into personal contact with simple people, all controversial barriers disappeared and he became the ministering priest and friend. His cheery greeting, accompanied by some shrewd and generally humorous comment on affairs, made his presence at all times refreshing to people who needed just such help in their ordinary daily routine. One of the signs of a rightly busy man is that he never gives the impression of being hurried. Whether he was playing with children, talking to the sick, or giving advice, the particular thing he was doing commanded his full attention and gave the recipient of his friendship the true impression that Marson had received pleasure himself. He succeeded in bringing great truths to simple people, and his success was due to his painstaking care to clear the path for simple truth and to avoid the snares of technical jargon. He had a way of putting things that stuck in the mind and often changed the outlook of the questioner.'

As regards his other parish work, Etherington explained: 'Charles attracted crowds of working people when he had the opportunity and was able to conquer the working-man's distrust of the priest, because he knew there was reason in this distrust. To do a service to one's neighbour in such a way as to establish a right to thrust religion on him was to Marson not only unfair to the neighbour but unfair to religion.' This altruism was particularly evident in his visits to the sick. Even when he was feeling low himself, he stirred himself for this work. Chloe records in her diary that he sometimes stayed up all night with poorly people. On December 11th he wrote to her: 'Yesterday I had to go to house after house for someone to sit up with a poor sick child. A working-man finally did it – other people refused.' There was a small community hospital of 13 beds in Farrell Street (built 1864, a maternity unit by the 1950s), but these were paying beds and thus avoided by many parishioners.

On another occasion (according to the testimony of a parishioner Mr Hughes) one of Charles's parishioners, a woman, was very ill and required to go herself into hospital but had eleven children of her own and refused to leave them. Charles found her wretched and hopeless but assured her that the Church was a family and would care for her children. He placed most of the children in various caring homes but two small boys he could not place, so took them back to his own quarters. They were squashed end-to-end in a bed and could not sleep because they were so excited. Charles went in to them eventually and said: 'I'm very sorry, little boys, but this must stop' – and pushed his knee into the bed between them and spanked it. 'Now next time it shall be the other one'. Each boy thought the other had been beaten and curled up at his own end of the bed and went to sleep.

12

Telegram – Coming May

Chloe began to receive some of Charles's depressing letters in early January 1890 and she was somewhat alarmed. On January 14th she sent a telegram 'Coming May' to Marson Glenelg Adelaide. Not receiving an immediate reply but only more downbeat letters, she wrote to Charles's father in despair. He replies sweetly on February 26th:

> 'I must put a consideration or two before you to calm your spirit. December and January are the hottest months and during that time the weather is most trying, especially to newcomers and more particularly to asthmatic persons. The boys have felt this and poor Frank very much so, and the more because he is so frightfully careless about himself. Unless telegraphing is resorted to, remember letters take six weeks to come and six weeks to reply. But the summer heats are over and I send you his last letter, which seems as if he were getting acclimatized to some extent. Consequently I should go on preparing for the voyage and be of good cheer. Steadily prepare for going out and assume that to be the right thing. God bless you, my little daughter 'designate', the girls join in love.'

Thus reassured, Chloe went shopping! Her diary records that in London in company with her Aunt Agnes (her step-mother's older sister, now 49), she went to Liberty's and Burnet's to get her wedding dress; to Schoolbred's for petticoats, aprons and frocks; to Silver's for pyjamas; and to Hanson Street for a lovely silver waist clasp and bracelet (a wedding present from Agnes's sister Constance). Next she goes to 2 Gower Street to say goodbye to Aunt Milly, who is not her real aunt but a close family friend. 'Milly' is Millicent Fawcett, mother of her school and university friend Philippa Fawcett. Then she travels up to Cambridge to say goodbye to all her Newnham friends. Philippa (always known as 'Chip') greets her and 'the dear Principal *(Anne Clough)* gives me a lovely little shawl'.

After tearful farewells, Chloe heads for Southampton by train to stay a few days at Highfield with Aunt Agnes and at last receives a telegram from Charles, saying 'Come'. Chloe records that she 'is awfully relieved'. So, more shopping for wedding shoes and a cloak, then a visit to the dentist: 'I go to Mr Bromby and have teeth tortured. He says my teeth are invalids and must often be attended to.' By mid-March she is in Clevedon to stay a few days with the Marson family and at Bristol she says goodbye to her Newnham friend Dora Pease (sister of the Fabian Edward Pease). All the goodbyes and the anticipation of a long (largely unescorted) journey, let alone wedding nerves, were bringing Chloe to a high pitch of emotion, so that on the return journey to Paddington: 'I fret over my trunk and lose my purse and am confused over getting my money out of the trunk. Sad letter from CLM which upsets me.'

She had final farewells to say to her father's Scottish cousin, Mrs Anna Scringeour (née Duguid), a stockbroker's wife, who slipped her a tidy £50 as a wedding present. She then spent a few days with her father Peter Bayne in West Kensington. Six years ago he had married his third wife, Marie Meuret, a French girl half his age, but Chloe doesn't seem to have been close to her. In her diary she simply says:– 'Dinner then Mrs Bayne plays.' Very formal. The support of all these relatives and friends in London was precious to Chloe and an important part of her life story.

Then it was back to Orlestone for Easter with her brother Ronald and her sister Janie, who was there to help with the final packing. A young man aged 18 by the name of Frank Etherington was a guest at the Rectory that weekend. He was at that time a lay reader in Ashford, but had known the Bayne family between 1883 and 1889 from Ronald's time as a curate at St Alfege's Greenwich. Frank's father James, an engine fitter, had brought up his family in that parish. Frank later studied at King's College London and was ordained in 1895. He became a lifelong friend and confidant of Chloe and assembled the collection of Charles's letters at Minehead Vicarage.

On April 10th 1890 Chloe set off from Dover on the boat train with Janie, bound for Italy where she would board the steamship Orizaba. Her brother Charlie met her in Florence with his new wife Gussie (Augusta). Charlie Bayne had left University College Oxford after just one year to enter the Indian Civil Service and was currently Secretary to the Government of Burma – he was later awarded the CSI (Companion of the Star of India) in 1901. Now he had a spot of leave and accompanied Chloe on her tour of the galleries and churches. She was ecstatic about so much of what she saw – frescoes, statues, paintings – and absorbed them all in the three weeks of her stay. She was due to visit Venice as well but unfortunately caught a chill and was confined to bed for nearly a week.

Charlie took her on his own for a few days each to Rome and to Naples but waved goodbye to her there on the SS Orizaba on May 4th. He did introduce her to the captain but she had no chaperone as such, making friends with several passengers as quickly as she could.

Chloe eventually arrived in Glenelg on Tuesday June 3rd and Charles met her off the boat. They were so overwhelmed to see each other again, after all the waiting and the long correspondence, that they could hardly speak. Two days later, on Thursday June 5th at 9.30am they were married at St Andrew's Church Walkerville in North Adelaide. Charles had made all the arrangements and had chosen St Andrew's for three reasons – firstly, it was one of the few churches with a peal of bells; secondly, Chloe was of Scottish origin; and finally, because he was friendly with its incumbent, Archdeacon George Dove. Cecil Sharp gave her away and the happy couple spent their honeymoon at Gumeracha, a lovely spot 20 miles north east of the city in the Adelaide Hills. The *Quiz* Newspaper reported the wedding:

> 'Mrs Marson is of medium height, is fair and wears her hair brushed smoothly off her face. She was attired in a simple cashmere dress, made with a short train and puffed sleeves and a large silver clasp at her waist. She also wore a plain tulle veil and carried a small bouquet of white flowers. The bridesmaids were the Misses Richardsons (2) and Miss Butler, who wore white cashmere gowns and white drawn silk hats. In accordance with High Church ritual – no gloves.'

It was at Gumeracha on Monday June 9th that Chloe received the great news that her dearest school and university friend Philippa Fawcett had come top in the Mathematics Tripos at Cambridge – the first woman to be placed 'above the Senior Wrangler'. This reminder of the intellectual potential of women, when they were neither admitted to Cambridge degrees nor entitled to a political vote, went round the world as headline news.

Towards the end of their honeymoon, the couple stayed at Kapunda with Canon Whitington and his wife. They had a jolly social evening there, at which Charles sang 'Oh Mistress Mine' (Shakespeare) and 'The Wearing o' the Green', a Republican song dating from the Irish Rebellion of 1798.

There is no mention of brother Frank at the wedding either in Chloe's diary or in Charles's letters home, so he must have headed back to England around April. In any event the couple moved into their first marital home at 18/- rent per week in The Broadway in South Glenelg, less than a half mile away from St Peter's. Perhaps for financial reasons, they started without a servant and this was very hard on Chloe, who was not a very practical person and had never cooked before in her life. She was not from a wealthy family but they had always had help. She records on June 14th: 'Long time lighting fire. At length sausages cooked. Enjoy this well-earned breakfast. Sally forth to pay bills etc. I buy a leg of lamb for 1/9d, thus begins housekeeping. Charlie makes and puts up lovely shelves and I arrange pots.' And on the 16th: 'Get breakfast and cook some sausages rather rawly! We hang the pictures, me dawdling terribly over the business. Terrible rainstorm. C & I make mince amid howls of laughter over the mincing machine and start reading *Modern Painters*'.

Charles was to be quite the 'New Man', cooking and doing household chores, supporting Chloe in her teaching and other duties. Chloe's entries over the next few weeks record their progress:

> 'I have a time lighting the fire which goes out to my shame; C stands on a kitchen chair and fabricates mince, while I laugh. C & I guess quotations and I win his boots; I cook a pudding and boil my first potatoes which I blush with pride to say are a success. The saucepan with the pud boils over; C cooks wonderful fry of fish, as Violet comes to dinner. C reads us "*The Scholar-gipsy*" and ballads; I kindle my colonial oven in trepidation of spirit and cook my first leg of mutton right. C is tremendously pleased and we eat in triumph; Fire lights and C & I begin sweeping house out. We go to Brighton by tram together. He preaches wonderful sermon on St Francis. Home and I read *The Church Reformer*. C sings me German songs. I

144

spoil omelette and make successful carrot hash. Goats eat dishcloths; Cecil Sharp comes in just as I am lighting the fire and we have tea and great fun. Talk about Cambridge & Crimea & Indian Civil Service & Bach Choir and I cook chops and have fun; C sits in the butter and the bottom drops out of the kerosene tin box! Miss Watts shows me how to make beef-steak pudding. We go to Mrs Beare where we make uproarious jokes while they are awfully solemn. Later C & I play on the harmonium at Brighton church; We go up to Adelaide to the University Reading Room and have dinner at Professor Kelly's. Go to tea in pretty room of Mr Sharp's. He plays us Schumann. C reads me Swinburne's "*Chapman*" and we have discussion; C washes up because I am tired. I read Tolstoy's *Sebastopol* and we make an omelette. To Duffields where I interview Geoffrey about his lessons. C has discussion with Mr Naish about blacks. I put on my pretty straw-coloured gown and we go up to an awfully dull dinner party at the Sells. C makes good jokes which I can't hear at the other end of the table.'

**Chloe
aged 24**

Such entries give us a great insight into the first month of their lives together – earnest intellectualising in sermons and books, in shared discussions and sharp opinions, which are combined with a freedom and independence of action, only punctuated on occasions by the chores of daily living. By coincidence they both wrote to their respective fathers on the same day, July 22nd 1890, Chloe thus:

145

'My dearest Father, I know you will be glad to know that my deep content and steady bliss at being Clotilda Marson increases daily and the sureness that I have obtained whom God ordained. Last night I went off to the Doves at Walkerville to read Portia at a Shakespeare Society there, and no-one knows the wild delight with which I got back home this morning. Sometimes I get very homesick and chivvied about by stress of callers and notes and my head has little rest from trying to take in new thoughts and aspects of life and work, and to be a really helpful wife but that doesn't last long and the sight of Charlie's strong shouldering of the burden of daily work and his unfailing unselfishness and energy pick me up and set me straight again.'

Charles was busy writing:

'Dearest of Fathers, Chloe is much tried by her culinary and domestic tripos but has thrown herself with real gallantry into passing and now that our dinners have been uninterruptedly successful for some time, my hard heart has relented and my tyranny (as the ladies here accounted it) is relaxed enough to give her the help of a servant maid. It was a bit of hard road, I confess and full of discomforts but most necessary to traverse and having done it ourselves, we have a tenderness for the little servant girl, which nothing else could give. But Mrs Chloe has got some pupils and is likely to have more, so the pot will not cease boiling.

'How do we get on? Well! We do get on but, of course, not without friction now and then, and yet are more en rapport than I supposed to be possible. She is considerably more at her ease than she was but being a hot-hearted little wife is always ready to do battle for her ideas. She finds it unexpectedly difficult that I am away so much and am tired (and unsociable I fear) after the day's work is over, for it is never done. I have seldom an hour to chat in and if I am at home, someone is sure to drop in and spoil our *tête à têtes*.

'I am glad Frank is better in body but sorry he is not yet at work. I hoped to have heard that he was at St Bart's working hard for his degree. We have been very full of sickness of late here and in the gray of the morning I was called up to give the viaticum *(last rites)* to my friend Mrs Bowen who was so kind to

146

Frank. Tonight she is still alive but the doctor gives very little hope and her poor husband is prostrate with grief. Her mother died a few weeks back and they have had a series of dreadful misfortunes one after another. I think I have had more private celebrations the last few weeks than at any time in my life.'

Chloe's first pupil at the end of July was Geoffrey Duffield. His age is not given but he studied many subjects with Chloe three mornings a week – Maths, English, History, French and Geography, but particularly Latin and Greek. The Duffield family were wealthy mill-owners and Walter Duffield had been a political figure as Treasurer in two State Parliaments. They owned a large estate at Gawler to the north of Adelaide but also had a house in Glenelg. They could have sent Geoffrey either to a private school or to an established private tutor, so it was a real vote of confidence in Chloe's qualifications that they chose her to be his teacher. If Charles had any misgivings about coaching a capitalist's son, he hid them and even took Geoffrey himself if Chloe was indisposed. They liked Mrs Duffield as a person anyway. The other main pupil was Arthur Sells, the son of Revd Alfred Sells. Arthur's father had been the curate of St Peter's before Charles but had died young at 30, while his mother was still an important figure in the parish. Chloe also began to give German lessons to various children and adults in Glenelg.

There is evidence that both Chloe and Charles were inspiring teachers. Charles's attitude was typically cavalier: 'The great educational secret is to pour the sunlight of good thoughts and the rain of good work upon souls and then leave them alone.' The gardening metaphor came easily to him, as he now embarked on great schemes of flowerbeds, vegetable patches and a chicken-house when the couple moved house again on August 4th to Rose Street.

The house was simply furnished. Chloe recorded her amusement when Annie Marson (Charles's sister) had written enquiring about the colour of their drawing-room carpet and furniture. 'We haven't got a drawing-room or a carpet and our chairs are all cane-bottomed. In this hot climate it's such a comfort not to have a carpet but only a few rush mats.' Chloe now had more room for her books and more space to prepare or give her lessons. They placed advertisements in

Adelaide newspapers for her next project – a series of Literary Lectures to be held at Glenelg on Mondays and at Walkerville on Wednesdays, commencing in late September. She admitted to being very nervous before them but all went well. Later one participant, Miss Edith Dove, daughter of Archdeacon Dove, wrote: 'My mother and I never missed attending a course of lectures she gave on some of the wonderful men of the Elizabethan age. She was a wonderful scholar.' Chloe's enthusiasm was infectious, as Charles explained to his father: 'It is most pathetic, the way in which some souls live, never seeing anything beautiful. Clo has a perfect mission for such people, with her boundless, intense, awful, tremendous, overpowering enthusiasm for Poetry and lovely thoughts. Dear Clo quite innocently and sweetly gives "literary" ladies a slight examination and recommends them some slim volume or author which they have not read but only talked about. They love her dearly all the same.'

Charles himself was in demand as a speaker-cum-entertainer at various gatherings:- For example, in July he recited a Lockhart ballad 'plunge the rowels *(spurs)* in his side, thy master dear I am' from one of his books *Ballads and Rondeaus*; in August he was busy trying out some of his own original fairy stories with children at Sunday schools and showed Chloe the manuscript; in October he recited in company the story of the Volsungs *(Old Norse Sagas)* and of 'The Daemon Lover' *(Child Ballad 243)*; and in early December at the Working Men's Club he sings 'The Wearing o' the Green' again; and for a Christmas presentation he and Chloe practise some songs from William Chappell's *Popular Music of the Olden Time 1858-59*. Chloe in her diary records instances of Charles's spontaneous singing and dancing at home, so it is clear that as well as his good visual sense and writing skills, Charles was blessed with a keen musical ear.

He was just a bystander, however, in the Anglican Church's big event that year, which was the laying of the foundation stone for the final phase (tower and Lady Chapel) of St Peter's Cathedral in North Adelaide. He was in the procession, however, and wrote the following amusing piece to his father on September 30th 1890:

'On Saturday there was an unimposing ceremony for the laying of the Cathedral stone. As one gets to expect in the Church of England, the Communion office was altogether left out and

148

instead thereof was a mongrel Masonic service. The clergy in every variety of headgear trooped out and three bishops led the rear. A huge lot of choirs in similar eccentricity of headgear went in front. The people (at 2/6d per seat) were seated in grand stands. A military band played out of tune. Masons, "not operative ones" but dining ones, in dress suits hung about with tinsel, came and talked about the "Architect of the Universe", performed their little ritualisms, put coins into the cavity, and then it rained. Heigho! How glad we were to escape!'

Amid all their activities and new projects, Charles and Chloe did enjoy socialising and cultural events. They saw Cecil Sharp informally and at several of his concerts: 'August 15 Charlie sees me off to Adelaide to the Norman-Neruda concert with Miss Singleton. Cecil Sharp meets us and we have immense fun. He introduces us to Herr Heinicke *(orchestra leader)*'; 'November 20 Charlie & I go up to Adelaide to the Philharmonic'; 'November 26 In evening go to Mr Sharp's concert, love the Grieg songs'; 'December 6 To "Sylvia", Mr Sharp's opera. Nice'; 'December 16 Charlie & I go up the Messiah which is most wonderful. He says goodbye to Mr Sharp'.

The reason for the farewells was that Cecil had decided to take 'his' opera 'Sylvia' to London to see if it could be successfully staged there. He was due to leave on the mail steamer the following week. 'Sylvia' was actually a joint effort with his friend Guy Boothby. Cecil had composed the music and Guy the lyrics. They had collaborated before in the production of a comic operetta *Dimple's Lovers*, a one-act play performed recently in September. The *Quiz* newspaper accounts of December 5th and 12th were confident of Sylvia's likely success: 'Mr Sharp's music is original – at least the suggestions of other composers are rare – and it has a bright sparkle that must make it popular' and 'there is no doubt that if his opera receives a fair show in the "big village", it will catch on'. Unfortunately it was not so. Cecil lost his main backer, Alfred Cellier, the English composer and director of many Gilbert & Sullivan comic operas, who was taken seriously ill and died a year later. Cecil returned to Adelaide in April 1891 to find either that some sort of coup had taken place or that his colleagues had given up on his returning and that he had therefore lost his co-Directorship at the Adelaide College of Music. He never recovered from these two disappointments and, though he found occasional work as a conductor and did a little more composing – a Menuet, two Preludes, a Reverie, a Mazurka and a Toccata – he would leave Australia for good in January the following year (1892).

Charles was also contemplating his likely prospects for the New Year. His two years at St Peter's Glenelg would be up in six months time and he was not at all sure that Canon French would offer him tenure. He and Chloe were financially improved by December 1890 – her diary has accounts showing that she earned £76 in the half year by her teaching. When Charles's father sent them a Christmas cheque, we 'then and there tore the cheque to little strips and decently burned it, so that you should not expend your substance, even out of love'. However, just as Charles had been badly affected by the hot weather in the previous December, so it was Chloe's turn now. Headaches, 'a sort of prickly heat in my calves', tiredness and depression are all recorded in her diary. December 27th was 'Still horribly and oppressively hot and the creek smells loathsome. Awful mosquito night.' But two days later by Proclamation Day (a public holiday), she feels a little better. They go for a trip on a steamer and there are great crowds. Her last entry for the year of 1890 reads: 'Thank God for the most blessed year of my life'.

What would 1891 bring to the young couple? Chloe extended her teaching hours in the New Year, after accepting an invitation to attend as a part-time teacher at the Advanced School (High School) in Adelaide. Sometimes they went into town together, Charles paying visits to the Royal Adelaide Hospital or the Children's Hospital – particularly the diphtheria ward. As a man prone to illness, Charles was always fearless about visiting workhouses and hospitals, where the risk of infection must have been high. He drove himself very hard, continuing to observe a fasting regime before communion services – he joked that he could not in all conscience administer and receive bread and wine with the taste of bacon still in his mouth. He did go for hours on a Sunday without food, as he often did duties at two churches. Chloe was concerned about this abstemiousness and also about his coughs that seemed to last for weeks. His pipe smoking and weird asthma inhalations would not have helped his cause either. Chloe wrote to her sister Janie that the stress of not

150

knowing his next posting was undermining Charles's health and that Dr Singleton was becoming a regular visitor:

'The people have been amazingly kind in sending us fowls and jellies and eggs and wine since he has been ill but somehow he doesn't get set up. I give him beef-tea at 11 and 4 , and eggs and milk and whiskey at 2, everything I can think of for the dearest old thing but still he doesn't shake it off.'

Although Charles sometimes felt undervalued at Glenelg, he was really beginning to enjoy his new life and England was fading in his memory. He wrote to his father on March 3rd 1891:

'I am very fond of Australia and am quite colonised among the kind and frank healthy folk here. One may just as well be buried as leave one's hemisphere – friends drop away, interests die, habits change, one becomes another being. Folks here are kinder than in England, at least I have been treated kindlier and fairer here, and so, except for one's relatives and a few faithful friends, I would rather pitch my wigwam here but Clo is all of another mind, being fresh imported.'

Another month went by and Charles was no further forward. He had put out feelers to other dioceses and even to New Zealand but with no sign of a clerical vacancy for him. Canon French was determined to replace him with a man of less original ideas and smoother temperament, even though a petition was going round the parish demanding that Charles be kept on (310 signatures 'for', 6 'against'). Again Charles wrote to his father on April 28th:

'I have treated French with courtesy and have strengthened the organisation not a little. I have worked like a horse and obeyed his orders like a spaniel for two years. The folk I have offended have nearly all come round to be my friends and quite all returned to the church (no! there is one exception to that). In return for this I have had the wages of an engine driver and no thanks and a marked desire that I should move on.'

Chloe had been unwell earlier in the month and this turned out to be morning sickness, as she discovered she was pregnant. This exacerbated Charles's dilemma as to whether to stay or return to England. The sea routes either via Cape Horn in midwinter or the Suez Canal in midsummer were most uninviting. Furthermore he was disturbed by fresh outbreaks of illness in the parish around them – particularly typhoid and diphtheria. He was anxious that

Chloe had been working too hard and imagined that she was desperate to return to have her child delivered back in England among her friends and family. He wrote so to his father on May 5th but interestingly Chloe many years later wrote an addendum in pencil: 'I was content to go or stay but now wish we had stayed.'

Charles's frustration boiled over in that same letter:

> 'I hate leaving the field. The Church here is fighting under asinine officers against terrific odds and my detachment has gained an unusual success. I cannot pretend that I think my brother officers have not been moved by jealousy to some extent . . . but French has very old-fashioned ideas about the relation of curate to incumbent. I have never refused to do as he told me, though he has, not seldom, knocked my pet schemes on the head and sided with dissenters or sanitary inspectors or anyone against me. Meantime the church is full when I preach and every kindness is showered upon us.'

Although this sounds a little arrogant, Charles was a very sophisticated soul, who tempered his drive and ambition with a self-deprecating humour. In a letter to his father he wrote: 'We have nothing much first-rate (in the church) here and mere nobodies like myself find small dunghills to crow upon and our crowing makes so much reverberation that we fancy the stars are listening and that the sun is getting up to hear us.' As regards his long-term prospects of high promotion, Charles wrote: 'I shall never have the chance myself, but if I stop on here for a long run of years without getting drunk, I may become a Canon.'

Although Charles had begun enquiries to book his passage home, his parishioners were adamant that he should stay. The petition had grown in size to 674 persons. They had set up a committee to lobby Bishop Kennion to find Charles an alternative curacy and had even raised a year's stipend £200 to support him wherever he went. Encouraged by this financial support, Kennion suggested the poor mission church of St Oswald's Parkside, a suburb of Adelaide, but this would mean that Charles would be directly responsible to Kennion himself. The two men did not get on and several weeks of negotiation followed, during which Kennion tried to insist that Charles give up some of his High Church ways, notably the use of the 'confessional box' and the sacring bell (rung when the consecrated bread is held up at the eucharist). In the end they agreed to disagree and a *modus vivendi* was drawn up between them.

So on June 29th 1891 Charles and Chloe left St Peter's Glenelg and moved to Parkside in south Adelaide. 'Parkside is a very artisan and shop boy suburb . . . my church is poor and in debt (£360) and behind hand, badly built, badly served, badly organised – generally in the ditch. It is a small stone building used as a school, club and service room all in one.' It proved to be just as challenging as he'd feared!

13

Parkside and Politics

Perhaps the main reason behind Canon French's desire to let Charles go from Glenelg was that for some considerable time Charles had been involved in Adelaide politics and had offered St Peter's schoolroom as a meeting place for social reformists. Chloe did not share her husband's socialist stance nor attend his meetings – she was a mild Liberal but did feel strongly about women's rights. In her 1890 diary she wrote on September 18th: 'Home to find C composing socialist letter with Mr Bickford'. On October 22nd she noted: 'C writes socialism article.' This may have been in preparations for *The Pioneer* newspaper, which was started in Adelaide in November 1890. It was a fortnightly socialist paper that reported on meetings and lectures in the area and also carried articles on the Single Tax League.

Henry George, the American author of *Progress and Poverty*, had visited Australia between March and June 1890, promoting his idea that a single tax on land values could eradicate poverty and rebalance economies. His lectures had received mixed reviews and he had been obliged to explain more clearly that he was not in fact proposing the confiscation or nationalisation of all land by governments. His tax would be imposed on basic land values excluding any buildings and improvements, because he did not want to impede landholders from developing businesses and jobs. The tax would be most effective against land speculators and large idle estates.

It's important to realise that George's proposal at that time was extremely powerful and many reformists saw it as the engine that would propel any country from crude industrialism to a more sophisticated and fairer society. There were Single Tax League branches in many parts of South Australia and the 'agent' for Glenelg was William Bickford, with whom Charles had been busy writing his socialist letter. In fact the Glenelg branch held its meetings every Thursday evening in St Peter's schoolroom, courtesy of Charles's support.

Charles's experience as Editor of *The Christian Socialist* newspaper for three years would have been most appealing to the editors of *The Pioneer* newspaper. Although many of its articles were unsigned, there are small clues that indicate that Charles was contributing to the newspaper. For example, in the following year a poem by E Nesbit *Song for Labour* and a review of her book *Lays and Legends* are printed in the paper as well as Fabian essays and an article by GB Shaw. These could just have been reprints, but Charles's knowledge of the authors and continuing Fabian membership suggest his hand was at work there. In November 1891 his name is certainly among the list of subscribers to a hardship fund for the widow of Revd Hugh Gilmore, an outstanding Methodist and socialist speaker who had just died.

Whatever was his role with *The Pioneer*, Charles now began to 'network' more earnestly. Two people whom he met in November 1890 were James and Louise (usually called Lucy) Morice. Chloe records in her diary that she and Charles went to tea with the Morices on November 1st at their house in Scarborough Street, South Glenelg. Chloe confided to a friend in a letter that day: 'They are interesting people because they have always been immensely proud of being agnostic and superior, and now they're beginning to be a little sick of it. Mrs Morice came and asked us if Charlie would give her <u>anything</u> to do . . . She didn't have a baby for several years after she was married and then, at the top of her hopes, it was born dead, poor woman.' Lucy had been married since 1886 and did go on to have one precious child, a son interestingly called John Patrick Spens Morice, to whom Charles was godfather. The name is a folk joke in that they all knew the Scottish folk ballad *Patrick Spens* (*Child ballad 58*) but Lucy was also related to the Spence family. Certainly Lucy's previous sad loss of a child explains why she devoted such tremendous energy later in 1905 as founder of the Kindergarten movement in South Australia and as a campaigner against high infant mortality rates.

The two couples got on well for several reasons. Charles at least was the same age as the Morices and all three shared an idealistic vision of a more equitable society. The Morices were Unitarians but also supported the ideas of the Forward Movement, a Methodist initiative started in London to reconnect with the problems of the urban poor – Charles could relate to that, of course. Chloe, for her part, had a link with James Morice in that both their fathers were Scottish and had attended the same University (Aberdeen). Finally all four were interested in women's rights. Lucy Morice (née Spence) was the niece and close companion of Catherine Spence, the author, reformer and feminist. Within a month of their first tea at the Morices, Charles and Chloe had been invited to lunch with the Spence family and visited them again to hear of plans to present a female suffrage bill to the South Australian Parliament. In March 1891 Charles wrote to his father that he had just sent off a letter in support of the bill and on June 15th he was still hoping for the bill to become law. It was to be another three years in fact, but South Australia was the second legislature in the world (after New Zealand) to give women the vote.

Louise (Lucy)
Morice

1859-1951

social reformer

The Marsons and Morices saw a lot of each other socially at this time. When Chloe announced her pregnancy, Lucy promptly made six little shirts for the new baby and when Charles went house-hunting for his move to Parkside in June 1891, Lucy went with him to advise. In the end Charles and Chloe took a three-month rented house on Alfred Street very near to St Oswald's church, where there was much activity to welcome the new incumbent after a gap of fifteen months with no priest in charge. The church was solid enough, having been built of stone six years previously to house 150 people, but with no vestry. Local men now volunteered to construct one of corrugated zinc and this was ready by mid-August. In addition there was a Church Day School, in the charge of Miss Neil, where

156

Charles visited and taught RE during the week. In return, he was able to use the schoolroom for his own purposes.

St Oswald's choir outside the new zinc vestry

Over the holiday period in December 1891, for example, following the Whitechapel model, he prepared a 'Free Picture Exhibition', borrowing paintings from friends and from galleries to show to the community. It was a worry from a security point of view in a schoolroom, and he admitted he would have liked a bigger attendance, but at least it was a stimulating idea. Within six weeks of his arrival, he gave a lecture in the schoolroom to the Federal Working Men's Association on 'Poor London', and followed it next day with a debate at the Democratic Club in Flinders Street upon 'The History and Aims of English Socialism'.

His first few months at Parkside were tremendously busy. First he had to revive the parish. He started a fundraising drive to reduce its debts (e.g. a summer fête in February produced £45); reinstated the choir; organised a team of home visitors; and set up his usual clubs. His sermons were now filling the little church to capacity. Three accounts of his activities are worthy of mention. First, Frederick Young, a graduate of Keble College Oxford and then a master at St Peter's College in Adelaide, wrote with hindsight twenty years later:

'The Revd CL Marson has made more difference to my life than anyone else outside my own family. It is owing to him that I am a Socialist and a clergyman . . . one incident I recall is when he had announced that he would give a lecture on 'The Masses and the Mass'. I arrived a little late and to my surprise the hall was packed with working men. What impressed me most was the bold way in which he preached Jesus Christ AND THEY DID LISTEN!'

Secondly, one of his Glenelg parishioners wrote, explaining that he had contributed towards Charles's stipend at Parkside 'just to keep this very delightful person in South Australia. I have never known anyone with such a power of inspiring affection and interest. There were High Churchmen and Ritualists doing the same symbolic acts but without that something which made those symbols living things.'

***Charles in biretta cap
1892***

***Photo: courtesy of the
State Library of South
Australia***

Finally, Arthur West, then vicar of St Augustine's (the neighbouring parish to St Oswald's), wrote:

'(Marson) preached right socialism as the essence of Christian teaching. He filled his little Mission Church with working men and had made the services beautiful with orderly, dignified ritual. Many leading men were attracted by curiosity to his preaching and a band of young men rallied faithfully round him. His uncompromising outspokenness and hatred of half-measures naturally brought him into conflict with Episcopal suavity and he had little use for assemblies and conferences.

158

'His appearance in the hot nights, a figure in complete white, striding the streets like a ghost, was often quoted to me, and his personal priestly influence was immensely strong.

'It was most interesting to note in Adelaide how hard-hearted businessmen, of the most Protestant persuasion, had very great regard and respect for his courage and devotion. Only one man, so far as I can tell – Canon Wise of St George's Goodwood – has made the same appeal to Australians.'

Three leading men that Charles met about this time were David Charleston, Robert Guthrie and John McPherson. Charleston had contributed an article to the December 1890 issue of *The Pioneer* and was a keen supporter of the Single Tax. He was a marine engineer, originally from Cornwall (born 1848), who had emigrated in 1884 and was President of the United Trades and Labour Council (UTLC) in 1889. Guthrie was a Scot (born 1857) who, as a sailor, had gone to work the South Australian coastal trade in 1878 and by 1890 was Secretary of the Port Adelaide branch of the seaman's union. McPherson, another Scot born 1860, had emigrated to Australia in 1882 and led the printers' union. He was Secretary of the UTLC. Whether through *The Pioneer* paper, through his sermons (Charleston and Guthrie were avowed Christians) or through political contacts, Charles drew these men into an important alliance between intellectuals and working people, when he launched the South Australian Fabian Society in September 1891.

For once, Charles was in the right place at the right time. He commanded respect as an early Fabian (since Oct 1885) and was indeed the only registered Fabian in Australia up till then. He had copies of the Fabian Tracts written by Shaw and others about socialism. In addition he had real experience of working-class poverty and issues. He had seen the Fabians in England duck the opportunity to support direct labour representation in Parliament (Annie Besant's ill-supported Fabian Parliamentary League of 1886). Indeed he was disappointed to see so few working people in a basically middle class club. The Fabian motto of 'permeation' (social evolution by education and persuasion rather than revolution) was 'a dangerous game', Charles said. 'Since we want working-class legislation, we had better get, as soon as we can, working-class legislators.' Labour members were essential, he said, because 'no-one else can be trusted to grapple with our plutocratic society; no-one else knows so well where the boot of poverty pinches the toe of labour.'

His socialist credentials and his inclusive message were bound to attract working people at this particular time for several reasons. An economic depression was now biting harder in the State and working people wanted representation. Secondly, State politics had hitherto been an unorganised business without constituted political parties. The majority of the 24 members of the Legislative Council (upper house) were rural conservatives, who were elected by a narrow property-owning electorate. However, the 54 MPs in the (lower) House of Assembly were elected by a free adult male vote and largely thought of themselves as Independents, clustering around particular leaders in rough 'conservative' or 'progressive' factions, as policies and issues unfolded. The way lay open for any disciplined group that could emerge with a manifesto which its members were pledged to support.

The failure of the Australian maritime strike of August 1890 had convinced labour activists that the best way to advance their interests was through parliamentary representation, especially after the law was confirmed that year awarding remuneration for MPs, so enabling working men to leave their jobs for a time. Thus encouraged, the UTLC (United Trades and Labour Council) set up a special committee in January 1891 to select and support labour candidates in the forthcoming elections. This committee became the United Labour Party (ULP) and it chose David Charleston and Robert Guthrie to stand in the two Adelaide seats for the Legislative Council. They were successful in May 1891, along with a third ULP nominee Andrew Kirkpatrick in the southern rural areas. Further success would follow in 1892 when John McPherson won East Adelaide in a by-election for the House of Assembly; and in the following year nine other ULP candidates became MPs in the Lower House, despite a belated effort by conservatives to form a counter-party 'The National Defence League'. This Labour block of ten MPs combined with the liberal faction, led by Charles Cameron Kingston, to deliver a progressive programme of legislation (including votes for women) during the six years between 1893 and 1899.

160

No wonder Charles was excited to gather together these newly elected ULP politicians into his new Fabian Society at such a promising time. They were keen, no doubt, to deepen their understanding of socialism and to feel part of a much wider movement. Given their support, the South Australian Fabian Society moved forward in numbers and influence. By April 1892, after just six months, there were 37 local members and several branches up and running.

The London Fabian Society had initially not been keen on the idea of branches outside London, let alone outside the country, and must have been amazed by this surge of interest overseas. The South Australian Fabian Society was the first constituted overseas branch and the 17th branch overall. It reported that it was busy adapting the London Fabian Tracts for publication in Adelaide, as well as promoting a series of Fabian lectures, very much along the lines of what London had done. In its own October 1892 membership list the London Society showed 368 London members; 137 local branch members and 121 'others' – a grand total of 626. The seven South Australians who had paid dues to London were – Charles Marson; James and Lucy Morice; William Bickford; Walter Baker; D Morley Charleston; Robert Guthrie; and Arthur Pearson. John McPherson joined in 1893. This group retained their membership for an average of ten years and clearly found it beneficial.

The South Australian Fabian Society was eventually wound up in 1902 and its members had mixed success in their parliamentary or reforming lives. But it clearly served a purpose and represents for Charles a considerable achievement as its instigator. The ULP (United Labour Party) morphed into the Parliamentary Labour Party after federation in 1901, and remains one of the main political parties in Australia today.

Alongside this political and parish work, somehow Charles found time to complete the drafts for his first book *Faery Stories*, which is considered to be the first children's book to be published in Australia. It was produced by local printers EA Petherick & Co in November 1891. There are nine original tales about trolls, dwarves and fairies, who hinder or help Nature and Humans in their lives.

The stories are set in Australia and Charles had been practising them in his Sunday school classes. Cecil Sharp had heard him reciting them to groups of children too. Finally he'd shown the manuscripts to Chloe and they were now ready for the printers. The book ran to one hundred pages with no illustrations, but the language is very visual. Fantasy worlds lie just behind the thin veil of 'reality' and the various children in the stories are transported there by magic boat or carriage, by flying hand-in-hand with fairies or just by wandering in the bush.

The stories are out of print now but they are exciting with nice touches of humour about teachers and other authority figures. They draw on European storytelling traditions and make no reference to Aboriginal 'dreamtime' stories but feel 'Australian' in terms of landscape and human interest. There is, however, no continuous 'hero' figure linking the stories – different children face danger on their own and find courage and special powers. The stories do not have obvious 'happy endings'. For instance, Roland, a young boy, rescues a magic fish stranded on the sands and in return is guided on a magic boat down to the bottom of the sea, where he confronts Yewli, the wicked Sea Troll. Rendered invisible by a magic flower (lily) that he carries, Roland is unafraid and blows pollen from the lily into Yewli's eyes and blinds him. Yewli's evil powers ebb away and Roland eventually returns home but finds that his parents and family are gone, because 30 years have passed during his short absence in fairyland. Only a (talking) magpie now recognises the hero's return. If you've ever heard the Australian magpie, you will know its splendid song!

Another extraordinary story is about Elsie, a young girl from the bush 'who never wore shoes, or hardly ever, but she could ride the wildest horse through the scrub, and she could track like any blackfellow.' One day she finds a white dwarf asleep under a tree and shares her food with him. He says his name is Treblekin and that he will return her favour by helping her just once in her life but only if she asks him. Much later, after various incidents in which Treblekin had not intervened to help her, she is riding in the bush when her horse throws her and runs off. She is by a lake and sees a boat in front of her. She climbs in the boat and falls asleep. Suddenly the boat shakes, the sail fills and she finds a tall giant steering her away on a whirlwind journey over hills and through clouds, until her nose and ear begin to bleed. The tall giant is Mukka, the Hill Troll and he gives her a tiny pebble to put in her ear to stop the bleeding. He kisses her on the cheek and lets the boat fall to ground. She returns home to her family but something is wrong – her cheek is scarred where he'd kissed her and her eyesight is such that it can no longer see beauty around her in colours, flowers, people. Curiously she now does brilliantly at school and becomes 'the best teacher' in the colony! But her unhappiness is only solved when she appeals to Treblekin and he releases her from the spell, by kissing her on the cheek himself and administering essence of the plant Fumitory (Charles was a keen amateur botanist and herbalist) in her ear.

A third story is worth repeating briefly in the light of subsequent events in Australia. This is the story of the Prickly Pear Hedge. Two children, Mary and Jack, are always asking their father awkward questions about the trees and plants around them and he replies that he is just a 'busy and stupid old fellow but you can learn all you want to know the other side of the prickly pear hedge.' Intriguing. Soon after, their Aunt Patience, who is a white witch and can cure people of their various ills, comes to stay and the children are frantic to know more about this magic hedge. She says to them: 'you shall go through the prickly pear hedge if you want to go and then you can see for yourselves; but I think you will be glad we live on this side of it, after all.' She whisks them away in a magic carriage and they come up to a massive screen of prickly pears (a kind of cacti). They each find their way through a hole and discover on the other side a mass of trees and plants rather like a huge Botanical Garden. Each plant has its name written on labels in Latin with great descriptions of its use and its origins. When the wind blows, all these plants sing out their names and details, 'all lecturing at once like learned professors'. And the birds sing out too, and the insects and all the beasts in a 'tangled and interminable chorus'. The frightened children run back through the prickled hedge and return home as fast as they can. Jack says that from now on he would just 'think about plants in peace, for when they all lectured like professors, I could not learn a single thing.' Aunt Patience says: 'If you go through (the prickly hedge), my dears, you will pass all your standards and be top of the school, but it hurts a good lot, and, as far as I am concerned, I like best the quiet, beautiful things on this side of the Prickly Pear Hedge.'

163

The footnote here is that the common prickly pear was introduced into Australia in the late 1800s and spread so fast that it colonised 25 million hectares of land. A law was passed in 1924 to ban it as a noxious weed and it was only controlled by a specially introduced biological parasite. Charles would have been fascinated by that outcome!

It's extraordinary to think that all this material was running through Charles's mind at the same time as the political and parish issues. One further concern for him was, of course, Chloe's imminent delivery. They moved house in a hurry in early October 1891 to Blackmore End House on Eastwood Terrace (now the busy A1 Fullarton Road out of Central Adelaide). The house is still there today – it's a Podiatry Centre! It is situated immediately opposite the old Lunatic Asylum (now the Glenside Hospital).

There was a wall right round the asylum. Many of its residents would probably not have been there, if modern psychiatric assessments and treatments had been applied then. Charles began to visit there one day a week and respected the doctor-in-charge Dr Cleland. On September 15th 1891 he wrote to his father: '(Cleland) never puts them in padded rooms but freedom in large ranging grounds and politeness and victuals are his methods.' Charles 'interviewed all the ones labelled Church of England, criminals, refractory (*unmanageable*) and docile. The refractory female ward is the worst I have seen yet but I am due again there this afternoon and new horrors await me.' He persevered, however, and a fortnight later comments that 'they seem to look forward to my pastoral visits and are to have Holy Communion on Saturday morning.'

The vestry minutes for St Oswald's show that Charles did indeed give regular services of mass there over this period and that no priest before or immediately after him did that duty. The little chapel at the asylum doubled as a female dining room and, as a consequence, Bishop Kennion had steadfastly refused to consecrate it but Charles ignored that ruling and carried on anyway.

Parkside Asylum (now Glenside Hospital) built for 700 patients and opened in 1870. Photo courtesy of National Library of Australia

While Charles had been heaping work and worries upon himself, Chloe had been reducing her commitments in October and preparing for her new baby. She was really pleased that Charles had written to her brother Ronald to ask him to be godfather to the child, 'thinking of their old friendship and forgetting the bitter things that Ronald had said sometimes'. She also liked their new house and all seemed well except that Charles 'doesn't get rid of this weakening asthma and cough, which he has had now really for months. I feed him with beef-tea and do everything I can to get him well but it seems impossible. He has very hard work and I think the climate really cannot suit him. It goes to my heart to hear him wheezing and he has to burn that dreadful Himrod.'

On November 3rd 1891 he wrote to his father: 'I am queer in the chest and have not had a decent night for weeks.' Then, of course, just a fortnight later on November 16th their baby Mary was born at home with ensuing nights of feeding and disturbance. She was a bonny baby 'nearly trebling her size and weight by Christmas'. The proud parents bought a 'perambulator with india rubber tires' to wheel her round the house and small garden. While Charles was

165

preparing his art exhibition over the Christmas period, Chloe took baby Mary down to Glenelg to show her off, but Mary picked up a tummy bug and they sped home to recover. Infant diarrhoea in the hot summer months was a major cause of infant deaths at this time and a real worry for parents. Parkside was one of four wards in the municipality of Unley (population 11,683) and its progressive Medical Officer Dr Wigg was pressing its Mayor to bring in regulations to regulate and improve the many dairies in the area. A total of 33,000 milch cows were kept in the whole Adelaide area. Impure milk given to children without the benefit of refrigeration in hot weather contributed to much illness; and tuberculosis was responsible for one out of every six deaths in Unley.

Charles and Chloe with baby Mary Dec 1891 outside their house in Eastwood Terrace

Chloe and baby Mary were both well and thriving through January of the New Year but Charles continued to struggle with his health. Another problem had hit him, namely that one of his churchwardens (Mr Ker) had been caught embezzling church funds to the tune of £50 (equivalent to £3,000 today). No wonder St Oswald's still had financial problems. Charles had not appointed the man himself but was upset at the ensuing scandal. Stress was definitely undermining his health. He wrote to his father on January 5th 1892:

> 'It seems really to be useless to stay on here, for this horrid asthma grows upon me, and the hot weather which I hoped and prayed would take it away only makes it worse. Every night I am awake with it and for weeks I have not drawn a single breath without whistling. I have discovered more

asthmatic people in South Australia than I could ever have imagined to exist in one community. If I jog on, I shall get angina pectoris or syncope. So we have almost resolved to book for home next April. It is most unhappy, for we had settled down to the Colony and I get on well with the people. The services are well attended and the support given me is warm.'

In the next month two doctors separately advised him in no uncertain terms to return home. On February 8th he wrote to his father:

'I have resigned St Oswald's but am heartbroken about it. The work exactly suits me and to·desert the post seems treason now. But it has been so hot here (104 to 111 degrees in the shade). This time Baby never had the 'dire-rear', as the people aptly call it, though three babies died in our street and Chloe was sick with fear.'

Although Bishop Kennion had not seen eye-to-eye with Charles, he did write him an encouraging letter:

'It is with very deep regret that I have received your letter informing me that on account of your health you must leave Parkside and return to England. That you would have accomplished much good work for Christ and His Church, had you been able to stay longer with us, I feel convinced. I am very sorry you are going and I know my wife will miss Mrs Marson very much. I shall be glad to give you a letter of commendation to any Bishop you may wish me to write to.'

Gradually Charles let it be known that he would be leaving after Easter – his last service at St Oswald's was Easter Day April 17th 1892. As a result he was even more in demand, writing to his father on February 23rd: 'I am very and horribly busy, for all the Colony and his wife seems to want a lecture, sermon or answer to some questions before I go.' On April 16th 1892 *The Pioneer* newspaper wrote: 'The second session of the South Australian Fabian Society was opened on Wednesday April 6th, when the President (Revd CL Marson) gave an address to the members and others at the Working Women's Trades Union Room, Victoria Square. During the six months of its existence four tracts have been issued and sixteen lectures given by various members in the city and suburbs. Mr Marson urged the members to renewed and redoubled efforts in spreading Socialist doctrines. The Rev JR Glasson moved a vote of

167

thanks to the President.' In a separate column it recorded: 'In spite of all his eccentricities and curious ritualistic notions the Revd CL Marson has done a good deal towards the awakening of the public conscience on matters social and his proposed departure for England will be sincerely regretted by many. The formation of the S.A. Fabian Society was an act of his that may yet bear good fruit.' The Society did indeed continue vigorously for a few years, reporting back to London of its achievements, but it gradually lost its dynamism without its instigator's vision and ability to draw together the different strands of socialist thought and experience.

His parish missed him too, because no priest was given to them for a whole year until Revd John Hussey took over in 1893. He worked tirelessly to erect the new and larger church building that exists today in St Ann's Place. Unfortunately he contracted tuberculosis and died before it was consecrated. The chances are high that if Charles had stayed, a similar fate might well have befallen him, given that his own health was precarious at best.

So ended Charles's and Chloe's Australian sojourn. They had both made friends there and Charles admitted as such back in England in a letter (June 25th): 'I wish I could tell you how dear and good and sweet and beyond all words kind the Australians have been to me.' One further reason for his departure may be that his friend Cecil Sharp had failed to find his niche in Adelaide and had left for England four months previously in January 1892. Charles no doubt thought that his three years there had been a time of mixed success. He had felt somewhat free from the class-based society of England and its complacent Established Church. The potential in the new colony was immense, if it could rise above mere individualism and the mad pursuit of material success, so as to build instead a more equitable society. He had shown great vision in setting up the South Australian Fabian Society and had been penetrating in his statements on education and other social issues. He had influenced many people, who were sad to see him go.

Top Left: Charles at Clifton College aged 15.
Top Right: Clevedon Vicarage where Charles grew up from age 12.

Left: Miss Sophy
Pedder of Clevedon,
Charles's guide and
friend.

Clevedon photos
courtesy of Cleve-
don Civic Society

Above: St Mary's Orlestone, where Charles was Rector for three years.

Left: Marble effigies in Brenzett church, as in the ghost story 'Man-size in Marble'.

Below: SS Austral in which Charles sailed to Adelaide. Photo courtesy of the National Library of Australia

Orient S. N. Cº   SS "Austral"   5588 tons

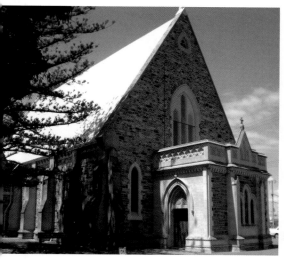

Above left: St Peter's Glenelg. Above right: Chloe and baby Mary 1891. Below: St James-the-less, Hambridge where Charles served for the last nineteen years of his life.

Above: Chloe and Charles with baby John in vicarage garden 1896.
Below left: Cecil Sharp (photo English Folk Dance & Song Society).
Below right: First book of Somerset Folk Songs published 1904.

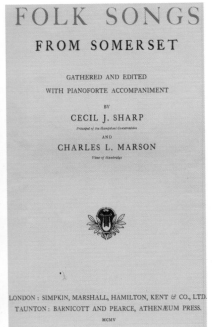

FOLK SONGS

FROM SOMERSET

GATHERED AND EDITED

WITH PIANOFORTE ACCOMPANIMENT

BY

CECIL J. SHARP

Principal of the Hampstead Conservatoire

AND

CHARLES L. MARSON

Vicar of Hambridge

LONDON : SIMPKIN, MARSHALL, HAMILTON, KENT & CO., LTD.
TAUNTON : BARNICOTT AND PEARCE, ATHENÆUM PRESS.
MCMV

14

Back to London Town

In early June 1892 Charles, Chloe and baby Mary found themselves back in London. The Bishop of Worcester had written to Charles, saying that he would be pleased to license him, if he could find a suitable curacy, but in the end Charles responded to an offer from his old supporter Brooke Foss Westcott. He had been promoted to become Bishop of Durham, while Charles had been away in Australia. Leaving Chloe and Mary with family and friends in London, Charles went to work on a trial basis at St Matthew's Church Silksworth near Sunderland among the 'sick and stricken' miners. This village had grown in size from just 400 people in 1871 to 4,707 by 1879 following the opening of the coal mine by its owner, the 6th Marquess of Londonderry. Workers from Ireland and Scotland as well as locals arrived in Silksworth, attracted by the new jobs and the new housing built by the coal company. The work, however, was arduous and dangerous for the 1,465 underground and 372 overground workers. Despite 'modern equipment' there were 37 fatalities recorded in the first thirty years of its operation. The mine was transferred to the National Coal Board in 1947 and eventually closed in 1971.

It seems that while the vicar Revd JJ Brown was away, Charles borrowed his carriage and gave drives to the miners. The carriage was badly scratched in the process by their boots and kit. Because there was no railway connection to the village at the time and exhausted miners had to trudge some distance to their homes or to catch a horse-drawn bus, Charles was no doubt trying to be helpful, but the vicar didn't appreciate the damage to his carriage and did not offer Charles a job as his curate!

So Charles returned to London and was pleased to land a job as curate under Revd Bradley Abbot at Christchurch, Clapham. To his surprise both Bishop Kennion from Adelaide and Bishop Roffen (Thorold), whom he had offended eight years before at Petersham, had written to support him. Abbot may have been sympathetic anyway, because he had himself been a curate in Whitechapel somewhat earlier at St Mark's between 1854 and 1855 and would have appreciated Charles's service there. Furthermore he approved of Charles's High Church style and had himself conducted services with vestments and full rituals for years. In fact Charles was initially shocked by Abbot's showy flamboyance and flagrant disregard of protestant rubrics.

Abbot had been vicar at Christchurch (population 4,600) for 36 years with a tidy salary of £500 (equivalent to £30,000 today) and was now nearing retirement at the age of 64. Born in Yorkshire, he had studied at Trinity College Dublin before coming to London for ordination. He was rather a bluff man, who enjoyed a good argument and was now rather portly and lame, walking with the aid of a stick. In a letter to his father (29 July 1892), Charles wrote that Abbot had 'built the church *(1861)* and vicarage and schools, spent freely and worked hard, and naturally thinks that he is entitled to do just as he likes. No-one will have me except him and I am far too grateful to wish to cross him for his anarchic views. He is a brave and strong man and says that he entirely disregards all socialist views, so I am at full liberty to preach these, to the top of my bent, if I think them right.'

The omens were looking good for Charles and he set about finding a house to rent in the area. Curiously he was now very near to his father's birthplace in Acre Lane, half a mile or so to the south. Indeed he wrote to his father to tell him that he had found his old school – Dr Charles Pritchard had been his teacher at Clapham Grammar – and that it was now a furniture shop! At last Charles found a small house in Christchurch Terrace (*now Place*) and Chloe and baby Mary could make themselves comfortable that summer. Their books had just arrived by sea freight and had a new home too.

Maybe recent stresses were beginning to affect him but Charles was enduring another bout of asthma trouble, lying awake three hours a night regularly. Baby Mary, on the other hand, was thriving, and Chloe had been showing her off in London to her sister Janie and her aunts Mary and Agnes, to her Newnham friends like the Fawcetts and to her father Peter Bayne. None of her brothers were available to see their new niece, however – Ronald was still in Orlestone and Charlie was abroad in Burma, having had to leave behind his wife Gussie soon after the birth of their first child, a baby daughter Alice. The good news, however, was that her other brother

170

Willie, who had just turned 30 and was a printer and compositor in Folkestone, had recently become engaged to be married.

There were a few more changes in family life for Charles and Chloe to catch up on after their years away. Charles's younger brother Harry Marson had got married in June 1891 to Katherine (Kitty) Powys Ker, daughter of William Palgrave Ker. William Ker's own father was for over twenty years a Collector of Customs in Clifton Bristol but the family had then moved to Clevedon, and that is where Kitty met Harry Marson. Kitty's father was a graduate of Christchurch Oxford but had no profession as such, living off private means. Whether the family thought that Kitty was marrying beneath her station or for some other reason, the wedding had had its tensions. Charles had written from Australia: 'It is a bother about Harry's wedding and rows with the Kers. Little good comes of such egoism à deux. He (Harry) never acknowledged my letter of congratulation on his engagement and has not taken the slightest notice of any letter I have written to him for years, so I do not feel inclined to write to him any more. It is very kind of Kitty to have him.' Harry was by then a Lieutenant in the 8th Bengal Native Infantry and the young couple promptly disappeared to India.

Relations with his youngest brother Frank had, however, been renewed on his return to London, for they had not seen each other since their Glenelg days together. Frank had enrolled as a medical student in London and was busy, according to his father, 'poring over dead men's bones and dissecting bits of the human form with much gusto'. When Charles had a break in his heavy workload – he had, he said, '3,300 folk to my share, four guilds, schools and heaps of societies' – Frank came over to visit, as he did at Christmas 1892.

Charles continued busily into the New Year, receiving invitations to preach and lecture outside the parish, particularly at branches of the newly formed Christian Social Union (CSU). The CSU had been started by Canon Henry Scott Holland back in 1889, while Charles was away in Australia. In a sense it was a revamp of Charles's Christian Socialist Society that had gone off at half-cock in 1886 and had recently folded (June 1892). Less overtly 'socialist', the CSU nevertheless appealed to a broad range of Christians, who demanded social reform through their newspapers *The Commonwealth* and *Goodwill*. Charles wrote several articles for those newspapers over the next few years and was pleased to lecture on subjects like 'The

171

Poor Law', which particularly exercised CSU members. At its height the CSU claimed 6,000 members including 16 out of 53 Bishops with Westcott as its President. It lasted for thirty years and was not wound up until 1919.

It was at this time too that Charles met the young priest Percy Dearmer (born 1867), who was working as a curate under 'Brother Bob' Morris among the gas workers at St Anne's Vauxhall, the neighbouring parish to Christchurch. Percy was Secretary of the London CSU and a member of both the Guild of St Matthew and the Fabian Society. He is best remembered today for his editing (with Vaughan Williams) of *The English Hymnal* (1906) and *The Oxford Book of Carols* (1928). In South London Charles also met and befriended Conrad Noel, the future 'Red Vicar' of Thaxted from 1910 to 1942.

Despite his claims of indifference to socialism, Father Abbot was put under pressure by members of his congregation over Charles's political views and he released him from the curacy after nine months. Charles wrote to an Australian friend in May 1893 that 'we were kicked out of Clapham, you know, for socialism'. Fortunately his friend Bishop Westcott intervened yet again to recommend Charles for the curacy at St Mary the Virgin, Soho. The Bishop of London, Frederick Temple, wrote to Charles on April 14th 1893: 'I have licensed you because I had a very warm letter from the Bishop of Durham in your favour and also because I thought you had been hardly treated. But your own account of yourself is not quite what I like, and I think you ought to try to learn to be a little less sure of your own powers and merits.'

So Charles and Chloe moved house again to a flat in 13 Soho Square. Frank Etherington, who had known Chloe when she was at Orlestone and he was a young lay reader nearby at Ashford, was now a student at King's College London and was one of many visitors to the 'white-panelled, lofty rooms in this seventeenth century house – the books in heaps all over the room, the teapot always going, people coming in and out all day, all the sound and surge of London round about the house'. St Mary's parish had been carved out of St Anne's Soho in 1854 and stretched from Tottenham Court Road in the north, along and a little either side of Charing Cross Road, as far as Leicester Square to the south. The church itself would later be demolished in 1934 but it was a historic church, as described by Charles: 'The church here was built in Charles the Second's reign and used to be a Greek church. It appears in Hogarth's print "Noon". It has a high, raised-up chancel and altar, and a side-chapel with a Lady altar in it, and a statue of the Blessed Virgin, and sanctuary lamps, copes and all sorts of Church Furniture galore, crosses and censers. The clergy go processing in copes or tunicles or chasubles, until any protestants who come in are carried out fainting and put under the pump.'

It seems that the Revd Robert Gwynne, vicar since 1874 and now aged 60, was often absent and left most matters in the hands of his two curates. Born in Ireland and educated at Trinity College Dublin, Gwynne had coincidentally served as curate to Bradley Abbot at Clapham in 1864 before settling in Soho. According to John Cardwell's 1905 book *Men and Women of Soho,* Gwynne was 'a distinguished Oriental scholar but of unobtrusive ecclesiastical views and of no aggressive energy'. Elsewhere in the book it implies that Gwynne actually suffered from dementia in his final years. In any event Charles now prepared to take over from Revd William Moll, who had been in post as curate for nine years and was about to move to St Philip's Newcastle.

Charles already knew Moll quite well. He was elected a Fabian member a year or so after Charles in January 1887 but more importantly they were both prominent members of the Guild of St Matthew. During his tenure at St Mary's, Moll had invited men like Stewart Headlam and Arthur Stanton to preach there, because they had no other pulpit. Moll had also been curate with Father Abbot at Clapham for a spell (from 1881 to 1882), so he and Charles probably swapped a few stories at their handover meetings. For example, on handing in his resignation at Clapham, Moll had heard Bradley Abbot say, 'I don't like you leaving this way – you are one of the only men who has left me without either my threatening a libel action or their solicitors threatening one.'

This was a good time in Moll's life. Born in 1856, the son of a linen draper from Norwich, he had done well at Worcester College Oxford and had now served for many years in City parishes. He was a tough character, who knew his own mind on matters and was ready for the challenge of a much bigger parish in Newcastle (24,000 people). He got married that summer and with his new wife Edith he travelled north. There he became a champion of the Tyneside labour movement and joined the Council of the new Independent Labour Party. Later in 1906 he would be a forceful member (with Conrad Noel and Charles) of the Church Socialist League.

Charles loved his work in Soho. Moll and his fellow curate William Busby had had the services of a Parochial Nurse Mary Simons as well as the usual team of visitors. Also at work in the parish, and quite prepared to help their Anglican colleagues, were a number of Catholic nuns – Sisters of Mercy. Charles was impressed by them: 'Nuns also belong, at least two unsworn and hard-working girls help us and wear white bibs and black streamers on their hats.'

Another team member was Henry Maskell, journalist, who wrote about Charles's rapport with his parishioners: 'No one won their hearts so quickly. He visited them all in their homes and his simplicity and natural sympathetic manner made them tolerate him where they would have flung most persons out. He always acted from impulse, but his impulses were kindly. Superior people were inclined to frown. Of course, he was born to be misunderstood except by children and the common people.'

So Charles happily went about his parish business throughout the summer of 1893 and into the autumn months. In fact he had the use of clergy accommodation in Charing Cross Road where he stayed sometimes 'so that Chloe and Mary cannot interrupt me in my studies'. He had now begun his next literary project – a book *Psalms at Work*, which was published by Kegan Paul in February 1894 and went through four editions. On September 1st he wrote to Chloe, who was on a visit to Clevedon: 'I have been doing too many hours at it and am grateful to the British Museum for saying "stop". I was at it last night till midnight.' The book selected a number of Psalms and supplied a textual commentary on them but also suggested practical uses for them in the daily life of a priest.

Another important development in 1893 was that Charles officiated at the wedding of his friend Cecil Sharp to Miss Constance Birch. Cecil had come back from Adelaide in January 1892 and spent much of that year teaching music to private pupils from rooms at Langham Street, just north of Oxford Circus. He had intended to take lessons in composition, because he was keen to extend the start he had made in Australia with his Nursery Rhyme Suite and operetta *Sylvia*. However, there was neither time nor money and he focused instead on securing several part-time jobs. He tried out as conductor with various choral societies and by June 1893 had a contract with the Finsbury Choral Association. Like Charles in his profession, Cecil was finding the whole business of jobseeking frustrating. In letters to Miss Birch (18th and 26th January 1893) he wrote: 'I shall soon get tired of these small societies. I want something bigger'; and 'I am itching to get work which I know I am qualified to do but people are so afraid of giving an unknown man a trial, and I am not good at advertising myself.'

Cecil had known Constance Birch since 1874 when he was about fifteen and she was about twelve. He had left Uppingham School to receive private mathematical tuition under Mr George Heppel in Weston-super-Mare. George was a great teacher, whose house was filled with his own children (seven at that time with five to follow) as well as two assistant teachers and four boarders. He had probably acquired his mathematical skills from his father, who was a fruiterer in the City of London. Educated at St John's Cambridge, George then spent two years as Principal of Nelson College in New Zealand. He later became a Vice-President of the Mathematical Association.

George must have been an inspiration to the young Cecil Sharp over the two year period of his stay at his school. His wife Catherine (née Corner) was born in Tooley Street Southwark, very near to the Sharp family business, and was a lifelong friend of Cecil's mother Jane – hence Cecil's complete trust in the Heppels. In particular Catherine was very musical with a lovely soprano voice and her family had frequent fun organising musical evenings and theatricals. It was to one of these that Constance Birch came.

Constance (always known as Connie) was the third child of Dora Hoghton (pronounced Horton), whose father was Sir Henry Bold Hoghton, 8th Baronet of Hoghton Tower near Preston. The family had owned land in Lancashire for centuries and represented the county as Sheriff or MP for most of that time but Dora's own fortunes had waned somewhat. Her husband Mr Priestley Birch (gentleman of Manchester) had died young in 1867 when Connie was just five and

Dora remained a widow for the next 35 years. Connie was actually born near Kingsbridge in Devon, and the family had then rented a house at Lyme Regis in Dorset where Connie was taught at home by a governess. She was described as a 'tall and beautiful girl with brown, wavy hair', who could 'sketch successfully, sing and play the violin'.

When Connie was 21, she received a modest annual income of approximately £140 (equivalent to £8,400 today) and lived with her mother at Clevedon in Somerset during the 1880s, where they would have bumped into Revd Charles Marson Senior. Cecil was away in Australia from 1882 to 1892 but did renew his friendship with Connie during a spell of sick leave in 1885, and the couple eventually became engaged in January 1893.

However, Connie still had some doubts. She was 30 and Cecil was 33 with as yet no settled prospects. He was just starting two days a week as music teacher at Ludgrove School near Cockfosters, a new prep school for boys wishing to go on to Eton, but it had only a dozen pupils and its future was uncertain. Its headmaster and owner Arthur Dunn, who had won four caps for England at football, was in a similar position to Cecil and only went ahead with his own wedding in December 1892 when his tenth pupil enrolled! But although Cecil had never taught this age group before, he was given freedom to teach piano, violin and singing in whatever way he chose and his gamble paid off. Pupil numbers increased quickly and by 1895 there were 44 on the roll.

Connie's doubts were then further relieved by the good intervention of Charles Marson. She had been writing to Cecil about her worries and he had written back: 'You are always wanting a sign . . . If you are continually cross-examining yourself and sifting and analysing your many feelings and thoughts, you will sooner or later muddle yourself. Life must be taken broadly, not minutely.' This is very similar to Charles's tone in his letters to Chloe nearly four years previously. Now that Charles was living in Soho, it was easy for Cecil to go round and ask him to intercede on his behalf. Connie had to come up to town anyway to see her older brother Lionel, who was also preparing to get married that summer to an artist friend. So Charles dispensed his advice to Connie, and perhaps she met Chloe for the first time too. The wedding went ahead on August 22nd 1893 at the church of All Saints in Clevedon with Charles presiding. The reception was held at Dora Birch's rented house The Wilderness nearby in Highdale Road.

So much was going right for Charles at this time – his Soho parish work was enjoyable; his wife and baby were happy and thriving; his second book was nearly ready; and now his good friend was married and settled nearby in North London. The only sad piece of news was that at the end of September Chloe's brother Willie lost his first child called Clotilda aged just 16 days. The funeral in Folkestone was a sad affair and Willie never really recovered from the loss.

It was just before Christmas 1893, however, when the serious news arrived that Henry West QC, patron of St Mary's and provider of Charles's stipend, had died suddenly. Effectively the money had stopped and Charles was out of a job.

15

Cabbies' Strike

To cheer them up, the Sharp family sent the Marson family a hamper with two fowls, ham, honey and eggs, and a Christmas pudding. On January 10th 1894 better news arrived in the form of a curacy position at St Mary's, Somers Town, a very run down parish squashed between Euston and St Pancras stations just south of Camden Town. Chloe was very relieved. She had only just nursed baby Mary through a bout of measles but set about finding a new house to rent.

Chloe looked at three houses and settled on 156 Seymour Street (*now Eversholt St*). On February 9th the Marson family moved in. In her 1894 diary Chloe describes the house as 'squalid' – it was uninhabited in the 1891 census and may have been in poor condition. The whole area was in truth dilapidated. A population of about 11,000 was housed in about 800 dwellings, many of which were later demolished as being infested with cockroaches, and the infant mortality rate was very high. Chloe did her best to scrub and keep the place clean, and had the stalwart help of a servant Lizzie Kowalska.

Lizzie Kowalska

With Mary

In 1894

Chloe had taken Lizzie on about fifteen months previously and negotiated a daily routine with her. The way you treated your servants was a sensitive issue with progressive people at the time and Chloe's 'system' was actually published in *The Girls' Own Paper* in 1894. Chloe got a guinea for it but it's not known if she shared that with Lizzie! In fact after Lizzie married Jack Chilman, one of Charles's acolytes, the two women stayed in touch for years. Lizzie had a sweet nature and looked after baby Mary very well in those first important years. She took her for regular walks in the pram to Regent's Park Zoo and sometimes bathed and dressed her in the mornings too. Chloe was a 'hands on' Mum but still wanted to have some independence to pay visits to her intellectual friends as well as taking up part-time work to boost the family income.

On March 1st Chloe walked down to the new Women's Hospital in Euston Road (between Churchway and Chalton St) to be interviewed for a job as a secretary. It was no surprise that she got the job, because the leading figure at the hospital was Dr Elizabeth Garrett Anderson (born 1836), the aunt of Chloe's close Newnham friend Philippa Fawcett. This splendid new hospital had been built just four years previously to enable women to receive treatment from qualified doctors of their own sex. It was a testament to the willpower and clout of Dr Garrett Anderson, who had been refused entry to medical training at various British institutions and eventually had to qualify at the University of Paris in 1870. For twenty years she had pioneered women's medicine and Chloe was inspired to join her team, even in this modest capacity. There was a link with Charles's work too in that the clergy of the local parishes would sign letters of recommendation most days of the week for their parishioners to receive free medical treatment at the Women's Hospital and at the nearby University College Hospital.

The very next day March 2nd Gladstone resigned (retired) as Liberal Prime Minister and Lord Rosebery was preparing to replace him. Less momentously Chloe took Dod (her pet name for Mary) by tram to lunch with the Sharps in their new house at 16 Manor Gardens, Holloway. Connie Sharp was expecting her first child that summer and the two women became good friends during this period together in North London. On March 10th Chloe started her job in the outpatients' department and earned 24/- that first week. She also took on five private pupils for Latin, Greek and German lessons at

5/- an hour as well as some locum teaching at Elm Park Gardens School. This was all very useful income on top of Charles's annual stipend of just £140.

Charles was hoping to earn a little more through his writing. His new book *Psalms at Work* had been well reviewed and his Australian book *Faery Stories* was being reprinted for sale in Britain. He had already hatched ideas for a new book of selected writings that he would edit himself: snippets of wisdom and inspiring thoughts by poets, philosophers and theologians of the day – from Matthew Arnold to John Stuart Mill, from Charles Dickens to his friend Bishop Westcott. Canon Scott Holland agreed to write the Preface. Charles began to write off for permission from the various authors. The book *The Following of Christ* would take a year to emerge before being published by SS Peter & Paul in 1895.

Meanwhile he had a lot to get on with in Somers Town. St Mary's had originally been carved out of the old parish of St Pancras. The church itself had been built in 1826 as a High Church to suit the many foreign (mainly Spanish) refugees, who replaced the well-to-do leaving the area. Its first vicar Revd Judkin stayed for forty years but ran out of energy. The parish was left depleted until the arrival of Revd Robert Reade remedied the situation. Reade, Charles's new boss, had commenced in 1887 and immediately set up Bible classes, various clubs, a Penny Bank and a Temperance Guild. A soup kitchen ran several days a week with soup at 1d a pint. A parish magazine had been instituted and the church itself had received a facelift with a new vestry, sacristy and side chapel. Unfortunately all this effort had undermined Reade's health and he was forced to rest and delegate to others. For example, Mr Howard Gilliat ran the club for working men at 80 Chalton Street which had a weekly membership of 70, enjoying games, lectures, debates and companionship. A locum priest and his two curates divided all the main parish duties between them, until Reade returned to lead the team again for a further four years in 1893.

So Charles arrived just as the parish was picking up speed again. Other forces were at work in and around the parish too. The Somers family, who owned most of the land, had promised to donate land for a new day school and parish hall for St Mary's. This plan had been held up for legal problems following the unexpected death of the 3rd Earl but his daughter Lady Henry (Isabel) Somerset had now given the go-ahead and Charles watched as the old buildings were demolished and plans for the new buildings were prepared.

Lady Somerset was separated from her husband, who allegedly had abused her. She had become a Methodist, social reformer and leader of the Women's Temperance Movement. It was no surprise, therefore, when she leased buildings off Chalton Street to the West London Methodist Mission to continue the spread of their social work. Their mission hall in Weir's Passage, opened in October 1892, was just to the south and technically outside St Mary's parish, but Charles very soon bumped into the 'Sisters of the People' operating from there. The hall had a street-level coffee bar, classrooms, a dispensary and accommodation for the sisters. One commentator at the time reported: 'Filthy hovels surrounded it where no policeman would venture, although the sisters were allowed to come and go.'

The instigators of the West London Mission in 1887 were Revd Hugh Price Hughes, his wife Katherine and his colleague Revd Mark Guy Pearse. Their main centre of worship was St James' Hall Piccadilly but their imaginative outreach work offered crèches and youth clubs, medical and legal support, second-hand clothes depots, soup kitchens and so on. Charles and Chloe went to lunch with the Hughes family in Taviton Street within six weeks of arriving at St Mary's and quickly got to know the Chalton Street Sisters Beatrice and Miriam as well as their leader Miss Kathleen Fitzpatrick. Katherine Hughes had sensed that there were many educated young women who were stuck at home and anxious to give themselves to important reforming work. From three 'Sisters of the People' recruited in 1887 the number rose to forty by 1894. Their uniform was black serge with white linen collars and cuffs and a long grey veil. One of these Sisters working not far from Charles in Cleveland Street was Sister Mary Neal, who ten years later had a most important contact with Cecil Sharp in the use of songs and dances in her girls' club, the Espérance Club. There's no actual record of Charles meeting her but (with hindsight) that remains an intriguing possibility.

☾━⚷

What should be Charles's own priority in Somers Town? St Mary's Church was situated right opposite the cab rank for Euston Station.

181

Horse-drawn cabs would line up all along Seymour Street. Charles estimated that he had 270 cabdrivers in his parish as well as ostlers, cabwashers and so on. Very soon Charles was drawn into their world. The two-wheeled 'cabriolet' (abbreviated to 'cab') with space for two passengers was quicker than the alternatives of the horse-drawn omnibus or tram and the newfangled underground – the Metropolitan and District lines were operational by then – but 'cabs' were expensive to purchase at around £85, with £40 for a good horse and a police license of £2 (a total of nearly £8,000 in today's prices). At railway stations the four-wheeled 'growler' predominated with its extra luggage capacity, but that too was beyond the pocket of any working man.

So the drivers rented their cabs from proprietors and paid them a daily fee of about 17 shillings (summer) and 12s (winter). There was too much competition for fares, however, with over 13,000 cab-drivers plying their trade and usually working long hours, often seven days a week. The Church had deplored this necessity to work on Sundays and had started a London Cabmen's Mission at King's Cross station as long ago as 1871. A network of shelters across the city existed for cabmen to get out of the weather and have a bite to eat. Furthermore they had their own Benevolent Association and the beginnings of a labour union. Their main grievance right now was that their proprietors were charging too much as a daily fee. As one cabby was quoted in the *Daily Chronicle*: 'What with bicycles, buses, the underground railway, people get about so cheap and so fast, they won't take a cab at any price.'

The bulk of the 2,000 proprietors, however, refused to accede to the cabbies' demand to reduce the daily fee from 17/- to 14/- and a strike was called for May 15th. Next day at least 6,000 cabs were withdrawn and pickets put on many yards. On May 20th in her diary Chloe records: 'I rush home and watch huge demonstration of friendly societies and C (*Charles*) preaches them a splendid sermon. Meeting of striking cabmen in our backyard.' Next day she says: 'Watch second huge strike meeting from our open window.' The union now claimed that 10,000 men had joined the union and 230 proprietors had agreed terms with them. But as deadlock set in, the families of the strikers were beginning to suffer and Charles met the men of the NW branch of the union to prepare a letter to send to Lady Somerset asking for her help. She was a practical person who had experience of supporting and feeding workers in their struggles – mostly with boiled rice!

The immediate task was to set up a relief fund for the strikers. Charles was, with Lady Somerset, the main contact person for donations in appeals run by the *Daily Chronicle* and other papers. Together they ran a relief kitchen for their local cabby families out of the mission premises in Chalton Street. The strike was co-ordinated by the union President Fredrick White out of premises in Long Acre. The main strike fund eventually received £8,202 to distribute as strike pay and to sponsor the soup kitchens. On June 1st Chloe went off with Charles to the Bedford Music Hall in Camden High Street where a 'benefit' evening was held for the cabbies – 'We are shown into the stage box and Charlie himself is put "in the chair" to host the evening's entertainment!' Another source of funds came by virtue of the fact that a large number of cabs (possibly 4,000) were still running 'by permission of the Union'. Special labels were issued to these cabs, who donated part of their earnings to the relief fund.

Charles's cartoon of the cabbies at a strike meeting with Mary

Money raised by public subscription depended upon public goodwill. Charles used his journalistic contacts to secure an interview with the *Westminster Gazette* and had lunch with its editor ET Cook, whom he knew from his *Pall Mall Gazette* days. He also wrote a letter to the *Daily Chronicle* (published May 26th) as follows:

'The friends of the Living Wage have an excellent touchstone in this cab strike and it is certainly time that they rallied in support of the men. One has but to live in a cab neighbourhood to see what need there is of strengthening the men's hands. Often for days together this winter the driver has only been able to earn the hire for his master, leaving nothing for himself. The men are tired of working for no wages, or next to none, and a cabman's day, I would remind you, often means as much as sixteen hours a day.'

The strike did not have universal support, however, with so many cabs withdrawn from service and some resulting inconvenience to the public (especially on Derby Day). Some people felt that there were too many cabs anyway and that sometimes they were overcharged for their journeys. However, on June 6th Chloe records: 'Dod and I have unspeakable treat of hearing C's glorious sermon to 500 cabbies – feel it an inspired moment.' Morale held and on June 11th, after four weeks, a settlement was reached when the Home Secretary announced a schedule of reductions in cab rents. Two days later the men went back to work and soon adopted the formal name of The London Cab Drivers' Union. They made a special gift to Charles of a large inscribed work desk and also a silver pyx (a vessel to carry the sacramental bread). Ever since that time St Mary's Somers Town has been called 'the cabbies' church'.

After a short family holiday on the Isle of Wight, Charles was approached by the omnibus and tram workers to draw up a petition letter on their behalf to summarise their grievances for presentation to the Home Secretary Herbert Asquith. They were unhappy about the licensing arrangements with the Police and about unfair deductions by their proprietors out of their earnings. Charles did his research and argued that wage deductions were contrary to the Truck Acts of 1831 and 1887, which did protect workers from unfair deductions, but had failed to specify the exact industries and categories of workers. He discussed his six-page summary with the men on October 2nd. Chloe wrote: 'C is bad with asthma but still goes out to the men's guild and on to bus men's meeting at midnight in Deptford. I read delightful *Church Reformer* until he comes in at 1.30 am to a fire and beef-tea.' On November 9th he had an evening meeting with the Busmen's Union at Waltham Green. This sort of commitment to the unions (especially on cold damp evenings) was, of course, over and above his clerical duties and was beginning to sap his energies, but it was practical local help that he wanted to give.

He had already this year given his attention to the new group called the Christian Socialist League. This interdenominational group was led by John Clifford, a Fabian and the foremost Baptist of his day. Charles was on the Executive Committee and the main speaker at the first public meeting held at Essex Hall on May 8th 1894. Initially 26 members signed up and a year later there were 80 members with the beginnings of a branch network. But the early leaders were not 'organisation men' and had their own interests and projects, so yet again Charles watched as a promising pressure group fizzled out. It only lasted for four years.

The one group that was still going, however, was the Guild of St Matthew, and Charles agreed to be the President of the Bristol branch of the GSM in February 1894, even though he was living in London. The branch secretary was a lay person, Hugh Holmes Gore, whom Charles had known since his Orlestone days and who pressed Charles to agree to the position. It gave him an excuse to visit his father in Clevedon and attend meetings at the same time.

Domestically, Chloe and Mary (aged two and a half) began to settle in the new house in Seymour Street that summer. It was a busy street, being a cut through to Camden Town. Their house was near to the offices of the Railway Clearing House where at its peak 2,500 clerks were employed, reconciling the accounts of the different railway companies, so that passengers could travel across the rail network without separate tickets and luggage systems. Next door to their house was a boot repair shop. Further up the street was the Euston Day School (capacity 400), which mostly catered for the children of railway employees. The children could often be seen "trundling' their wooden hoops along the street with their sticks. This old pastime was back in fashion and Chloe records in November: 'I go out and get Mary a new hoop but she cannot manage to bowl it and gets upset.'

158 Seymour Street in 1904. Charles's house was to the right at number 156

Courtesy of Camden Local Studies & Archive Centre

The Marsons saw a lot of the Sharps that summer – not only Cecil but also his younger sister Evelyn aged 25, who was just commencing her writing career as an independent woman. She was soon to contribute to the *Yellow Book* periodical and also write a book of fairy stories, which would have certainly interested Charles. Evelyn later became involved in the suffragette movement, which became important to Chloe.

Connie Sharp was delivered of her first child Dorothea on September 19th in Clevedon where her mother Dora lived. Charles was asked to be her godfather. Chloe immediately sent off a 'monthly robe' for the baby and went round to see the baby when the family were back in London.

The two men met sometimes to discuss their work concerns and in May Charles even composed a poem for Cecil to use with his pupils at Ludgrove School. Cecil was always on the lookout for new teaching material. He taught piano to a dozen pupils himself and oversaw the violin teacher Mr Halfpenny in his tuition, but his chief interest was in the teaching of singing. Shane Leslie in his autobiography recalls that when he went to Ludgrove as a boy in 1895: 'Cecil Sharp taught us music, singing, catches and chanteys, glees and madrigals. When CS was about, everybody had to sing.'

186

Despairing of the usual patriotic and rather conservative songs taught elsewhere, Cecil had the freedom to experiment and began to use folk songs in the classroom and in the end-of-term concerts that he organised. Perhaps he consulted Charles over this development. There is no record of this but he did at least know that Charles already had a considerable knowledge of ballads and had lectured in the subject as early as 1889.

Certainly Cecil began to use the 1893 book *Songs of the Four Nations* with the boys, as shown in a photo in the school archives. This book had 50 English, Irish, Welsh and Scottish songs with piano accompaniment. Its preface refers to folk music authorities of the time – Revd Baring-Gould in Devon and Mr Fuller Maitland among them.

Cecil Sharp with Ludgrove pupils July 1894
Photo courtesy of Ludgrove School Trust

Charles had ballad books of his own that he could lend to Cecil and knew where to direct him to go in the British Museum for reference works, so that Cecil could easily set about his own research. By March 1896 Cecil had sourced five folksongs that were

187

not in the Four Nations Book and taught them to his boys in time for the two end-of-term concerts at Ludgrove. These were 'Barbara Allen' (*Child Ballad 84*); 'The Miller of the Dee' (*Roud 503*); 'Early one morning' and 'The Leather Bottèl' (both from Chappell's book *Collection of National English Airs* 1840: Cecil had his own copy of this book); and 'The Maid of Islington' (more likely to be 'The Bailiff's Daughter of Islington', *Child ballad 105*, rather than the bawdy 'Fair Maid of Islington'). It would seem, therefore, that Cecil's 'conversion' to folk music took place in 1894-95. After several years of practical teaching, he went on to produce his own selection *A Book of British Song for Home and School* in 1902. Of the 78 songs in that book, 31 are described as 'traditional folk songs'.

16

Poor Frank

Charles had had a busy year and was due a break. On December 22nd 1894 the Marson family assembled at the Sharps' house for a jolly Christmas celebration and two days later had another party with Chloe's father Peter Bayne, his (third) wife Marie and Chloe's brother Ronald. This party was a mixed affair. Marie was only 40 years of age but was already showing signs of the mental disorder that would lead to her death the following year. The stress upon Peter Bayne (then 65) would bring him down too. Ronald, on the other hand, had recently left the rural isolation of Orlestone and was happily back in London as vicar of St Jude's Whitechapel. He was replacing Revd Barnett in the parish where he and Charles had been such good friends before their ordination twelve years earlier.

The final Christmas get-together was at Clevedon vicarage with Charles's father (now 72). All his children attended – his spinster daughters Annie, Edith and Grace with their two younger brothers Harry and Frank, and Charles himself – but Chloe and Mary decided not to go, partly because the vicarage was full up! Harry had come back with his wife Kitty from serving with the 8th Bengal Infantry in India 'and filled the house – even the organ room is blocked with their boxes'. Charles went off to find a room with his old friend Sophy Pedder at Tickton Lodge. Harry's news was not good really, as Charles explained to Chloe:

> 'Harry has done most nobly in India but his Colonel came into his (civil) court and thrashed Harry's chief clerk before him. Harry then severely reprimanded and reported his senior, and for this – which was his plain duty and honest defence of the native – he has been dismissed from his magistracy. The papers have warmly espoused his cause and the English at Barrackpoore (*Barakpur, 30 miles north of Calcutta*) have petitioned for his reinstatement. He has been peculiarly successful as a judge and all the appeals against his verdicts have been decided in his favour. Meantime he has a year's leave and is on half pay.'

189

Charles, who had rather lost touch with Harry in recent years, was clearly impressed by his brother's good 'moral compass' in his dealings in that far-flung corner of the Empire. Bucking at the arrogance or complacency of high authority was clearly a Marsonian trait!

Frank's situation was equally precarious and had been worrying Charles all year for different reasons. He was still a medical student at the Middlesex Hospital in Mortimer Street (*now part of University College Hospital*) but had been falling deeper into drug dependence, enrolling in August at the Keeley Institute at 6 Grenville Place, Cromwell Road in an effort to find a cure.

Dr Leslie Keeley was an American doctor who had in 1880 opened in Dwight Illinois a sanatorium for alcohol and opium addicts. He claimed 'Alcoholism is a disease and I can cure it!' He had developed a secret preparation that he said contained bichloride of gold. His 'gold cure' treatment took four weeks and consisted of four hypodermic injections per day plus tonics every two hours. It was so successful that by 1893 there were 92 franchised Keeley Institutes around the world with further expansion planned. The attraction was that alcoholism was no longer portrayed as a moral vice but as a medical problem. Patients attended the Keeley clinics of their own free will and were free to come and go as they pleased. But the treatment was expensive – Dr Usher in his report to the British Medical Association in 1892 gave an account of his visit to Dwight, where patients paid $25 down and anywhere between $5 and $25 a week after that. Dr Keeley was already a millionaire by all accounts.

The British Medical Association, however, had come out in July 1892 by condemning the treatment. Their researchers had carried out an analysis of the secret preparation and found it contained no gold at all and was in fact 27.55% alcohol. This result fortunately had scotched a resolution, prepared for a special meeting of the Church of England Temperance Society, that £150,000 should be raised to purchase the right to use this 'gold remedy' in the UK. However, desperate people seek desperate measures – the Keeley advertisements of their success rate ensured a steady flow of customers, and Frank was one of them.

Charles visited him at the Keeley Institute on August 21st and found him ill in bed. He was little better three weeks later and seems to have discharged himself. On October 13th Charles went to see the

Warden of the Middlesex about 'poor Frank'. In the end Charles's father came up from Clevedon to escort Frank back to Somerset and wrote to Charles on November 16th 1894:

'Our poor Frank bore the journey well and has had no asthma and so far as I know has not had any morphine but of course it is not easy to tell. Dr Davis came yesterday morning but seems quite incompetent to do anything – asked no questions but felt his pulse and stared at him and I fear as morphine goes, is no use at all. One comfort is so far as I can see he has no money so unless he has a stock of the drug with him, which I doubt, he cannot easily get at any, as we have warned the chemists. He is really better and more cheerful and eats and sleeps well, so we must hope for the best. One must not look beyond the present just now – thanks for getting him under weigh so nicely.'

What great common sense! There's no doubt that Frank's addiction was at least partly traceable to his treatments for stomach complaints as a child. Laudanum (10% powdered opium) was frequently prescribed by Victorian doctors as an anti-diarrhoeal treatment.

The Himrod 'burned powder' inhalations for asthma that Frank, Charles and even Cecil Sharp took over many years may not have done them much good either. It has extracts of the plant Datura Stramonium (common name Jimson Weed or Devil's Snare). This plant contains atropine, an alkaloid that does reduce secretions and bronchial constriction but may also have side effects including hallucinations and blurred or painful vision. Charles never complained of eye trouble, but Cecil Sharp certainly did. He was still using Himrod for asthma as late as 1909 (as he told Chloe). As a child Cecil had not enjoyed good health and had bouts of hay-fever. At Ludgrove he had more respiratory problems and was absent for most of the summer term 1897 'recovering from a serious state of prostration'. He complained for many years about sensitivity to light and painful eyes and Himrod may have been a contributory factor. How all their lives would have been transformed if salbutamol had been available! Insomnia and irascibility would have been greatly reduced.

Chloe headed into the New Year 1895 in good spirits. Not only had she consolidated all her family links in London in the last year but she had kept her intellectual life going too. In her diary Chloe records all the books she was reading and all the discussions on social affairs of the day, although she was not really interested in national politics. She regularly attended concerts and visited art galleries, making acquaintance with the artist Holman Hunt and visiting his studio one day in October with Mary to see the painting *The Lady of Shalott* in its slow gestation (as shown in Charles's cartoon).

"I go to see Mr. Holman Hunt and turn my back upon Art."

Twice she returned to Cambridge to see her Newnham friends Mary Bateson, Edith Sharpley and Philippa Fawcett, corresponding with them regularly. Philippa came to London frequently because her mother Millicent Fawcett lived not far away in Gower Street and so Chloe visited them there often. It was encouraging that on October 14th 1894 Chloe received a letter from Millicent (always called 'Aunt Milly') saying that she and other friends had been lobbying the Lord Chancellor to give Charles a proper living instead of the endless curacies he had endured.

Charles continued to drive himself hard – too hard – at the start of the year. On March 9ᵗʰ 1895 Luke Paget (Vicar of St Pancras from 1887 to 1901) wrote to him: 'Dearest Marson, Two independent witnesses have told me that you are keeping Lent in such a way as to really endanger your health and seriously weaken yourself. I can't believe you are right in going so long without meat.' His fasting and his asthma difficulties, which always increased in times of stress, were beginning to undermine his health badly.

The stress he was experiencing was due to an impending row with his erstwhile mentor Revd Stewart Headlam, leader (Warden) of the Guild of St Matthew. Charles had been a member of the GSM for over ten years and had seen its membership quadruple to 364 by 1895. He had written for its newspaper *The Church Reformer* many times and introduced Headlam into membership of the Fabian Society in 1886.

However, there were problems within the organisation and these centred upon Headlam's maverick and autocratic style of management. While Charles was away in Australia, for example, there had been a split in the membership when in 1891, without consultation, Headlam tried to impose a GSM manifesto that advocated the abolition of voluntary (church) schools. The Forster Education Act of 1870 had set up school boards across the country to build new (State) schools where needed and to supervise the existing schools, many of which had been started by the Church. The immediate problem arose: should religious instruction be given in schools and if so, by whom? Nonconformists were not happy that their rates would go to support an Anglican programme in schools. On the other hand, many clergymen wanted to continue visiting and teaching in their established church schools. The question would rumble on for years, but Headlam wanted to impose his ideas on the GSM, especially after he was elected to the London School Board in 1888. He had always advocated the Disestablishment of the Church from the running of the State and the logical extension of this (he felt) was no church schools and no religious instruction at all – a purely secular system – with free competition in the Sunday schools to attract the next generation of believers.

Headlam had survived this 1891 GSM split, but when he stood for the Progressive Party in the London Board elections in 1894, he dragged out the religious instruction issue again, suggesting this time that schools and teachers should take over religious instruction from clergymen. Charles was unhappy about this 'compromise' and wrote on October 19th to his friend Percy Widdrington, undergraduate and Secretary of the Oxford GSM: 'Can your branch pass a resolution that the State is not the organ for giving instruction in theology?' In the end Headlam was elected and the issue was shelved, but the disquiet persisted. Headlam had also angered Charles back in February 1894 by attacking Bishop Westcott in his newspaper, and Charles immediately ran to the defence of his friend and supporter.

Now a year later Charles was locked on a collision course with Headlam over the future direction of the GSM. On January 25th 1895 the GSM council met and a request was made for the GSM to produce a new tract with revised policies and philosophy. Headlam 'pooh poohed the proposal and said the old tracts were not yet sold out' but Charles with the support of Revd Percy Dearmer persuaded the council to prepare a new tract and promptly set about writing one. When they presented their draft at the next meeting in February, it caused 'a fierce dispute'. Charles felt that Headlam had never really moved on from the ideas of Henry George and his Land Tax. He wrote to Widdrington again on February 15th: 'The fight came over the last bit, when the land maniacs began their assault. If the GSM finally decides against Socialism and for Henry George, I shall have to resign, I'm afraid.'

Nothing in his letters indicates that this struggle with Headlam was a personal or 'ego' battle. It was a policy battle. Charles was the younger man by twelve years and dearly wanted this enduring socialist group to develop and grow. In March 1895 he drew up a comprehensive critique of the GSM and had it published in *The Church Reformer*. He complained on several counts:

> - the GSM had done more work with fewer members twelve years before ('the troops are good enough now but the handling of those troops is inefficient, careless and disgraceful')
> - the GSM (like the Fabians) had never really supported the growth of branches ('the country member is ignored')
> - the GSM rules needed revising ('we are strangled in our own red tape . . . and the Council nominates itself in the most oligarchic way in the world.')

194

- the Council was lazy and inefficient (the Guild 'is being unnecessarily and gratuitously killed by mismanagement')
- In short, the GSM needed new blood and new ways ('Have we no gospel except the London School Board, the Empire Promenade and the Ballet?')

This last dig at Headlam's support for education and the performing arts was a little glib, but Charles's case that Headlam mixed up his personal interests with his official duties was suddenly and surprisingly strengthened, when Headlam stepped forward to put up £1,250 of the £5,000 bail for Oscar Wilde, a man he had not even met before, at the end of his first trial in May 1895. In April, Wilde had unwisely taken out a libel case against the Marquess of Queensberry, father of Lord Alfred Douglas, Wilde's gay lover. He had lost the case, been required to pay costs and thus been bankrupted. A warrant was then issued against him for 'sodomy' and 'gross indecency'. The Press whipped the nation into a 'moral hysteria' but the first jury failed to reach a verdict and bail was agreed. Headlam clearly felt that Wilde had been unfairly treated and showed great courage in escorting Wilde to the Old Bailey every day at the second trial later that May. Wilde was sentenced to two years imprisonment and never really recovered, dying in exile in Paris in 1900.

Headlam was heavily criticised for his intervention and there was a spate of resignations from the GSM that summer. Charles, usually of tolerant and independent mind, was scathing and said that he was 'all for building a New Jerusalem but not for wading through a Gomorrah first'. Perhaps he regretted these unkindly words, for when a vote of censure was suggested in July against the Warden, Charles replied that there should indeed be a new Warden but that he entirely opposed a vote of censure upon Headlam as 'a thing ungrateful and ridiculous'. 'However', he asked pointedly, 'is the GSM a socialist body or not?' He was referring to Headlam's refusal to back the emerging Independent Labour Party (ILP), which had been established by Keir Hardie in January 1893 in Bradford. By 1895 the ILP had 300 or more branches, mostly in the North. The Fabians also misread the rise of the ILP and Headlam continued to back the Liberals as the best-placed party to deliver change.

Charles, therefore, challenged Headlam's judgement and at an Extraordinary Meeting in September 1895 proposed a rule amendment that the GSM Warden should seek re-election every year. Headlam brought out all his old followers and the motion was badly lost. Charles was thus humiliated, but Headlam never recovered his old authority. His newspaper *The Church Reformer*, which he continued to publish at his own loss, could no longer compete with the bright new labour newspaper *The Clarion* (produced by Robert Blatchford) and it folded in December 1895. The GSM continued until 1909 but Charles and others quietly switched their energies elsewhere. It had survived longer than most reforming groups and later Charles was gracious enough to dedicate his book *God's Co-operative Society* to Stewart Duckworth Headlam.

All this in-fighting took a lot out of Charles that summer. In addition he was still worried about Frank, who had returned to London and needed his support. On April 26th he wrote: 'I have still much to do on Frank's account' and four days later: 'I saw poor Frank yesterday. He seems to suffer very little on the whole.' Not surprisingly, Charles's own health was affected and he was advised to leave London, if possible. On May 10th 1895 the *Daily Chronicle* announced his appointment to a Crown living in Hambridge in Somerset. It was one of Lord Rosebery's last acts as Prime Minister, because the country went to the polls in August and the Conservatives won with a landslide.

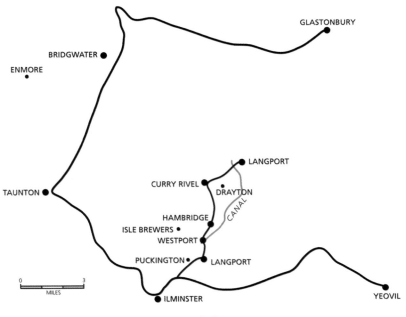

17

Marson the Parson

The Hambridge appointment came at an awkward time for Charles and Chloe. Charles was in the middle of his clash with Headlam and had left a lot of unfinished business in his old parish but he needed to rest and went home to his father in Clevedon for much of June 1895. Chloe and Mary stayed on in London with friends in Gower Street but Charles missed them badly, writing to Chloe for their fifth wedding anniversary on June 20th: 'I am wonderfully better and as much in love as ever with Chloe.'

He had at least begun to make arrangements to take over at Hambridge. The previous incumbent was the late Revd Charles Stephen Grueber, who had died in September 1894, and the parish had been without a priest for over nine months. His widow Catherine had meanwhile moved with her son and three unmarried daughters to Clifton in Bristol. Either she left behind some furniture that Charles agreed to buy or some other liability of £30 was due to the Gruebers. As usual, Charles had no money, but eventually he settled with them, moved in and could see what sort of parish (population 554) he had inherited – situated halfway between Taunton and Yeovil on the southern edge of the Somerset Levels. The landscape was of low, flooded wetlands by winter, rich pastureland by summer.

The first thing for him to realise was just how long Grueber had been in charge. St James-the-Less church had been built in 1844 to serve the two villages of Hambridge and Westport, as they expanded with the building of a new canal – the transport system of the future until the advent of the railway. Charles Grueber was its first and only incumbent to date. For fifty years he had held sway, delivering a High Church style of service and writing 22 learned but esoteric treatises – Grueber had been influenced by the Oxford Movement during his time at Magdalen College. Quite what the agricultural workers of Hambridge made of his doctrinal arguments is not recorded, but they had a choice and could attend instead with Thomas Spillett in the Bible Christian Chapel (founded 1855) or try the Gospel Hall in Westport.

If Charles thought that he could slip easily into this safe enclave of Anglo-Catholic worship – the Revd Stuckey Coles, chaplain at Pusey House Oxford was a strong figure in the area, as he was also Rector of nearby Shepton Beauchamp – then he would be disillusioned when the Ritual Commission began its work in later years. But that was still to come – now he had to get to grips with his new flock and his new responsibilities.

First, his vicarage was a large barrack-like house, expensive to maintain and much too large for his small family. Charles Grueber, of fourth generation German merchant stock, was wealthy and could afford to put on a third storey in 1866 to accommodate his eleven children, three servants and a governess. The Ecclesiastical Dilapidations Act of 1871 made clergymen directly responsible for the upkeep of their vicarages, with occasional visits by surveyors and the repairs schedules that followed. This was to trap many men like Charles in their houses. He couldn't afford to leave and he couldn't afford to stay. His stipend of £268 was inadequate, and he would have to continue to supplement his income by doing book reviews for papers like the *Saturday Review*, by taking on private pupils and by producing more books of his own. He inherited a gardener and handyman called John England, who was then 30 and married with two young sons. John was also the sexton, lived in the cottage at the back of the church and sang in the choir. Charles sensibly agreed to keep him on at 14/- weekly.

Hambridge

Vicarage

Next he paid a call on the local squire and churchwarden, Richard Thomas Combe JP of Earnshill Manor. This large country house in

198

the Palladian style was built and completed by Henry Combe, a Bristol merchant in 1731. Set in a park of 67 acres, the estate owned a number of houses in the village and a further 375 acres of farmland for lease to any of the seven farmers operating over the years. Unlike his previous situation in Orlestone where Charles fell out with the landowning patron Mr Oliver, he was not beholden to Richard Combe for his stipend, which was largely guaranteed by the Church Commissioners. It was a Crown living and Lord Rosebery could make the appointment, even when there was no bishop in post at Bath & Wells following the death of Bishop Hervey. It was a nice moment of irony, however, when the new Bishop was none other than George Wyndham Kennion, Charles's former adversary from Adelaide, whose first task it was to license Charles. They were to cross swords again in Somerset.

On July 5th Charles put in his first appearance at the village school, which was built next to the church in 1844 but had been extended three years earlier to a capacity of 130 to meet demand. At this time 45 % of the village population was under the age of twenty, with only 9% over the age of 60 – quite a different demography to today. Fortunately Charles always got on well with children and was soon telling them stories and showing them his special skill at cutting out black paper silhouettes of people; but he was disappointed with the standard of teaching that he saw in the school (especially in arithmetic). The Attendance Officer had been the week before and reported an average attendance of only 98 out of 130, which was partly due, no doubt, to the opportunity to pick up seasonal work on the farms. School was then closed for a few days 'for the village clubs'.

When Charles visited again on July 22nd he found a new headmistress – Miss Alice Mary Tanner, aged only 20 but the daughter of an experienced infant teacher – and from then on things began to improve. Alice, a gardener's daughter, was from Dorking in Surrey. She had taken the chance of an education in Ilminster and was now a certificated teacher. Attendances improved and Charles visited frequently in his official capacity as Correspondent for the School to the Education Department and as RE teacher. With her energy and his encouragement the school flourished and was used by Charles for evening classes for older children, who could not receive a secondary education unless they won a scholarship to Ilminster or Langport Grammar Schools.

Next, as he had done in every single parish he had been in, Charles began his visiting rounds. This is when the parishioners really began to notice a difference. Grueber had been a kindly and generous priest by all accounts but he had spent increasingly large amounts of time away at Burnham-on-Sea. He was 79 and very tired at the end. In fact between July 1891 and June 1894 he had performed just one baptism in three years. But here was Charles, aged 36, full of commitment and energy, keen to give the rural life another go. He had already put several new plants and trees into the vicarage garden and was no doubt discussing the heavy clay soil with anyone willing to give him advice.

For the male workforce of the village was quite tied to the land – of the 144 working men, 59 were agricultural labourers working for 7 farmers, along with 2 dairymen, 2 shepherds and 6 grooms/carters (i.e. a total of 76 or 53% of the workforce). A further 13 men worked in support services (3 blacksmiths, 3 wheelwrights, 4 carpenters, 2 sawyers and 1 thatcher comprising another 9%). However, agriculture was only just coming to the end of twenty years of depression. Cheap imported grain from the USA and refrigerated meat from Australia and New Zealand had deflated prices for the UK farmer, who responded by taking land out of production and laying off workers. Winter work like ditching or hedge-laying might be neglected and tied cottages not well maintained. It has been estimated that one third of agricultural labourers were laid off between 1871 and 1901. Young men particularly drifted to towns to find work or responded to agents offering emigration deals. Wages fell too. The average weekly earnings of a Somerset labourer in 1894 amounted to 11/8d (equivalent to perhaps £50 in 2010). Out of this sum, the family might expend 4/- on bread, 2/- on meat and cheese, 6d on candles or lamp oil, 6d on coal, 2/6d on tea, sugar and so on. Perhaps 6d might be put aside for the Friendly Society that would help you in times of illness or great need, leaving just 2/8d a week for boots, clothing and such expenses.

However, there were other sources of employment. Hambridge had grown up along a ridge flanking the turnpike road (now B3168) from Curry Rivel to Ilminster, but as you go down the hill at the north end (now called Underhill), you cross the River Isle and find the old mill and brewery on your left. There's a record of a mill (and fishery) there as early as 1252, grain being brought to be milled by boat and by road. Throughout the 19th century this was an important business, run by the Lang family of Bowdens Farm. At its peak in 1881, Henry Lang employed 27 men and 8 boys – millers, maltsters, brewers, carters and barrelwashers. Henry diversified too, setting up as a wine and spirit merchant. His son Joseph still employed 15 people in 1901 and presumably his beer was sold at the three pubs: the New Inn in Hambridge, run by James Alfred Brownsey; the Westport Inn (now demolished), run by John Male; and the beershop in Westport, run by James' father William Brownsey. This beershop was later called The Clarence and is now called the Old Barn Owl. The last two pubs had been particularly profitable when the Westport Canal was being built between 1836 and 1840.

This two mile waterway to the east of the village linked up with the River Isle and then the River Parrett at Langport. It enabled coal from South Wales and salt from Cheshire as well as building materials to be shipped via the Bristol Channel up the tidal river to Bridgwater and then on by barge for the 14-mile trip to Langport. There cargoes were unloaded into smaller craft for the five mile journey across the moors to a terminal and warehousing at Westport. A toll of up to 4d per ton was charged by the Parrett Navigation Company for the right to navigate the canal. One of the company's directors was the young Walter Bagehot (1826-77), future economist and journalist, who clearly learned much from his father's shipping and banking business. So the navvies, boatmen and coalmen could quench their thirst in the Westport pubs, at least until the railways took their business away. Once the Langport to Yeovil line was completed in 1853, and the Taunton-Ilminster-Chard line in 1861, the canal was no longer competitive and the company was wound up in 1878.

The canal's legacy to the two villages, however, was a tradition of shops and suppliers – a Post Office, baker, draper, grocer, coal merchant, cheese dealer, newsagent, fishmonger and a fruit dealer. It also left a good stock of coarse fish for Charles to exploit! From his vicarage he could just cross the fields opposite or else walk to the New Inn and down to Westmoor Bridge to spend a happy hour catching carp or pike. He also learned how to catch eels. He taught his daughter and some of her friends how to fish and bought a great Canadian canoe to paddle about in. He soon made the acquaintance of Job Gillard, the oldest man in the village at 89. Job had lived with his wife and seven children in Water Street down by the weir on the River Isle and earned a living as a fisherman. He was quite a character, resourceful and independent, raising his children on his own when his first wife died in the 1850s, until he remarried in 1888. Living just outside the parish bounds, he was not entitled to any poor relief but managed quite well without. Six years later (June 1901) Charles attended a Friendly Society meeting at which Job Gillard was invited to sing: 'The vigour imparted into the song was astonishing, considering that he has reached his 95th year' (*Langport & Somerton Herald*). Job died in June 1904 and was perhaps one inspiration for Charles to write his book *Super Flumina – angling observations of a coarse fisherman,* published in 1905.

✎——☙

The other important sources of income for the villages in the 19th century were gloving and shirt-making. It was very important for women to add to the family budget, if they possibly could. Yeovil had been a centre of the leather tanning and glove trades for several decades. A number of satellite factories were set up in Martock, Kingsbury Episcopi and Langport (i.e. within four or five miles of Hambridge). In return for 2d or 3d a week per outworker, a 'glove carrier' would deliver the cut-out leather for women to stitch gloves by hand in their own homes, whenever time allowed. The glove was turned inside out and placed in a clamp called a Donkey, which enabled the worker to stitch round all the fingers (32 stitches to the inch). Turned back out, the gloves were taken back for quality checks and then payment was made. A competent glover would take perhaps two hours per pair and turn out 15 pairs a week, receiving about 5/- for her efforts. In 1841 in Hambridge there were just two glovers listed but by 1851 this had risen to 59 (out of a female workforce of 86) and again to 80 (out of 120) by 1861. That was the

202

peak, however. By 1871 the number of glovers was down to 36 because of the arrival of shirt-making.

In Kelly's Directory of 1875, Charles Brownsey (then aged 29) is listed as keeping a shop and 'collar works'. In the previous census there were already 16 collar makers and 10 buttonholers shown for Westport village. Most men at the time wore detachable starch collars with studs back and front. Charles Brownsey's older brother John was a glove carrier and may have had contacts to start this new line of pieceworking. For example, Welsh & Clarke opened a linen collar factory in Somerton in 1866, while James Cook & Co opened a collar works in Chard in 1870. By 1881 Charles Brownsey, now a widower without children, had been joined by his niece Emily Dudman from London and together they built a small workshop space next to his house. In time 34 women worked there (as well as 10 outworkers). Sewing machines were being mass-produced by the American Company Singer in Glasgow from 1869 and by a host of UK manufacturers (mostly in Birmingham). These machines were not cheap (about £2 for a basic model, more for a table and treadle) but they could be bought by instalments. As at Somerton, there is evidence that Mr Brownsey used steam engines to power part of the production process.

This re-skilling of the workforce was a sign of change in the sleepy village. It was estimated that a shirt required over 20,000 stitches, which might take twelve hours by hand or just one hour by machine. By the 1891 census there were already 16 machinists at the workshop. Emily Dudman was 25 by then and probably related well to the young workers. She was still in charge of the operation in 1911 and the building with its belts and pulleys intact was only demolished in the 1940s.

One person to experience this skill change was Louisa (Louie) Hooper née England (no relation to John England). She was born in 1860 in the village of Puckington, one mile south of Westport. In 1855 her mother Sarah Bridge had married William England, a shoemaker and agricultural labourer. She brought her illegitimate child Lucy Anna aged six to the marriage, while William brought his two boys Walter (ten) and James (five) from his previous marriage to Harriet, Sarah's cousin. Sarah was a glover and Louie would have watched her working away at the hand-stitching process. Louie spent extra time with her mother, because she had a lame leg and could not walk to school like the other children. Often the glovers would meet up in each other's houses, the hostess supplying the candle, fixed and lit on the central gloving stool, round which they would all cluster to do their stitching. These friendships helped to overcome the isolation of outworking and the tedium of the work. Often too the women would sing to pass the time. Sarah was a fine singer, and both Louie and her half-sister Lucy (married name White) learned a complete repertoire of songs this way. In 1871 Louie and parents are in Westport and she is a 'collar maker'. By 1881, at age 21, she is a 'buttonhole worker' and in 1891 she is a 'shirt maker'.

Shirt-makers outside the Westport manufactory

This is what Charles learned about his parishioners and their activities, as he went about the two villages in those first months in summer 1895. He watched the harvest being brought in and the celebrations that followed, but he certainly felt strange away from the bustle of city life and Chloe was very sad to have left all her family and friends in London. He received a kind invitation from the London Cabbies to attend a Grand Concert on October 24th when the banner of their new trade union would be unfurled by Thomas Lough (Liberal MP) and by John Burns (Independent Labour Party MP). Sadly he had to decline. The journey would have been a long one – pony and trap to Langport (West) Station, GWR train to Yeovil Town, change to LSWR train to Yeovil Junction and on via Salisbury to London Waterloo.

It was just a week later that Charles received a massive blow, when news came of his father's sudden death (at the age of 73) in Clevedon on November 1st 1895. His father had been vicar there for 24 years and the whole town stopped for his funeral. Charles, of course, dropped everything and went to help his distressed sisters Annie and Grace, who would not be able to stay on in the vicarage. Effects were divided up between siblings (Charles getting most of the books!) and the two sisters left for a new life in Bournemouth.

Charles did not offer to take them to Hambridge for two reasons. Firstly, Chloe had announced that she was pregnant again, with the baby due in April. Secondly, Charles was just agreeing terms to take on a private pupil. He wrote to Percy Widdrington on December 2nd: 'Of course, I shall be delighted to have you but do you know that our table is a very lean one and that though we can give you a bedroom and sitting room and bare subsistence, you will have but scant entertainment? C says she can do it on 15/- weekly including service but not including washing.'

Percy had met Charles in London by chance. They quickly realised that they were both members of the Guild of St Matthew and got on well together. He was 22 and an undergraduate at Oxford, but was spending his time there editing the Isis magazine and not studying. Here's his version of events in a letter much later (Feb 21st 1934):

> 'As my tutor despaired of me ever doing any work for the History School, I was sent down. Luck was in my way, for Stuckey (Coles) insisted on my spending the Long Vac at Shepton Beauchamp in the very year that Marson went to Hambridge. Then came that experience which I look back upon as the only real education I profited by. I must have spent 18 months or more under that wonderful roof. (He was) one of the most fascinating and wittiest men I have ever known and the best friend of my most difficult years.'

Percy returned to Oxford and completed his degree and ordination, going to serve as curate with Revd Moll in Newcastle. In the interim he asked Charles to officiate at his wedding to Enid Stacy, the sister of Revd Paul Stacy (also a good friend of Charles). Enid was born in Clifton, Bristol and educated at the University of London where she became committed to feminism and socialism.

She was involved in strikes by women workers in Bristol in 1889 and 1892. Then she moved to Manchester where she met Emmeline Pankhurst and participated in some of the early organisations for women's suffrage. Enid was a good public speaker and travelled widely lecturing and campaigning. When she was first considering marriage, she had written to Charles in September 1895 to ask his advice on two counts – firstly, she was an agnostic and unsure about a church wedding, and secondly, as a feminist, she had misgivings about vows of obedience and the institution of marriage per se! Charles wrote back frankly and cheerfully: 'You are quite right when you say that I also want the emancipation of women. I have constantly fought for it, because I think the whole world waits for women and what they represent.' But, he went on, he would not cut out any words of the marriage service for her or for anyone else and that 'if you don't want children, for God's sake, don't marry.' Enid and Percy did marry in May 1897 with Charles officiating, but Enid's tireless campaigning took its toll on her health and she died in 1903 aged only 35.

With his parish sized up and his new paying pupil in place, Charles was looking forward to the new year 1896 but it was to be a very mixed few months. Chloe had three deaths to contend with in her family. Her stepmother Marie had become insane and died at the end of 1895 and then her father Peter Bayne died on February 10th of 'senile weakness and nervous prostration' aged 65. Finally on March 20th in Ramsgate her younger brother Willie died of 'heart and kidney disease' aged just 33. On the other hand, Chloe was pleased that her brother Ronald, a widower for nearly nine years, was married again on February 5th to Helen Offord in Dover. All these events meant a lot of travelling and upset for a heavily pregnant person, but Chloe was safely delivered of her second child, a son John, on April 15th. James Marsh, the second oldest man in the village and resident poet, composed an ode in honour of the new birth.

Despite growing signs of acceptance in the village, Charles was really struggling to adjust to the slower pace of life and new patterns of speech and thought. On February 27th he had written to a friend: 'A country flock is hard for me to understand. Chloe is well but depressed, but I am busy as usual over water, school and parish council.' Although the vicarage had its own water pump at the back of the house, Charles well knew the importance of clean water from his experiences in Whitechapel and in Adelaide, so he made sure to survey the village and report problems to the newly formed Langport Urban District Council.

He was also a Trustee of the coal charity in the village. The sum of £300 had been left by George Grueber, a relative of the late vicar, for bread and two hundredweight of coal to be distributed to poor people over the age of 40 on Christmas Eve. This money had been running out but had been topped up by a further £183 after the recent death of Catherine Grueber. The money was invested by the Charity Commissioners and interest drawn from Stuckey's bank in Langport, enough to supply 25 recipients. Louie Hooper was a regular beneficiary over the next few years.

As regards parish poor relief, Hambridge was now part of the Langport Union and a sample record from one week in April 1899 shows 27 claimants for 'outdoor relief' (i.e. not workhouse provision) in the village. A total of £3-12-6d was distributed (an average of about 2/6d each). Eighteen of these claimants were over the age of 60. Charles would have been involved in this administration.

His concern for the 'have-nots' extended to the gipsies who occasionally visited the village. On January 26th 1896, Charles wrote to Chloe (who was away on family business in London): 'A gipsy was discovered today dying on the moor in a van. I fetched him in and he is now in the nurse's bedroom, better', and next day: 'I shall try to have him moved to the Infirmary, for you must not have the burden of him when you return.' On a separate occasion Charles apparently rescued a poorly and pregnant gipsy woman and took her into the vicarage. Emma Fox, a parishioner of Revd Etherington at Minehead, was told about this rescue by Charles's own sister and described it to Etherington in her letter (Feb 21st 1934): 'He took her in at the vicarage, where her child was born and where she stayed till she was well. I think Mrs Marson was away at the time.' This use of Church property as a sick bay was entirely in keeping with Charles's outlook, ever since his Whitechapel days when Revd Barnett opened his house to the people.

Charles obviously continued this rapport with gipsies, because Douglas Goldring (who had been a pupil with Charles for a whole year in 1906/7) wrote the following amusing piece in the *West Country* magazine in 1946 –:

> 'In pursuance of his belief that the pub and the parish church should be regarded as the communal centres of village life and that the villagers should be equally at home in both, he encouraged the gipsies in winter time, to come in and warm themselves round the stove at the back of the church. They were glad of the opportunity and brought their frying pans and eggs and bacon with them, so that in the middle of the sermon suggestive sizzling could be heard by occupants of the rear pews. In return, the gipsies used to humour the kind gentleman by letting him baptise their babies.'

A gipsy child enrolled in his evening classes too. In his annual report Charles wrote that on January 26th 1897 'a boy named Andrew White attended but being a gipsy he was totally ignorant of everything but he perseveres and shews great capacity for learning.' These classes had commenced in November 1895, and on average 13 boys and a few girls attended on Tuesdays each week at 7.30pm in the first year. When the school was too cold, the class relocated to the Long Room, a kind of conservatory running along the side of the vicarage. It was here too that Charles started the village library and conducted choir practices, confirmation classes and sundry parish get-togethers. Here he led the youngsters through a variety of tasks and experiences – from letter-writing and composition exercises to extracts of poetry (e.g. Coleridge, Tennyson) and prose (Dickens, Grimm, King Arthur); from botany (using a microscope) to history (Life of Raleigh); from astronomy to the principles of wireless telegraphy. Once he used the ballad 'Brave Lord Willoughby' as a dictation piece. Whatever they enquired about, he would research and prepare a session. Always the evenings ended with games. The report concludes on February 16th 1897: 'The vicar was called away to attend a dying person. In his place Mr Frank Marson and Mrs C. Marson took the class.' Obviously brother Frank was on a visit from London at the time.

All this close contact with the young villagers began to pay off when Charles asked them to write their own nativity play in Somerset dialect for Christmas 1896. Being country folk, the children focused on the role of the shepherds, who took their own simple gifts, rather than on the Three Kings and their rich gifts.

Charles organised a proper set and the shepherds were dressed in the smocks that had not yet quite gone out of fashion. The play was a great success and was repeated every year for the next twelve years. Charles had it published in the *Goodwill* magazine in 1898 and in *The Daily Mirror* in 1908 with photographs of the various scenes. His respect for the villagers' own language and sentiments gained their confidence. His desire to showcase their talents was an important precursor to his later folk song work and he had no trouble justifying his experiment: 'The result was astonishing. It interested everybody. Is it the worse for the fact that English shepherds found an English Bethlehem, and angels sang in our modern tongue of a modern Saviour?' Their efforts were years ahead of all the primary school plays enacted in modern times.

His first two years at Hambridge represented a good start for Charles but he'd been in that position before and not gone on to glory for one reason or another. Chloe was hoping for better this time.

John Marson's Christening (May 1896): John England seated on ground left: godparents incl Philippa Fawcett and Kitty Marson

18

Trouble and Strife

In June 1897, Chloe took the two children off to stay with Miss Sophy Pedder at Tickton Lodge, 8 Bellevue Road, Clevedon, for a 'buckets and spades' holiday. They were there for Queen Victoria's Diamond Jubilee celebration and enjoyed the extra festivities. Chloe went out one day to Clifton to see some friends, including Cara Pease, and they all went bicycling, no doubt in the new 'Rational Dress' outfits for women rather than their voluminous skirts. Charles had bought a 'safety bicycle' the year before, as an alternative form of transport to their donkey 'Sarah Grand'. She had been acquired from the local greengrocer and pulled the bright-yellow dogcart that was bought off a Langport bookie. Charles drew the bicycling cartoon below.

June 1897: The broken bicycle: Mary: 'Daddy, how I wish I could have a bath in that tub of yours. It is so hot.' Charles: 'Why not? Mother is out.'

Chloe's hostess, Miss Pedder, was the daughter of Revd William Pedder, the vicar who had preceded Charles's father at Clevedon for over forty years (from 1830 to 1871). She was 63 now but had known Charles as a boy and acted as a kind of grandmother figure to his two children. In a letter to his daughter Mary, written on October 4th 1901, Charles described her as 'quite the best woman you will ever meet this side of the Resurrection'. She was one of the first female 'Guardians' in the West and had done great reforming work for the 300 inmates at the Flax Bourton workhouse eight miles distant from Clevedon. Charles's own commitment to visiting workhouses came from her. She had great energy and spirit and would come down frequently in the next few years to help out at Hambridge or would invite the family to her home for a break.

That same summer Charles saw his fourth book come out – *Turnpike Tales*, published by Elkin Mathews. These eight original short stories are 'psychological' tales about people whose lives are changed or challenged by sudden twists of fate. The stories are unusual, indeed a little quirky. There is the bishop who reconnects with ordinary people when he gets stranded one holiday by the sea; the bachelor who rediscovers his zest in life, when asked to look after his young niece and show her round London; the country spinster who is drawn into a plot to set fire to a farmer's hayricks as an act of revenge; an Oxford academic who travels to Arabia to trace an antique document and dies in the quest. The story with just a hint of autobiography about it concerns a country vicar called Mr Lavender. He arrives from a slum parish and begins well in his new environment, but then marries a woman who is proud and hates labourers at meals and the smell of tobacco smoke. When she dies, Mr Lavender lets his parish go to ruin and does not even redeem himself when given the chance to look after and raise his little grandson. It's not a happy ending, for the villagers give up on him and he dies friendless.

Charles was also busy with two more pupils, but at the end of 1897, he had to drop everything and go up to Clevedon again to console his sister-in-law Kitty, when it was announced that her husband Harry had died of a fever out in Peshawar, India. He was only 31. Charles wrote to Chloe on December 21st: 'Poor Kitty is in a dreadful state. The poor old boy left all in most perfect order, his debts all paid', and a few weeks later: 'KM is not beautiful (as reported) but plays deftly and sings in a pretty, chippy voice. She has lived in some dismal eggshell and can't burst it, nor wishes to burst it.' Kitty had no children and was at a bit of a loose end, so spent some of the next spring in Hambridge, taking walks, playing whist, reading and helping with the children. In the end she based herself with her father William Palgrave Ker in Clevedon, but enjoyed visiting Hambridge on a regular basis.

Immersed in their new lives, Charles and Chloe had not neglected to keep in touch with the Sharp family back in London. Their news was that Cecil was still enjoying his work at Ludgrove School but had taken on a new job two and a half days a week as Principal of the Hampstead Conservatoire at 64 Eton Avenue (Swiss Cottage). The contract was worth £100 a year plus a house. Soon afterwards their second child (appropriately named Charles) was born on October 31st 1896. Cecil was busy putting together a good staff team over the next year or so, but certainly did get down to see his old friend Charles in Hambridge sometime in 1898. Revd CW Hutchinson wrote to Etherington in 1934: 'I am sending herewith a photograph (*of the church choir*) taken by myself at Hambridge in 1898. Cecil Sharp was also there at the time, and as a young man interested in music, I had a delightful time which I have never forgotten, although I regret that owing to 30 years' absence in India, I never had the opportunity of repeating it.'

Hambridge Choir 1898 Charles in centre at back, John England on his left

Chloe was away (with Mary) for several weeks in May and again in August 1898 with terrible dental troubles, which eventually required a minor operation. Charles coped at home with Kitty's help and the assistance of their new maid Amy Day. He looked after chickens, guinea pigs and all other pets but more especially focused with tender care on toddler John's progress with his bedwetting problem. He wrote regular reports to Chloe on the child, for it must have been stressful for her to be away for so long from her young son. Chloe was highly strung and did not enjoy practical matters – at one point Chloe suggested that Kitty should take over the keys for the house but Charles dismissed the idea. Chloe had clearly lost inner confidence somehow and Charles wrote on June 23rd:

> 'I suppose Miss Lawrence or your dear Aunts have been explaining your many wrongs to you and furthering the cause of a general sex war *(ref to the Fawcetts and emancipation issues)*. As for believing that I don't love you, you are a goose indeed to harbour such foolish thoughts. If I did not, I assure you I would have bolted years ago – for I am often sick enough of my priestly duties and have no moral sense to speak of and can break a commandment with as much ease and delight as a breakfast egg but tchut! I have always been true to you and gravitate homewards as naturally as rooks to their elms.'

An honest reply perhaps but not quite the romantic reassurance she might have craved. Domestic tensions would in fact increase over the next few years, particularly when there were doubts about what they were or were not achieving at Hambridge. For example, Charles wrote to his former pupil Percy Widdrington up in Newcastle on December 26th 1898:

> 'We are doing poorly, less than 60 communicants this Xmas and no advance in friendliness among the rustics. No sign of the higher life anywhere. I don't know how to speak any message to these folk. Surely folk ought to relieve us after 3 or 4 years from these lonely sentinels, before we run amok? I would bolt with an heiress if one there were, when Chloe is in a slight taking.'

He wrote again a year later on 30th December 1899:

> 'I am most unsettled in H(ambridge) and long to go. Domestic difficulties and acute friction are the chief reasons but this is only a hint in your ear. I tried to exchange into Birmingham

but Bishop Knox jumped heavily upon me and refused to allow it at all. As to the War (*Boer War began in October*) I am for it. Although there is much rotten on our side, yet on the whole we stand for more right and police the world as no others do. I only wish I could help the carlin' wife by going out myself.' (*carline: Scots word 'old woman'*).

Charles wasn't the jingoistic type but the Left were divided over the war. The Fabians did not oppose it but many in the ILP did. Perhaps Charles suspected that business interests and European mischief-making were at play behind the Boer uprising, so he backed the war despite his misgivings as to its likely progress. As for his dispiriting and uncharacteristically ungenerous words about Chloe, these indicate that something had obviously gone wrong that year between them. No letters between them survive unfortunately for this period, so one can only speculate. Charles had just turned 40 and 'mid-life crisis' might aptly describe his frustration at lack of promotion or recognition. For the next three years (1900 to 1903) he worked away in the parish but also rather 'did his own thing' – writing more articles and one book; taking up photography by setting up his own darkroom; and doing lots of fishing. He looked after John when Chloe went away, as in February 1900 when he wrote to Mary on the 15th: 'Thank you for your kind letter. It is raining furiously and the snow is melting. John is rather hard to dress and I have to chase him into his clothes. Yesterday we went out in the snow and John snowballed me while I made paths. Poor (John) England is sick with influenza. We live in the nursery now because it is much more light and cheerful and there is less to smash.'

It sounds like some romping and father-son bonding was well in progress. In June 1901 he wrote again to her: 'John does lessons with me now.' The following month, while Chloe took John off on holiday to Nottingham, Charles went on an enjoyable fishing trip with Dr Taylor of South Petherton to Benson, a village on the Thames near Wallingford. So it seems that Charles and Chloe had worked out a *modus vivendi*, creating a little space and freedom for each other.

For some time Chloe had been feeling trapped in Somerset, far away from her London relatives and friends – there would be no telephones in country vicarages for another 20 years. She could not develop her teaching work because there were no paying pupils around and she could not easily get about and find intellectual friendship. No doubt she was reading as voraciously as ever and in 1898 she did join the Somerset Archaeological and Natural History Society. Presumably she attended their meetings and made some contacts, because in March 1902 she joined a party on a five-week trip to Italy. Subsequently in February 1903 she delivered a series of six lectures in various drawing rooms in Taunton entitled 'Italian Towns, their literary and artistic associations'.

But, unlike Charles, she actually had no useful role back in the village and did not much enjoy the rustic festivities on offer. Chloe did not enjoy domesticity and the practical side of housekeeping, so when her husband breezed in with extra people for meals, her budget and larder and patience would all be sorely tested. To cap everything, in 1899, at the age of eight, her daughter Mary had gone away, to boarding school with Miss Florence Porter of St Aldwyn's, Hallam Rd, Clevedon – a grand name for a tiny school (with just seven boarding pupils). It's likely that Miss Sophy Pedder had recommended Miss Porter. Mary could stay at weekends or during holidays with Aunt Kitty as well as Miss Pedder, so this may not have been such a wrench for young Mary, but Chloe may have felt it deeply and this may have been a bone of contention between her and Charles. Despite their keen support of universal education, they both agreed that the primary school at Hambridge would not be right for their own children. There would be no Latin and Greek, no French and German – all subjects dear to their hearts.

One person who would immediately have noticed this change in atmosphere was their mutual friend Frank Etherington. He had known them well at Soho and Somers Town, when he was a student at King's College. He used to drop in to their North London home quite often and the Marsons all called him Pank (because Mary could not pronounce the word 'Frank'). He had then gone as curate under

Chloe's brother Ronald Bayne to St Jude's Whitechapel and so came to understand Charles's socialist beginnings. But in 1899, at the age of 27 and newly married to his wife Diana, he had landed the job of Vicar of Minehead and now saw Charles as a colleague, with whom he could correspond and discuss local issues. In March 1902 he invited Charles to come and lecture at Minehead. This first visit was not a complete success, as Charles wrote amusingly to his daughter Mary on March 8th: 'I have finished lecturing at Minehead and so mine head is empty, like mine pocket.' However, he was invited again in November 1904 for a series of six talks on 'Ballads', 'Matthew Arnold', 'Rudyard Kipling' 'Anthony Wood' and other subjects.

Despite the personal and professional worries indicated earlier, Charles was actually beginning to settle in the village by 1901. The longest he had stayed in any of his parishes was the three years at Orlestone and here he was 'six years in' at Hambridge. His ready wit and easy manner had at last won him a place as guest speaker at agricultural dinners, May Queens, ploughing matches, Friendly Society annual feasts and so on. For the latter occasion in 1901 the 70-odd Society members met in the church where prayers were said for the new King Edward VII. Then, headed by the Westport Brass Band, they processed with their banners through the village. The idea was that every member paid a subscription and, if sickness, unemployment or bereavement hit them, they could draw out compensation. The scheme's doctor was Dr Richard Vereker from Curry Rivel. As an insurance scheme for the whole community, it enjoyed good support and its festival was an important celebration at the New Inn, where Charles and others made toasts and speeches at the dinner. In one of his reports later to the Bishop, Charles wrote cheerfully that his parishioners were 'backward to the altar, forward to the public house'. He was behind the change of name from the 'New Inn' to the 'Lamb and Lion'. Noticing that the pub sign was dilapidated, Charles agreed to paint a new sign with a lamb on one side and a lion on the reverse, saying that you went into the pub like a lamb but came out like a lion. The name still stands.

ϑ—⌐

As his confidence recovered, Charles began research for his next book, a study of St Hugh, Bishop of Lincoln (1140-1200). Hugh was an exemplary monk and bishop, who stood strongly independent of the monarch of the day (Henry II et al) and did good works for church and country. Charles was particularly keen to write this biography because his daughter Mary was born on St Hugh's day (November 17th) and was ten in the year it was published (1901).

The other piece of writing produced in July that year was *Huppim and Muppim*, an article published in *The Commonwealth* magazine. This witty piece was reprinted several times, because it was a topical criticism of the dry and aimless religious education going on in some schools at the time. The Conservatives had got in again in the 'khaki' election of 1900. Balfour had just brought forward an Education Bill to promote the formation of more secondary schools and to offer rates support for the many struggling Anglican primary schools – a move that was described by upset nonconformists as 'Rome on the Rates'. But this, of course, reopened the old question of what kind of religious education should be taught in all the nation's schools. Charles poked fun at the irrelevance of learning the names of the sons of Benjamin (Huppim and Muppim were two of them: see Genesis chapter 46:21) or the actual route of St Paul's sea journeys. Memory tasks, ancient history and distant geography were teachable and testable, but were not to his mind as useful as discussions on faith, moral issues, the meaning of the sacraments and so on.

Charles was very confident now in his own style of ministry. Miss Pedder recorded her impressions of him thus:

> 'He rarely used the pulpit but delivered his sermons directly from the floor. His manner in church had great natural dignity. He was tall with a kind face and very blue eyes. He had a very musical and sweet-toned voice. Every gesture was natural and instinctively matched the thoughts behind the service or the sermon in process. It was a rare combination. Every service, including Baptisms, Marriages and Funerals, was made as impressive as possible with all that ritual, light, music, flowers and incense could do to open the sense-doors.'

One annual event that he instituted in the church was the Maundy Thursday washing of the feet. Louie Hooper described it thus: 'He used to have three little boys and wash their feet by the font in church. He chose my boy one year, as I was a widow, and another widow's boy and a little boy without a mother. He used to clothe them from head to foot with lovely suits of cloth and shoes

217

and stockings. The choir used to bring the garments through church and lots of good things he did for the poor. Every little child loved him.' Louie had wed her husband George Henry Hooper back in February 1884 and lost him all in the space of four weeks – he died of double pneumonia on March 14th. Subsequently she had two children by unknown fathers – Flossie born on December 13th 1885 and Archie born in August 30th 1892. From early in his ministry Charles obviously gave considerable support to Louie, a single mother.

The truth is that by 1901 Charles was becoming resigned to his lack of promotion. Miss Sophy Pedder records him quoting from Plato: 'Where the Gods have posted a man, there I think he should remain.' Perhaps being a big fish in a small pond satisfied him, but Charles really had run out of any worldly ambition. Like most people, however, he still liked appreciation of his work, some kind of a spark reaction. At last he was receiving that from his country flock and he began to value the strength of the community – contrasting it with 'the absolute inefficiency of the individual to help himself by himself – the consequent need of a society, a club, a country, a church.'

He had also learned patience. Both Sophy Pedder and Kitty Marson would accompany him on fishing trips. Sophy records one such outing: 'I came home in the canoe in the dusk down the river, such a starlit path, with bats and wild duck and strange calls from bank and break, not hurrying so that I saw and heard more. It was CLM's conclusion that if one cannot find God by searching, at least one finds something. Just as we saw gems of kingfishers and pale dragonflies when we could not get the fish to nibble. At least we get some hush and patience into us.'

Charles's cartoon of him paddling his canoe with Mary

This patience was carried through into Charles's daily life. He began in his study, planning out his day with his pupils and with John England, his general 'factotum'. He was happy to change his plans, if something cropped up – a sickness reported, an unexpected visitor. Otherwise the work of the parish went ahead in an orderly way. It is not fanciful to say that Charles's attitude to his work was very much along the lines of the Buddhist concept of 'samu' or 'right livelihood', though he may never have consciously embraced that doctrine. He felt that you must invest every piece of work, whether 'important' or mundane, with your full concentration. He wrote later to his friend Bertha Clarke (December 26th 1906): 'Life is a most interesting game to watch and play in, and the size of the board does not matter, nor what colour the squares are. If we can manage a scullery well, we could manage a fleet or a University or vice versa. It is all really the same game.'

In 1902 Charles actually increased his workload when he took over care of the neighbouring parish of All Saints, Isle Brewers. Their vicar, Revd John Cole, had been taken seriously ill and took no further part in parish life until his death in 1907. He was 72 at the time of his illness and had spent many years in India before taking over at Isle Brewers in 1884. For five years, therefore, Charles conducted their services too and was a manager at the little school run by Miss Rachel Kiddle for 40 pupils. Responsibility for several rural parishes at once is commonplace today but that was not the case in Charles's time.

Charles used to ride over to Isle Brewers on his new horse Ladysmith (so named after the relief of Ladysmith garrison in the Boer War). It was only a mile, and his son John went with him sometimes. Sophy Pedder recorded: 'Once young John, only six, set off on his own to see if Isle Brewers was allright. When he returned after four hours with gory legs and very muddy, his mother rebuked him but he replied: "Mother, what you say is very true but I think it would be better to give me some dinner."' He was an adventurous little boy, and now that Mary was continuing well at Clevedon, plans were put in hand for John to go to Miss Willis's school there in September 1903. Before he went, he was allowed to stay up for the first time for the annual choir supper that took place after the commitments of Christmas services were over in early January. The supper took place in the Long Room along the side of the vicarage

219

and over 60 guests would be invited as well as the choir members for music and dancing afterwards.

The vicarage would seem much too big for Charles and Chloe once the children were away at school. They only had the one servant now, a village girl called Alice Barrett, while John England maintained the house and two acres of garden. Sarah the donkey pulled the mower to cut the grass and lived in the adjoining stables, while the dog Judy, a cat called Hodge and numerous rabbits and chickens added to the inhabitants. Even so, the house was too large, and Charles began to look around for more pupils to fill the rooms and help pay the bills.

This then was the state of the Marson household when Cecil Sharp next came visiting in his summer holidays in August 1903.

19

Discovering folk songs

'Cecil Sharp was sitting in the vicarage garden talking to Charles Marson and Mattie Kay . . . when he heard John England quietly singing to himself as he mowed the vicarage lawn. Cecil Sharp whipped out his notebook and took down the tune (The Seeds of Love)'

Cecil Sharp had spent a busy few years after Charles's departure from North London in 1895. As Principal of the Hampstead Conservatoire, Cecil had enjoyed the use of a house in Eton Avenue, where his third child Joan was born in July 1898. He visited Charles in Hambridge that year but may have lost touch with him somewhat over the next few years. One reason for this is that the Sharps lost the Clevedon link with the Marsons, when Connie's mother Dora Birch left there in 1896 to move to Oxford.

The only compensation was that it was during a family visit to Dora in her new home on Boxing Day 1899 that Cecil Sharp met the Headington Quarry Morris Men. They were out dancing to make a few bob, while their winter work was short. They wore white flannel trousers with red bell pads below the knee and white shirts with wine-red and dark blue baldrics (cross straps from shoulders to hips like sword belts). It was a very cold day and Cecil's eyes were paining him so much that he was wearing an eyepatch to reduce the sensitivity to light. This eye trouble was probably a consequence of the 'colonial fever' (paratyphoid) which he had contracted out in Australia but it may have been exacerbated by his 'Himrod' inhalations for asthma – a problem which had begun to afflict him in earnest that year.

Cecil was so intrigued by the sight of the men's costumes, their movements and catchy tunes that he went outside immediately and persuaded the concertina player William Kimber Junior to return next day to Sandfield Cottage to give him the tunes again. The tunes were 'Bean Setting', 'Laudnum Bunches', 'Constant Billy', 'Blue-eyed Stranger' and 'Rigs o' Marlow'. With his acute musical ear, Cecil wrote them down and played them back to Kimber, who was amazed at this easy expertise. The two men would meet again nearly six years later, but for the time being Cecil did not know quite what to do with the morris tunes and the experience as a whole. He did orchestrate the tunes for strings, bassoon and horn, but beyond that he could do nothing.

He was still experimenting with folk songs in his singing classes at Ludgrove School, and in May 1901 joined the newly-formed Folk Song Society. This decision was probably to boost his confidence and his contacts, before compiling his selection *A Book of British Song for Home and School* (published by Curwen the following year). The Folk Song Society (FSS) had held its inaugural meeting back in May 1898 and within a year had a membership of 110, including Edward Elgar and Sir Hubert Parry, Director of the Royal College of Music. Elgar successfully launched his 'Enigma Variations' in June 1899 and was then asked somewhat to his surprise a few weeks later to give a paper to the Society on 'the songs collected by him in Worcestershire'.

The secretary of the FSS was Mrs Kate Lee, a successful concert singer, who had recently been meeting and collecting directly from singers in Norfolk and in Sussex – most notably from the Copper brothers James and Thomas, farm bailiff and pub landlord, whom she seems to have persuaded to join the Society. FSS members were split between those who were interested in a scholarly approach to the subject and those who were keen to find living examples of song for performance and for dissemination. The Society's stated aim was 'the collection and preservation of Folk-Songs, Ballads, and Tunes, and the publication of such as these as may be deemed advisable'.

Folk songs and melodies were 'in the air' again internationally. The previous generation of composers – Brahms, Dvořák and Tchaikovsky, for example – had occasionally incorporated folk tunes in their music. Now, by the 1890s, Edvard Grieg, who was much influenced by folk melody and spirit, was recognised as Norway's primary composer; and within a few years Kodály and Bartók would set off collecting folk songs and tunes in the villages of Hungary. In England Gustav Holst joined the FSS, as did his friend Vaughan Williams, who would begin collecting folk songs in Essex in December 1903, using them to develop his own pastoral and rather mystical style. Strong and simple melodies, if combined with nationalism, made a powerful mix, especially in an England just recovering from the disappointments of the Boer War.

Unfortunately just when Cecil Sharp joined the FSS, Kate Lee fell ill. She later died of cancer in July 1904. The energy temporarily went out of the Society and its *Journal* ceased production. Subscriptions were not even collected in 1903. Nevertheless Cecil was fired up and could now sense a wider ambition beyond the confines of his classroom. He felt that he too could be involved in the rescue and revival of English folk song and follow the example of other FSS members like Lucy Broadwood and John Fuller Maitland, whose book *English County Songs* (1893) he knew so well.

So, once his own British songbook was out, Cecil was primed and ready to go collecting, while Charles was sitting in Somerset with a good knowledge of likely singers. When Cecil had visited Hambridge before in 1898, he had enjoyed a good musical time but there was neither the motivation nor the knowledge to scout round for folk songs. This time it would be different. There is some dispute as to exactly who invited whom to the first song event, namely the noting of 'The Seeds of Love', sung by John England, the faithful gardener at the vicarage. Perhaps Charles, aware of song potential, invited Cecil. Or maybe Cecil, anxious to impress his new friends at the FSS, invited himself. In any event towards the end of the summer 1903 Cecil arrived in Hambridge with his protégée, the contralto singer Mattie (Martha) Kay.

Cecil had been visiting his wife's younger brother Walter Birch in Preston, Lancashire, when he 'discovered' Mattie at an amateur concert in Walton-le-Dale. She came to London in 1899 at the age of just 16. She was a humble cotton-spinner but had a particularly pure voice that Cecil wanted to train for the concert platform. He gave her a scholarship at the Conservatoire and she stayed with two other students in the Sharp house for several years.

꩜───⚓

It seems that Connie and the children were not with Cecil on the 'Seeds of Love' occasion – their fourth child Susannah was just a year old and perhaps the logistics were too difficult. In a letter to his friend Thomas Lennox Gilmour dated Sunday 23rd August 1903 Cecil wrote:

'Mattie is singing away very successfully here. We went to a mild At Home yesterday afternoon where she made a great success with the 'Earl of Moray' (*traditional Scottish song)* and in a folk song which I took down yesterday morning from the lips of the gardener as he mowed the lawn and arranged for her afterwards. It is a (new to me) variant of 'I sowed the Seeds of Love'. In the afternoon at the Vicarage I secured a wassail song peculiar to that village, so yesterday I did not draw a blank.'

This implies three things: firstly, Cecil had come with a plan to collect folk songs; secondly, he already knew the 'Seeds of Love' song (it's in *English County Songs*) but did not know John England's particular tune; and thirdly, he had prepared himself to sing for the 'At Home', which was hosted at Drayton Vicarage two miles to the north. This last event happily provided Cecil with a second song, namely the 'Wassail Song', which is still sung today on a torch-lit tour round the village in early January every year.

The vicar at Drayton, Revd Henry George Quick knew Charles quite well. They were the same age and had both recently arrived in the area. Revd Quick's previous appointment was at Westbury-upon-Trym, which Chloe knew well as the home of her Newnham friends the Pease family. Cecil was clearly made welcome at their party for his musical contribution and chose the Scottish song in deference both to Chloe's Scottish pedigree and also that of his hostess – for Mrs Quick's maiden name was Lucy Anne Cameron MacDonald.

Cecil continued in the same letter to Gilmour: 'This afternoon I am going in quest of an old and decrepit man of the age of 93, whose one and only accomplishment is the singing of a song about a sow. It lasts, I am told, many hours and consists of innumerable verses and up till now no-one has been able to catch the tune or distinguish the words!' These somewhat disparaging words refer to Charles's angling friend, Job Gillard, and the song is 'Gossip Joan' (*Roud folk song index 1039*). This is probably the same song Charles heard Job sing so lustily in 1901 at the Friendly Society dinner. Cecil duly collected the song and even used it later in his lectures.

Charles then introduced Cecil to Louie Hooper and her half-sister Lucy White from Westport village. This was the real breakthrough for Cecil, for he collected 23 songs from these two women over the next three weeks or so, before he had to return to London to start the new school term. They launched him on his mission by the sheer size of their repertoire and their enthusiasm to share it. He began to see what to collect and how to collect. Charles's role in introducing Cecil to these two women should not be underestimated. Not many vicars of that time would have embraced these two characters.

Left Louie Hooper; Right Lucy White. Photos courtesy of the English Folk Dance and Song Society

Lucy White was 54 by now and had had a troubled life. She was born out of wedlock (father's name not given) on September 14th 1848, daughter of Sarah Bridge of nearby Puckington village. Sarah then married William England in 1855 and had Louisa (Louie) as her fourth child in 1860. Lucy had two illegitimate children herself, the first child Arthur John dying as an infant in 1869 when she was just 20. The second child John, born in 1873, was by Jonathan White, an agricultural labourer whom she married in 1875. Together they had nine children. Lucy certainly had a tough life, working as a collar worker to bring in extra money. In 1899 her husband is recorded, along with Louie Hooper, as a recipient of the Coal Charity administered by Charles and it's clear that Charles knew the family well.

Louie Hooper, as we have already seen, was a single mother with two children, by now aged 17 and 11. In 1903 she was 43, the same age as the two men who were now soliciting for her songs. It's clear that any social barriers were cast aside in the joys of music-making. The two women were invited up to the vicarage for impromptu song evenings along with Tom Sprachlan, a cowman from Earnshill, who contributed nine songs. According to WA Newall, writing forty years later from his conversations with the elderly Louie Hooper: 'if Mrs Marson was out, there would be great foraging in the pantry for a scratch meal, Sharp's contribution to the feast usually being a bag of doughnuts which he christened "sudden death".'

The working relationship that developed between the two old friends was that Cecil would notate the tunes, while Charles wrote down the lyrics. In total that summer they collected 42 songs, which Cecil took back to his Hampstead study to arrange for piano. It must be remembered that though Charles had a good working knowledge of ballads with a small library of relevant books and though he had written poetry and prose for publication, he did not have access to the British Museum and London libraries to help him in any editing work that Cecil would soon propose. He simply said goodbye to his friend at Langport station on September 11th and returned to Hambridge to prepare for his son's departure to Miss Willis's boarding school in Clevedon on September 17th. It had been an exciting few weeks and the significance of their finds would be more apparent to Cecil than to Charles, who did not join the FSS till the following year.

When Charles would later write that for many years he had been unaware of folk songs in his community, this was a little disingenuous and made rather for literary effect. He certainly knew of Job Gillard's singing and Louie Hooper was such an exuberant personality, singing at every opportunity that it is hard to believe that he had not heard some of her songs. John England was close to Charles on a daily basis and a stalwart member of his choir at weekly practices. Charles's account that he first heard John sing 'The Seeds of Love' at a choir party in January (probably 1903) is corroborated by Chloe and Mattie Kay in subsequent interviews for Sharp's biography in 1933. The conclusion is that Charles already knew all these singers and did invite Cecil down to Hambridge.

Over the next few weeks Cecil corresponded with Charles about the exact texts of the songs. He wanted to be sure of his ground, because he was planning a lecture (according to his publicity poster) 'at which several unpublished Folk-Songs, recently discovered by the Lecturer in Somersetshire, will be sung'. Charles wrote back on

October 13th 1903: 'Dear old fellow, I am most interested in your comments upon these pretty texts and much I wish I could help in the shikar-spooring out the originals (*ref to Rudyard Kipling* 's *'Plain tales from the hills' stories 1888: shikar is Hindu word for hunting: spoor means trail*). But 'The Oak and the Ash' I think to be really quite simple, clean and gentle poetry. I should only suggest one or two simple touches and then give it boldly. Louie certainly said "he hath beguilèd me" first verse third line.'

This short statement implies three things. Firstly, Charles kept his own copy of the lyrics he was recording from singers, so that he could recall exactly what Louie had sung six weeks beforehand. From April 1904 Cecil developed his own notebook system for words and tunes. Secondly, Cecil valued Charles's comments and advice at this early stage. Charles knew this particular song well, because a version of it is in the Roxburghe collection of ballads – a book that he used in his lectures in Adelaide. The song was in fact widely printed on broadsides and Cecil would come across it several times more in Somerset. Thirdly, Charles is not afraid of any censorship issues. The song is sometimes called 'Rosemary Lane' (Roud folk song index 269) and is about a young serving girl, who is seduced by a sailor. She becomes pregnant and he pays her off with gold, so she sings in the final verse: 'With gold in your purse and milk in your breast, And you see what you are come to by a sailor in the west?'

In this letter Charles goes on: 'I can't imagine how anyone could mind it. I would teach it to Mary as soon as I had it, certainly.' His daughter Mary was nearly twelve at this time and Charles didn't feel that she needed protecting from these lyrics. He was no prude. This is an important point because Charles Marson has been caricatured as a bowdleriser and a timid textual editor. The more timid of the two was likely to be Cecil in fact, since his *Book of British Song* had been criticised by some reviewers as unsuitable for children. Even his friend Arthur Somervell, Inspector of Music since 1901 and co-author of *The Songs of the Four Nations* book that Cecil used in class, was unsympathetic: 'I think the critics were right in saying that the words were not such as should be given to young children to sing.' References to alcohol and to sexual licence simply presented difficulties for editors at this time. Nonconformists were upset enough about their rates going to Anglican schools without 'vulgar' folk songs being taught in the classroom.

Cecil pressed on with his lecture plans and booked Mattie Kay and other singers to demonstrate the sixteen songs he had in mind (including 'The Oak and the Ash'). The date was fixed for Thursday 26th November 1903 at the Hampstead Conservatoire. Proceeds would go to the choir fund of Cecil's own parish church, St Mary's Primrose Hill, just round the corner from him in Elsworthy Road. The vicar there was Charles's old friend Percy Dearmer, who had taken over in 1901.

Just before the event, however, on November 1st, Cecil's father died at his home at 83 Brook Green, Hammersmith. Cecil had been nominated as an Executor of the first will signed in 1891 but was released from those duties in subsequent codicils, his sister Evelyn taking his place. His father had left an estate valued at £41,335 (equivalent to over £2 million in 2010). As a self-made man – he had been a slate merchant benefiting from the building boom in London – James Sharp left his house and £300 a year to his wife Jane but expected his sons to make their own way in the world. His will is full of restrictions, including a codicil added in 1896 to exclude any family member who adopted the Roman Catholic faith – a move against his youngest son Algernon, who in that year married Rosina O'Callaghan. Cecil, along with his three other brothers, was now to receive a modest annuity of £30. His four sisters received slightly more. Notwithstanding this family upset, Cecil went ahead with his lecture to good reviews and considerable public interest. He also made one good contact in the form of Revd Alex de Gex, rector of Meshaw in Devon, who invited him to visit and scout for songs there.

Cecil had probably discussed journalistic contacts with Charles but in the end he used his friend Gilmour to publicise his efforts to save English folksong. Gilmour was a leader-writer for *The Morning Post* newspaper. Cecil planned to repeat his lecture on his next visit to Somerset that Christmas and did so at the Municipal Hall, Taunton on December 31st. By then he had already spent a week in Hambridge collecting twelve more songs from Louie Hooper and Lucy White. This time, however, Connie and all four children went with him. Chloe was away at Clevedon with Mary and John, who had had a good first term at boarding school but was ill over the festive period. Charles wrote to his children on January 7th 1904:

> This is a letter to tell you about the choir party and what fun we had at it. The girls were all as pretty as girls always are.

Ernest Willy danced the monkey's horn pipe. Father danced with alacrity and badness to the horror of every rightly minded person. Mr Templeman *(tenant farmer)* came and sang most beautifully. Mrs Sharp saw to everything and everybody just as if she had been Mother. The fiddlers sat on the desks and scraped away from nine till twelve quite merrily.'

Perhaps it was a good thing that Chloe was away, because tensions between her and Charles had not eased that autumn. Cecil knew all about this and Charles wrote to him on October 13th:

'Poor C(hloe) has been very much on the war-trail since you left and Janie *(her sister)* was exceedingly rude both to me and my friends. I simply clear out all I can and keep my mouth sewed up with surgical stitches. It is not heroic but the best I can do. The worst of it is that now no-one is stopping with us, her hunting season begins briskly and she is much inspirited by an unimpeded view of the game at feeding time. Petty *(Chloe's aunt Agnes Mayo)* meantime blows the cheerful horn by every post. PS Much track of (song) game visible all about. There is a big bag to be made at Curry *(Curry Rivel, village two miles north of Hambridge).*'

Charles had obviously been scouting for more singers and the duo did travel a little further afield this time. First they cycled over to Isle Brewers to visit William Spearing, the miller. Charles knew him, of course, through his parish work in that village. Spearing later recalled that Cecil had been learning to fish with Charles and they both came over to fish in his millpond. Spearing had recently had a bad accident and lost his right arm but he was a most convivial character and an excellent singer. Farmers would call in on their way back from market, and singing and drinking would go on. He sang three songs that January and another six at Easter.

Next Cecil set off by train (possibly without Charles) from Taunton thirty miles across country on the old Devon & Somerset Railway line towards Barnstaple. This line had recently been taken over by Great Western Railway and delivered Cecil to Bishops Nympton station in deepest Devon countryside, where he was met by Revd Alex de Gex, his new contact. Fifteen songs were collected from two singers –

John Edbrook and William Nott – a rich haul. Cecil stayed five days in the Rectory and would return there again in the summer.

During the Easter holidays Cecil visited Charles for another two weeks of hectic collecting. On bicycles they went over to the village of Muchelney Ham (four miles north-east) to see Mrs Elizabeth Lock, aged 63, who sang them four songs. Her husband George was a small farmer (six acres) and he, like his grandfather before him, lived in the same honey-coloured, rose-covered cottage for years. The next singer was Frederick Crossman, a small market gardener, aged 58, from Huish Episcopi near Langport. Back home in Westport, Lucy and Louie contributed again with another nine songs and then Charles called upon their neighbour Lizzie Welsh.

Lizzie Welsh of Westport, whose mother-in-law Emma Welsh sang 'The Keys of Heaven' song

Photo: EFDSS

Lizzie was aged 35 and a machinist like Louie. Charles took a special interest in her because she too had spent a short time in Australia – in Brisbane on the east coast. She had emigrated with her first husband Walter Barrett and her second child William was born there. However, when her husband died, she returned to the village and was married again in 1892 to George Welsh, a farm labourer. He was a widower with three children and together they had another four, so the little house was absolutely full of children. She gave Charles and Cecil six songs and recommended that they visit her mother-in-law Emma Welsh (Welch) in Isle Brewers. They did this and obtained their first version of 'The Keys of Heaven' song.

Finally Cecil headed off northwards by train from Taunton to try to get to East Harptree, which was only 30 miles as the crow flies but with the Mendip Hills in the way. He was going to meet Colonel William Kettlewell and his wife Florence, whom he had met at his Taunton lecture. They lived at Harptree Court and were wealthy people with nine servants and perhaps even a motor car to pick him up from Yatton station. It was a long way to go at his own expense but fortunately he collected nine more songs. Five of these were from a farmer William King in the (wonderfully named) local pub 'The Castle of Comfort'.

Heading back to London two days later, Cecil now had another 43 songs in his notebooks to work on and he suggested to Charles that they really ought to produce a collection of the best songs in a single volume. He was already confident of 15 songs but needed a few more. He asked Charles to write the preface, while he would write a section on the source and history of the songs. After his appeals in the Press for funds for a systematic collection of folk song material, Cecil was now co-opted onto the Folk Song Society committee. This picked up new energy and new members, especially when Lucy Broadwood took over as Secretary.

In addition on May 16th Cecil received a letter inviting him to attend at Marlborough House with a view to his teaching music and singing twice a week to the young children of the Prince of Wales (George V to be). The two young princes (Edward VIII and George VI to be) were just nine and seven at this time. Cecil was recommended because of his progressive work at Ludgrove School. His own son Charles was nearly seven by this time, so no doubt he used the songs and games that worked well with this age group. It wasn't very onerous work, nor particularly prestigious. He kept on with his school and Conservatoire work exactly as before.

For his part Charles was not to be outdone on the lecture side and delivered a talk 'Folk song collecting in Somerset' to the Fabian Society in London on June 24th 1904. Although Cecil had joined the Fabians in December 1900, Charles was the senior member and led the talk, although it was his first direct address to the Fabians for years. The talk had been scheduled for April but Cecil had needed to go to Wiesbaden for eye treatment. As might be expected, Charles spiced his talk with social comments about rural poverty and of 'a musical heritage being destroyed by schoolteachers, deacons, and now forbidden in the shirt and glove factories, surviving only in the taproom'. Mattie Kay and Walter Ford were asked to demonstrate the songs for him. Mattie was never involved in the song-collecting trips and was trying to build her own career as a singer. She gave a good performance for Charles that night and he promptly returned to Somerset to prepare for Cecil's imminent visit in July.

This time Cecil brought his camera as well as his bike. He had probably used his recent inheritance money to purchase a new camera – a Kodak No.1 folding camera, to be precise, which cost two guineas. Maybe he was inspired by Charles's recent photographic hobby. Certainly his subsequent lectures benefited from the new technology of 'Magic Lantern' slides which he could then show of his singers. He turned out to be a good photographer (*see Bibliography*). Cecil was the first collector to record the image and brief biographical details of his singers, and it shows the respect that he felt for them. This was learned from Charles, who by this time truly appreciated and empathised with his parishioners.

In the summer of 1904, Cecil was free to focus completely on his collecting, because Connie and all the children went for seven weeks to Clevedon, where they rented The Wilderness, a large detached villa in Highdale Road about a mile from the promenade. Behind it there was a large fir wood to play in and explore. This must have been a sentimental time for Connie, because this was the house where her mother had lived for several years till 1896 and where she and Cecil had held their wedding reception in 1893. The children loved their holiday here and saw a lot of Sophy Pedder, who described them as 'interesting-faced and nice children'. Dorothea Sharp was now nearly ten, Charles nearly eight, Joan six and Susannah two. Mary and John Marson, aged twelve and eight, no doubt met them sometimes at 'Aunt Sophy's'.

⟨key⟩

Chloe was ready to receive Cecil in Hambridge on July 27th 1904, but he came and went in a frenzy – meeting new singers and collecting 102 songs in 11 different places. Of this total, 71 were collected from women and 31 from men. New singers included Mr Harry Richards from Curry Rivel, Mrs Emma Glover from Huish

232

Episcopi and Mrs Anna Pond from Shepton Beauchamp (all nearby villages). Cecil then went to stay for the first time with Revd Frank Etherington in Minehead where he met Robert Lewis, formerly a master mariner in Porlock, now aged 68 and always called 'Captain'. Cecil would go back to him on four more occasions for songs.

However, the most important 'find' of the summer was to be Mrs Emma Overd of Langport, the 65-year-old wife of an agricultural labourer, who gave them 20 songs including the well-known 'Wraggle Taggle Gypsies' and 'Bruton Town'. On July 30th 1904 she sang a song 'Our Captain cried all hands', which, by coincidence, Vaughan Williams collected that same year in another version in Monk's Gate village near Horsham and adapted for the hymn 'He who would valiant be' in the *English Hymnal* of 1906. Charles recalled the excitement of meeting Mrs Overd in a letter he wrote to Sophy Pedder on August 17th 1904: 'Such fresh hauls of Folk Song! One especially good today "I'll plead for the life of Georgie!"'. Charles knew this as one of the Roxburghe ballads and Cecil duly wrote it up as 'Geordie' in the new book, which emerged in draft form over that autumn.

Emma Overd was quite a character. She had had a hard life, bearing nine children, three of whom died young. For a time she was a withy stripper – willow stems are boiled to strip away the bark for use in basket-weaving. When Cecil first enquired for her outside a local pub and said he was hunting for old songs, she stepped forward, flung her arms around his waist and danced him round, shouting 'Lor, girls, here's my beau come at last!' This was somewhat to the amazement of Revd Joseph Stubbs (vicar of Huish Episcopi) and his daughter, with whom Cecil was staying for a night or two.

Rewarded with so many new songs, eleven of which would find their way into the new book, Cecil was careful to write to Chloe on September 13th to thank her for her hospitality and wish her a good holiday with her children down at Seaton:

> 'My holiday has been the best I have had for years. How much of the success of it is owing to you, it would be hard to overestimate. I can never thank you enough for all the pains and trouble which you take to make me comfortable and to feed my inner man with all its fads and idiosyncracies (*Cecil was a vegetarian*). I am afraid I used your house very much as an hotel sticking to my song business without regard to anything else in a way that one could do only with old friends! I

233

wish I could return your kindness by doing something to lighten your burdens but that I fear must be left to more than human power. Courage and patience and confidence in the real and ultimate rightness of things, is the only mainstay to cling to when matters go awry.'

These last lines show great sympathy and sensitivity over the marital difficulties that he could see in his two friends. More patience would be needed all round, as the book was prepared for publication. One publisher (Clarendon Press in Oxford) had turned down an early draft of the book back in July but Cecil was hopeful that local printers Barnicott & Pearce of Taunton would take it. Cecil already knew Miss Ethel Barnicott, daughter of Reginald Barnicott, the managing director of the firm, for he had asked her to demonstrate songs at his Taunton lecture the previous December. She was a young teacher of singing (aged 30) and may well have been a pupil of Cecil at Hampstead at some point, because her uncle Adolphus lived nearby in Finchley.

In any event the various draft manuscripts would need to be proofread and returned to Taunton in time for a Christmas launch. Charles had already written his preface. It's a nine-page criticism of the English for ignoring their folk music (unlike the Scots or the Germans). It is written in rather arcane (to our minds) language but as a summary of the changes in our rural and community lives, these extracts stand up well enough:

> 'Folksong, unknown in the drawing-room, hunted out of the school, chased by the chapel deacons, derided by the middle classes . . . takes refuge in the taprooms, poor cottages and outlying hamlets. It comes out very shyly, late at night when the gentry have gone to bed, when the barrack-room has exhausted its Music-hall menu . . . But Hambridge is not peculiarly a nest of singing birds. On the contrary we hear that most of the villages about already boast that they can out-sing us. But it will not be so for long. It is the last lingering remnant of the old village life; a survival of the times when the village had more or less an independent existence, built its own church, hanged its rogues, made its own boots, shirts and wedding rings, and chanted its own tunes. All the rest is gone. We cannot call our souls our own now. We create nothing. We cannot even sell our own trees without an auctioneer from

town. The people are going away fast, and in a couple of generations of such progress, there will be neither songs nor singers in the silent fields.'

Just at this crucial time for the book, Charles became busy with a series of six lectures that he gave at the Minehead Institute, commencing on November 16th 'Ballads' and ending on December 21st 'Rudyard Kipling'. In addition he prepared to repeat his ballad lecture to an audience in Langport on December 8th and submitted his article on the same theme to be published in *The Commonwealth* magazine (Feb 1905). Communications with Cecil suffered as a result of these distractions and Charles wrote to Cecil on December 2nd:

> 'Of course you are reasonable about seeing revises but you forget that you instructed Barnicott direct and cut to pieces my whole instructions to him, which were to send all proofs round to me first, I to you and you to him. You did not tell me of this. So I have assumed that you got proofs by my post. Your letter this morning seems to say you have not and I have wired to Barnicott to post them all today. I am to blame for this muddle, for I foresaw it and did not get a plan down in black and white before we parted. But the egg is hatching now and we must make the best of a horrid welter and try to keep our hair on in the pains of parturition and not upbraid each other for the difficulties.'

Obviously the triangular nature of communications was proving problematic and Charles was being quite conciliatory in response. He was the more experienced partner in publishing matters. Furthermore he had needed to encourage Cecil to publish at all by offering him financial backing, as shown by a letter that he wrote later to Miss Trask dated October 28th 1910: 'In fact to induce him (*Sharp*) to collect, I promised to bear half-loss-and-no-gain.' This is ironic in that Cecil's income was probably twice that of Charles's at this time. Fortunately the book *Folk Songs from Somerset* was a success and a second edition was printed six months later in June 1905. However, the communications issue was to surface again later with heavier consequences.

20

Under Investigation again

Charles and Cecil had worked well in their first collaboration and the book was a success, encouraging them to plan a second volume, but it must be remembered that they were still rather feeling their way in song collecting. Some academics in the last forty years have been overly critical of the duo's efforts in terms of their treatment of the material (e.g. reconstructing or bowdlerising lyrics) and in terms of their motives ('stealing' ownership of the songs). Textual scholars have written papers on the former charge. The temptation to reconstruct a song when a singer gives you a fragmentary or obviously corrupted version was an issue for Charles in 1903 as much as it is today.

As regards motives, there have been arguments over the class profiles of the singers, their urban/rural backgrounds, their literacy levels and other 'definition' issues. As for 'stealing' the songs, we should judge Charles by his actions as a committed socialist and local priest. He felt that just as the villagers created and took pride in their dialect Nativity Play, so the singers would be uplifted by recognition of their songs. We should accept his preface at face value: 'Song is really communal. We do not rob the poor man when we take his song. It is not like buying away his ancestral chest or his grandmother's tea-pot. Rather we enrich him by making him more conscious that he owns treasures.' Certainly Charles made little or no money out of the folk song venture.

All these long-running academic arguments resemble two dogs fighting over a bone that neither particularly wants. As a result, the authenticity of English folk song (and dance) is steadily undermined by intellectuals, which is exactly what Charles warned against in his first preface. Fortunately folk musicians just get on with enjoying music (and dance), just like Louie Hooper or Emma Overd or Charles Marson or Cecil Sharp. Perhaps with hindsight and government funding and computers they could have done a better job and expressed themselves more carefully in their ideas of what they thought they were doing. At least they thought they were being accurate, as Charles wrote in the preface: 'The collection here made is presented to the public as nearly as possible just as it was taken down from the lips of the singers; in the tunes with exact fidelity. In a few instances the sentiment of the song has been softened, because the conventions of our less delicate and more dishonest time demand such treatment, but indication has been given, and we plead compulsion and not desire in these alterations.' At the end of the day we still have all their original field notes to enjoy or criticise as we wish.

At any rate in January 1905 they were still excited about the work and prepared to spend their own time and money on it but had no idea how long it might go on and where it might lead them. Cecil came down to Hambridge, as before, over the Christmas holidays and collected another ten songs. He wrote to Chloe on January 1st 1905 when he had gone down to stay with Revd Sabine Baring-Gould:

'A Happy New Year to you and all your household! I am always a little sad when I leave Hambridge. I missed your choir supper on Thursday but ran into the same function down here. It has been very jolly here and we have got through a good deal of work in connection with the book. Please give my love to Charlie and the children and with many many thanks for all your kindnesses, Believe me, yours affectionately, Cecil J Sharp.'

The book referred to was a new edition of Baring-Gould's *Songs and Ballads of the West* (1889-91) to be re-titled *Songs from the West* and published in 1905. Cecil arranged 83 of the 121 songs in this volume. Baring-Gould was 71 by now, an acknowledged novelist and folklorist, and was parson and squire in Lewtrenchard in mid-Devon. He had briefly met Cecil there the previous summer to discuss the new book. They were both alumni of Clare College, Cambridge and would co-operate again in 1906 with their book *English Folk Songs for Schools*.

Just as Cecil had this solo project, so Charles was considering his own – a book on fishing. This was not a technical manual but an appreciation of the art of fishing, with references from history and literature. It would come out in the autumn called *Super Flumina* and was dedicated 'To the kind and wise companion of so many angling excursions, my friend and sister, Katherine.' This was, of course, Kitty Powys Marson, his brother Harry's widow. Kitty (38) was a year younger than Chloe and came to stay at the vicarage again in February. She obviously went out fishing a lot with Charles and in one of his letters that month (February 27th) Charles mentions to Etherington that he had confided in her over a work worry. She clearly did not side with Chloe and other female relatives against Charles. As his relationship with Chloe was under strain, it would be understandable if such a charismatic man did attract the attentions of an unattached woman and perhaps be flattered to do so. There is no evidence of anything but a platonic relationship but some soul-sharing went on, as can be seen by the dedication in another book by Charles – *Village Silhouettes* written in 1914 and dedicated 'To KPM in grateful memory of her unflagging help and encouragement, not least in helping me to spell out some of the charms of mystic England'. Kitty was a bright and practical woman. She had had no children by Harry but greatly enjoyed being with Charles's children, who spent so much time now in Clevedon. Kitty lived in her father's house, Melbourne House in Wellington Terrace, overlooking the sea and just north of the pier.

Still Charles and Chloe rubbed along together that spring. Charles continued a series of charming, funny, love-filled letters to his daughter Mary (aged 13), updating her of the progress of her pet rabbits and of his fishing trips. He drew little cartoons for her and she must have looked forward to these lovely letters (example is dated 1906 but is typical of his style and is of Mary learning to ride).

Chloe, on the other hand, was writing anxious letters to her 'dear, dear John' (now 9), encouraging

238

him at school and giving him home news, as on April 5th 1905: 'I have had two very delightful letters from you this week and I do thank you so much. Poor Sarah *(the donkey)* has been very ill, but she is better today but not well enough to mow. Judy *(the terrier)* and I are in the long room enjoying the sun.' How much she must have wished to have the children with her, perhaps even to teach them herself! To keep her skills up, she gave a lecture in Langport the following week on 'Siena and its associations' but probably felt under-used most of the time.

Cecil came to stay in April but only for a few days (just four songs). After that, he was busy moving house in July 1905 to 183 Adelaide Road, Hampstead. He had lost his previous house when he resigned from the Conservatoire, after an acrimonious dispute with its owner Arthur Blackwood over contract terms and salary arrears. The Conservatoire was then sold to another concern and is now the base for the Central School of Speech and Drama. Cecil still had his Ludgrove part-time salary but this job loss was a financial blow for him. He began to consider a side income from lecturing, publishing and sheet music. By 1910 these elements would constitute over half his income – royalties £230 and lectures £120 out of a total of £603.

However, by July 28th 1905 Cecil was back in Hambridge, collecting again for a period of seven weeks. As in the previous summer, Cecil dashed around, going to 21 different locations to collect from 45 singers, a total of 80 songs. Nine clergymen helped him this time with information and accommodation. He went from East Harptree and Priddy in the north to Lewtrenchard in the south, from Minehead in the west to Marston Magna in the east. In Hambridge he collected just one song from Lucy White, though he did also see Louie Hooper and took her to Ilminster Fair on August 30th. There was an eclipse of the sun that day and Cecil 'smoked a piece of glass for me to look and see it through.' It was about that time that Cecil gave Louie a concertina as a gift.

Charles was not, therefore, so closely involved with this second full summer of song. One reason for that was that he was greatly distracted by the goings on of the government's 'Royal Commission on Ecclesiastical Discipline'. He was under investigation along with

21 other clergymen in the diocese for possible 'irregularities' in their church services. Potentially he could be struck off and lose his job altogether. Charles, of course, saw this as a challenge, not a threat and responded vigorously.

The Conservative government elected in 1900 determined to have one more go at ritualist priests. The Oxford Movement under Cardinal Newman and Edward Pusey in the 1830s and 1840s had argued for the reinstatement of certain traditions lost at the Reformation and they brought the Eucharist back as a central form of worship. A few prosecutions were made against some 'popish' priests in the church's own courts and then in 1874 the Public Worship Regulation Act was passed, allowing for priests to be examined in a secular court for any use of roman practices. However, the attractions of mystery, movement, colour and ceremonial grew among rich and poor alike. Some of the rich in the suburbs liked sumptuous decoration in their houses and in their pre-Raphaelite art, while, as Bishop Blomfield of London observed, in the dirty cities 'Matins and the litany with a sermon lasting the best part of an hour, in a cold gloomy church, was not the kind of worship to appeal to a man or woman with no education or little imagination'.

In 1882, therefore, it was reported that out of 903 churches in London, 37 had vestments, 10 used incense, 45 had candles on the altar and 270 used the eastward position for the celebrant at communion. The Book of Common Prayer (in its various versions of 1549, 1559 and 1662) was quoted in argument and counter-argument by The Church Association (Protestant wing) and the English Church Union (Anglo-Catholic wing). A few more test cases and prosecutions only increased public sympathy for the ritualists.

Nevertheless the new Royal Commission began its work in May 1904. It conducted 118 sittings and examined 164 witnesses. Mr Henry Webber, an agent (Charles called him a 'spy'), visited Hambridge Church on November 6th 1904 to watch the service and reported back to the Commission on January 23rd 1905. Charles's own practices are revealed in his robust reply to the Commission, which is worth quoting here at length:

'Hambridge, Feast of St Matthias (*May 14th*) 1905
Dear Sir, I beg to acknowledge your letter of the 22nd of February 1905 with the report of a spy, concerning the High Mass at Hambridge Church on the Sunday within the Octave of Hallowmas

1904. I gathered from the copious conversation bestowed upon me by your agent (while I took a much-needed breakfast after my third Mass) that he was a Donatist heretic, and no doubt belonged to the sect of Anabaptists. May I protest against the employment of an agent of this sort? It was a great indecency. It was also unnecessary, for I always shall be delighted to give to any serious persons a full account of our public doings; but your agent supplied you with an ignorant and inaccurate account of the services he witnessed. Perhaps the church can best be described by a photograph, and I beg to enclose two. From these you can see not only all that the report alludes to in the way of candles but even more, for the altar is dressed in its best in the photographs. The particular service mentioned was the High Mass for All Saints at 11 am. I sang it myself and the Revd A Lethbridge preached the sermon. The ministers were two acolytes, a thurifer *(carrying the censer)* and a boatbearer *(carrying supply of incense)*. Before I began the Mass I confessed my sins to the acolytes; else I should have been the only unforgiven person in the church. Incense was also used ceremonially, as it is in heaven. Also we used unleavened bread and wine mixed with water (publicly mixed of course) according to Christ's own custom. We rang a bell at the Sanctus and at the Sacring. I was clothed in a vestment and washed my hands after the oblation. At the consecration I elevated each species of the Blessed Sacrament for worship of Christ. I hope I put in the right number of manual and general acts and also signed the people with the holy sign when I forgave and when I blessed them . . . If the Commissioners wish for any further information as to our clothes, chandlery, or as to which of our joints we crook in worship, I shall be delighted to give them any information. But I beg leave to point out that the lives of Christ's poor people are starved and stunted; that their wages are too low; their houses often bad and insanitary, and their minds full of darkness and despair. These are the real disorders of the Church, and not any faults in my stage management, which is perhaps amateur.'

In one fell swoop he undermines the credentials of the 'spy', outstrips the latter's report in a brave show of transparency and mocks the aims of the Commission, whose energies should be directed elsewhere. Furthermore he was in touch with his other threatened clergy colleagues and insisted they make a stand

241

together. The Bishop of Bath and Wells (George Wyndham Kennion) was not himself a member of the Royal Commission but might make a move against them individually. However, Charles argued that the Bishop could not act on a whim but required the support of the whole synod. He wrote to Etherington on February 4th 1905: 'Without synod he cannot even tread flat a nine and sixpenny censer.'

Charles must by now have made peace with his former mentor Stewart Headlam, for his advice came in a letter of February 15th: 'If my Bishop was to ask me in a friendly fatherly way not to kiss the altar, I would probably do as he wished but until he acts synodically with the priests of the diocese, he has no right to <u>command</u> in these matters. From all I hear, the Commission funk the Report.' Bishop Kennion had clashed with Charles back in Adelaide and again at the Diocesan Conference of 1898 when Charles's motion 'that this Conference holds that Socialism is to be welcomed by Churchmen' was only lost because of the Bishop's casting vote. But everything went quiet that summer and Charles's job was safe for the time being.

∽—⚿

On June 29th 1905 Charles wrote to his son John that Chloe and Mary had gone up to London and he was taking the opportunity to go off on a fishing holiday to Donegal, Ireland 'where no-one cares if we wash or don't wash.' He sounded a little lonesome at the time: 'I have to cook and wash up, if I want anything'; but he returned refreshed in the summer to meet Cecil and plan the second selection of songs. In fact only a minority (nine songs) of the second volume were newly collected that year, and this may reflect the fact that Cecil had been distracted by his collaboration with Baring-Gould. He was not yet ready with many new arrangements and fell back on work he had started in 1904. Charles seems to have lost focus somewhat too. His second preface is much shorter than his first and speaks of less patience with his textual editing:

> 'The words in this series have been rather more freely dealt with. They have sometimes survived only in mutilated form. People remember short tunes more faithfully than long sets of words. The ballad-mongers supply the defect, but they often

242

edit the words out of all vigour and vivacity. To restore the original is hardly possible, or if possible can only be done by a bolder treatment than we ventured upon in the First Series. The words have been re-cast without hesitation where they were mere doggerel or obscure.'

This less careful and more cavalier approach to the texts by Charles has been criticised in two songs in particular – 'Dabbling in the Dew' and 'The Drowned Lover'. Fox-Strangways in his 1933 biography of Sharp says: 'Marson set out with the same conscientious purpose of keeping as close as possible to the original oral texts but occasionally his poetic mind was too much for him.' The criticism here is that, in order to repair a fragmentary text, words or phrases were inserted too freely and of an inappropriate literary tone. Despite its flaws, however, the book was soon ready and came out by Christmas 1905.

That autumn Charles took the opportunity to take on two new private pupils – Maurice Child and Cecil Salt. Charles wrote to Etherington on October 20th: 'I have the very nicest man possible reading with me for Mods but he is also the very idlest (*Child*).' After eighteen months of intermittent help from Charles, Child went on to pass his degree at St John's Oxford and become an Anglo-Catholic priest. He developed a reputation as a great socialite and probably enjoyed his time with the outgoing and outspoken Charles Marson.

Charles was still much involved in the life of Isle Brewers parish, particularly its school. On October 21st he wrote to the headteacher:

> 'My dear Miss Kiddle, The Managers hear with deep regret that you think of leaving us on Dec 31st next. During the four years you have been Head Teacher at Ile Bruer's school you have done a great deal more than satisfy us. You have delighted us with your faithful, intelligent and kind work and you have endeared yourself not only to the children but to all the parish. I have felt that the children learnt well and with a minimum of punishment and have been proud of the School and I only hope you will not give up a work to which you are so admirably fitted and which, next to that of the Clergy, strikes me as the most important possible, that of School

teacher. I am, dear Miss Kiddle, your sincere friend, Charles Marson'.

What a splendid testimonial and such a fine summary of his educational approach. The very next month he went to the school to give his usual RE lesson and told the children the story of St Peter, fisherman and apostle. As a follow-up activity Miss Kiddle asked the children to make their own miniature nets and send him a sample with a short note of explanation. He immediately wrote back a puzzle letter with phrases arranged criss-cross in the shape of a net. Such care and imagination! No wonder children loved him.

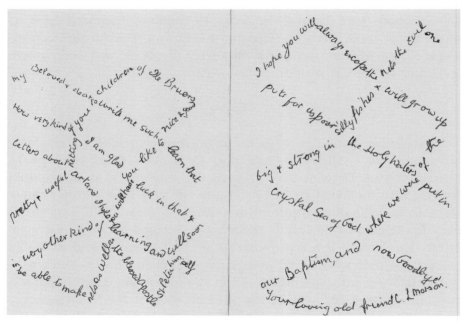

'My beloved and dear children of Ile Bruers,

How very kind of you to write me such nice and good letters about netting. I am glad you like to learn that pretty and useful art and I hope you will have luck in that and in every other kind of learning and will soon be able to make nets as well as the blessed Apostle St Peter himself.

I hope you will always escape the nets the Evil One puts for us poor silly fishes and will grow up big and strong in the Holy Waters of the crystal sea of God where we were put in our Baptism and now Goodbye, Your loving old friend CL Marson'

Meanwhile, one development that autumn back in London would have important consequences both for Cecil and for Charles. When Cecil had surrendered his house and job at the Conservatoire back in July, he was understandably at a low ebb but had been cheered by the visit of Mary Neal, who ran a girls' club not far from him in the St Pancras area. She was very keen for her musical director Herbert MacIlwaine to teach folk songs to her girls in their evening singing class. He had seen a report in *The Morning Post* newspaper about Cecil's Somerset songs and thought such material might be very suitable for his winter programme with the girls. Cecil knew the songs worked in his classroom and was intrigued to see how they might go down in a different setting.

It wasn't long before Mary Neal came back to confirm the success of the songs and ask if he had any folk dances. The club had already experimented with Scottish and Irish dances but would try English dances, if any were suitable. Her girls were mostly seamstresses who worked long hours but were nevertheless lively and boisterous at club time. Cecil remembered his contact with the Headington Quarry Morris Men six years previously, and Mary Neal immediately left for Oxford to persuade William Kimber and his cousin to come to London to teach the girls. As working men, they obtained leave and made their way to the Espérance girls' club at 50 Cumberland Haymarket, Regent's Park. The girls really responded – two in particular, Florrie Warren and Blanche Payling, showed great promise. It is ironic that Kimber did talk to the boys' club that Neal also ran – the St Christopher's club at Fitzroy Square – but it seems that the boys didn't take to the idea.

Mary Neal 1860-1944, leader of the Espérance Club and early instigator of the morris dance revival Photo EFDSS

MacIlwaine learned the tunes and dance figures to keep the club's new interest going. He was a competent pianist and the girls were able to perform some of the Headington dances at their Christmas party on December 15th 1905 at the Passmore Edwards Settlement. This venue was chosen because MacIlwaine lived nearby at Powis Place and had been a member or volunteer at the Settlement. Mary Neal had come to this part of London as a 'Sister of the People' doing unpaid social work as early as 1888, so she had a lot of local contacts and supporters in the area too.

The Settlement was a brand new building in Tavistock Place (near Russell Square) and was the brainchild of Mrs Mary Ward, the novelist. It was a community centre with lectures, concerts, adult skills training, play centres and a variety of self-help groups. The Espérance girls impressed the many invited guests, some of whom suggested that further performances should be arranged. Mary Neal was a good publicist and began to send her best girls out across the country as instructors. Perhaps Cecil's dream of a national folk revival had indeed begun. As well as his friend Vaughan Williams, other song collectors were busy – Henry and Robert Hammond in Dorset and George Gardiner in Hampshire. Percy Grainger was making contacts in Lincolnshire and planning to use a phonograph to make wax cylinder recordings of his singers. Lucy Broadwood had taken charge of the Folk Song Society and Anne Gilchrist was ready to do great work for its journal.

Now Cecil could at last see a means of transmission for the morris dances, which he had not previously known how to exploit. He could also see that the dances seemed to be popular across the social divides. Furthermore Cecil liked Herbert MacIlwaine, a genial but sensitive man, son of Revd Dr William MacIlwaine, Canon of Belfast Cathedral. Like Cecil, Herbert had spent eight years (1885 to 1893) in Australia. He had set up in partnership with his older brother Arthur in a horse-breeding venture at Mullaburra, near Mount Garnet 100 miles south west of Cairns in Queensland. It was a lonely existence and eventually the business failed. However, he was a shareholder in the *Townsville Herald* Newspaper Company and got a job there as a journalist before returning to London, where he worked as a reader for the publishers Archibald Constable & Co. He then wrote a number of thoughtful stories about the colonial experience, particularly describing bush life and aborigine/pioneer relations (e.g. *The Gulf Pioneer*). These fourteen stories were published in both countries. Cecil was thus impressed with Herbert's publishing experience and contacts, and saw him as a suitable partner in developing and publishing the morris dances.

Herbert MacIlwaine
(1859-1916)
who co-wrote the
Morris Books Pts 1-3
Photo: EFDSS

Herbert had not married and was looking for some sort of social reform work through the new 'settlement' projects, when he applied to be musical director at the Espérance Club in 1901. The previous director was Emmeline Pethick, Mary Neal's co-worker at the club and her partner at Maison Espérance (a kind of Fairtrade business producing fashion garments but with fair wages and conditions). When Emmeline got married, however, Herbert took over the musical training. His knowledge of the dance steps and figures that Florrie Warren had learned and developed were now invaluable to Cecil. Herbert may have bowed to Cecil's superior musical abilities but his contribution at the start of the morris revival was crucial.

Impressed, therefore, with the personnel and enthusiasm of the Club, Cecil quickly volunteered to give an introductory lecture at the next Espérance concert on April 3rd 1906. For the next two years he and Mary Neal would co-operate closely to promote folk song and dance. Charles perhaps knew little of these developments but he would soon be affected by them – positively, in that he would quickly meet the Espérance dancers himself in Somerset but negatively, in that Cecil had now embarked on a completely new line of research that Charles could not follow. New collaborations would soon take over.

21

Conflicts of Interest

Charles went into the New Year of 1906 with another flourish of his pen. He had been revising an article (originally printed in *The Commonwealth* magazine in November 1904) about the recruitment and training of the clergy. For years he had felt that the Church was recruiting from too narrow a band of candidates. As long ago as January 1888 at Orlestone he had written to the Archbishop requesting a dispensation for his friend Hugh Holmes Gore to be ordained despite his lack of a university degree. In 1899 at a diocesan conference he had confronted the Headmaster of Eton Dr Edmond Warre, a great rower and sportsman, who had been holding forth about the disappointing decline in the number of public school men putting themselves forward for ordination, especially in comparison with those going into the army. But Charles intervened that he was grateful for this, 'because what the Church needs is not so much young gentlemen but holy and efficient bounders and cads like the Blessed Apostles'.

His new article was entitled 'And Ard' (another of the sons of Benjamin, like Huppim and Muppim, title of his previous article on religious education). It came out in January 1906, and although many of its witticisms are lost on us today, it had considerable impact at the time in its attempt to expose the stiff and out-of-date methods and mentality of the Church of England. After 24 years of hard graft among urban and rural poor alike, Charles felt he could talk with authority about the attributes and skills needed in a good parish priest. He begins: 'Assuredly there is something wrong in the clergy, and evidently that something is not a question of character or of general intelligence. In spite of all the overmuch blaming to which they are subjected, there is no body of men who so pathetically and rapturously long to do right.'

The first problem actually was their training (or lack of it). Their job requires many skills – conducting services, managing buildings and committees, engaging with parishioners (especially the poor) and especially 'a capacity to talk sense if loosed upon a congregation'.

248

But as things stand, he goes on sarcastically, 'the first qualification for the office of a deacon is to have been educated in a public school and to have graduated at a University, where none of these things are learnt. There is no body of boys so flagrantly ignorant of Christian learning as the students of our Public schools (where) religious training is relegated by perplexed parents to still more puzzled pedagogues . . . The playing fields of Eton have a real place in history: most of our battles have been lost there.' Next Charles quotes from an actual examination paper for ordinands – questions like 'Where was Nob?' 'Examine the foreign policy of Ahab' 'Comment upon "Moab is my washpot".' 'Not a word about reading, voice production, music,' he says, 'not a suggestion of slums, sweating, soup kitchens, balance sheets, truck acts, sanitation, allotments, diseases, and school teaching.'

The article ran to ten pages and Cecil certainly enjoyed it, writing to Charles on February 18th 1906:

> 'Thanks for Ard. We both of us have read it and agree that it is quite first rate. Bravo! I have been at home this week with a very mild attack of the flu. I have used my spare time in working away at indexing songs and 2 or 3 days ago began harmonising for 3rd series. I have done six – 'Whistle daughter whistle'; 'A farmer's son so sweet'; 'Admiral Benbow'; 'Watchet Sailor'; 'American Stranger'; and 'Ship in Distress'. We must hammer out some of the words in the Easter holidays, if you can spare an evening or two. I wish Hambridge could be moved about and placed for a while in different parts of Somerset, so that I could dig for songs in the day in fresh soil and do words with you in the evenings.'

Clearly Cecil still valued Charles's contributions to the folk project. The last two of Cecil's song list were actually collected in the previous summer of 1905, but the other four were gathered just five weeks prior to the letter, so Cecil was a quick worker! In fact he had gone back to five locations in particular that Christmas – Priddy, Haselbury Plucknett, West Chinnock, Bridgwater and Minehead – collecting over 50 songs. He therefore stayed only a few nights in Hambridge but displayed a determination in the hunt that winter, which surprised even Charles. For example, on January 16th Cecil wrote to Mrs Etherington after his convivial stay in her house: 'I arrived here at Enmore yesterday quite safely after a three and a half mile (*cycle*) ride from Bridgwater over very slippery roads. Today we have spent at Spaxton but to no result, although we were away about 5 hours! This is, however, no uncommon experience in song collecting.' It was no surprise then that he caught the flu!

Cecil was still doing three days a week at Ludgrove School, cycling there and back but he worked steadily away at song arrangements, so that by March 3rd five more songs were ready for *Series Three*. He gave his lecture at the Espérance concert at the Queen's Hall in London on Tuesday April 3rd and dashed off next morning to meet Charles at Minehead for more songs from Captain Lewis. This time it was Charles who caught a chill. Chloe wrote to her son on April 7th: 'Father's cold is a good deal better, but he is not strong yet and is having a very busy time. Mr Sharp came back from Minehead with him on Thursday and they have been busy together over folk songs.' This shows that close co-operation was continuing and that Charles was still accompanying Cecil on some (if not all) his song trips. This is confirmed by Douglas Goldring, who had recently joined the Marson household as a pupil. He was preparing to go up to Oxford and later became a journalist. He confirmed that in 1906 he often went on the song expeditions with both men.

Cecil left Hambridge on April 12th, so that Charles could carry out his Easter duties that weekend. Charles wrote to Frank Etherington on the 15th: 'Sharp left me on Thursday in great woe about his eyes. He fears blindness with an absolute panic.' But at least Cecil found a new singer in Bridgwater, Jack Barnard, with three new songs just right for *Series Three*. In all, that Easter, they had another 31 songs from which to make final choices for the next book.

Soon after that, while Charles stayed at home with son John, Chloe took Mary (aged 14) on a journey to Berlin to see their German relatives – Chloe's mother's maiden name having been Klothilde Gerwien. Charles wrote three amusing letters to Mary, for example on May 17th: 'I hope you got over all well and found the 'Herrs [*sic* Hares] on the Mountains' (*folk joke*) all fairly sober and the Fraus not in the least frau-sy'; and on May 23rd in Somerset dialect: 'Mollie, How be'e? How do 'ee like them furriners? Have 'ee forgot we to Hambridge yet? I sim 'ee be long whiles gone, that 'ee be. Have 'ee spent all thee money? Tell Mother that there be an Aliens Act, as says volks must have £5 afore they comes to England, else they be shipped whoam, so arst her if she do want £5 from I'; finally on May 31st: 'John is pinkily well and asked me to advance 13/6d which his Mother has of his money. I did so and he skipped off to buy a camera with plates and all such things at Marks the Chemist. He is going to develop everything himself. So your Mother owes me the sum, please tell her.'

Charles was rather relieved to have some peace at home, because he was preparing to give a series of six lectures on Plato in June at Clevedon. Plato was his hero, to whose thoughts and ideals he constantly referred. A few years later he would write an original translation of Plato's *Crito*. However, things were obviously still not right between him and Chloe, as we see from his letter to his former pupil Percy Widdrington on May 19th: 'I am going on feebly as usual, but just alive in mind and body. My domestic difficulties are Alpine. They grow. They blot out the sun both from my soul and from the parish, and fret me frantic. How insuperable are such difficulties, particularly in a country vicarage.' The couple must have felt quite trapped, as divorce for any clergyman at that time would have been very difficult. Goldring, in a letter to Etherington dated April 4th 1934, remembered 'the strained domestic relations at the parsonage. Poor dears, both'.

Several factors may have increased their difficulties during this year. Chloe was a Londoner who clearly missed the bustle and stimulation of city life. Her old diary of 1894 described her visits to galleries, concerts and to friends but now, after nine years in Somerset, it must be said that she had never adapted to country life. There's no mention of her enjoying riding or any country pursuit such as fishing. She liked the idea of gardening but left the work to Charles and to John England. For solace she had her books, it's true, but the nearest library (built in 1889) was five miles away in Ilminster, and there was no-one with whom she could discuss the latest novel or exchange opinions. She had been prepared to 'make do' in the early years of their marriage but she liked nice things, which they could still hardly afford. Her children were now away from home for long spells and she was probably lonely, while Charles was so busy around the parish. Furthermore, apart from hosting

Cecil on his flying visits as best she could, she seems to have taken little or no interest in folk songs.

Above all, she had been ambitious for Charles. When his first books came out, she read all the reviews – her 1894 diary recorded that on April 1st the *Spectator* review of *Psalms at Work* sent her into 'a war-dance of joy'. Her hopes rose with every invitation to a curacy and fell back with every refusal because of his socialism. He had become resigned to his lack of promotion and was determined to be the best priest he could be in the situation. But she was disappointed for him and by him. He was so obstinate with his opinions and schemes.

She was a Liberal by inclination and he a Labour Party man. Now that the Conservatives had lost the general election in January 1906 after the best part of 20 years in power, both of them saw different possibilities. The Liberals under Henry Campbell-Bannerman had a large majority and could perhaps at last undertake some social reforms. Chloe was hopeful that a women's suffrage bill might be forthcoming, as she did feel strongly about that issue. After all, for over 20 years she had known Millicent Fawcett (Aunt Milly), who was President of the National Union of Women's Suffrage Societies (NUWSS). In her youth Chloe had spent hours discussing the issue at Newnham and at the Fawcetts' house at 2, Gower Street. Back in February 1897 when an early women's suffrage bill was talked out in the House of Commons, Millicent wrote to Chloe: 'I don't wonder at your feeling discouraged. We have had so many bad blows lately; still I think it is only a backwater, and that the mainstream is going on undisturbed. The House of Commons really disgraced itself on the 7th. Moral courage is very scarce; there is not much among women and next door to none among men.'

Over the years Chloe met other activists like Dr Elizabeth Garrett Anderson and Isabella Ford, although it seems she did not know the Pankhursts. To try to get some action rather than warm words and vague promises, Emmeline Pankhurst had started the Women's Social and Political Union (WSPU) in October 1903, which from 1905 onwards used more 'militant' tactics. Her so-called 'suffragette' group would (from 1906) include Evelyn Sharp, Cecil's youngest sister, whom Chloe had entertained on several occasions before the move to Hambridge.

Unlike Chloe, however, Charles distrusted the Liberals, as can be seen by his reply (March 11th 1904) to Arthur Ponsonby, proposed Liberal candidate at a Taunton by-election, who sought his support. Charles wrote: 'I don't think that I could be of much service to you. Personally I think the Liberal Party is directly across the path of Social(ist) advance. So how can an old Socialist like me help in a Liberal candidature? If I came and stumped for you, I should probably do you more harm than good.' Interestingly, Ponsonby did become an MP in 1908 but became disillusioned with the Liberals and was returned as a Labour MP in 1922. He did remember Charles's advice.

The return of 29 (outright) Labour MPs in the January 1906 General Election was a major breakthrough and that did excite Charles. He felt a surge of political adrenalin and can be found on May 1st preaching about Socialism with renewed fervour at St Agnes Church, Bristol. When an Independent Labour Party was inaugurated in Langport in July 1906, Charles was elected Chairman and it was decided to hold meetings every Wednesday evening to 'educate the community in the principles of socialism and the needs of the labour party'.

In the same month he was doing practical politics in making complaint to the Sanitary Inspector over the inadequate water supply to two cottages, one of which was rented by Lucy White. According to the *Langport and Somerton Herald* (July 14th): 'Revd Marson said that the only drinking water, or water for any purpose, came from a grey and fetid ditch. Mrs White was dependent on the charity of neighbours for an amount not exceeding two quarts a day. Mr Priddle, of Hambridge, the owner of one of the cottages, carted at intervals of about three weeks a barrel of water from a source with which he (the Inspector) was unacquainted. The Inspector was instructed to take the necessary steps to secure a proper supply.'

Another development that stimulated Charles in June was a conference in Morecambe, Lancashire, at which sixty priests and a number of laymen came together to form a new body – the Church Socialist League (CSL). Charles did not hesitate to join it, because he knew most of the leaders – men like WE Moll (whom he knew at Soho but who was now at Newcastle); Percy Widdrington (Charles's former pupil, now at St Mark's Coventry); Conrad Noel (whom he knew in London 1893/4, now Moll's curate); James Adderley (now at

253

Birmingham); and Frederick Donaldson (champion of the Leicester unemployed). Its first President, from 1906 to 1909, was Revd Algernon West. Most of these men had experience in London but were now inspired by the upswell of the labour and co-operative movements in the North. They were dissatisfied with the 'milk and water' ideas of the Christian Social Union and the rudderless state of the Guild of St Matthew (GSM), where Headlam was distracted by his educational work for the London County Council. The GSM in fact folded in 1909, by which time the Church Socialist League had recruited about 1,000 active members and set up 25 branches.

Charles was active in the Bristol branch, for example pledging League support for the Labour candidate at the Taunton by-election of February 1909. The League lasted until 1924, but there are few records extant of its activities. However, Professor John Saville of the University of Hull wrote in 1979: 'All the veterans of the CSL I knew in the 1920s talked incessantly of Marson and with enthusiasm. I should say that he was one of the 3 or 4 best known and loved of the CSL leaders.'

$\longleftarrow$ ⛓

Buoyed by these fresh political hopes, Charles nevertheless found time in June to work with Frank Etherington on an event for the Somerset Archaeological and Natural History Society, of which the latter was the Local Committee Chairman. For the Society's 58th Annual Meeting, a large number of people assembled in Minehead for their AGM on Tuesday June 26th and then enjoyed a mass outing by charabancs and 'breaks' to Porlock on the Wednesday morning. That same evening a *conversazione* of English folk song and dance was held at the Public Hall in Minehead.

It was while Charles and Cecil were staying with Frank at Easter that they had all planned this event. Revd Baring-Gould was invited to talk, and Cecil recommended that the Espérance girls should come down from London to teach local children three or four morris dances, because Kimber and the Headington morris men would not get the time off work. Mattie Kay was unfortunately unavailable to sing, because on April 2nd, aged 23, she had married Algernon Lindo, a piano accompanist twenty years her senior, and perhaps preferred to stay in London in her new home. Miss Barnicott was asked as substitute but in the end Revd Gerald Peppin agreed to sing four songs. Cecil could not attend either, due to a lecture commitment at the Aeolian Hall on the 28th, so Charles gave the introductory talk on folk song in his place. Peppin sang 'I'm Seventeen come Sunday', 'Brave Benbow', 'The Trees they do grow high' and 'Midsummer Fair' and the local children performed their dances to everyone's delight. The evening concluded with a short address from Baring-Gould and a final encore of the dance 'Country Gardens'. It was a great success.

The morris dances performed that evening were 'Beansetting'; 'Rigs o'Marlow'; and 'How d'ye do Sir?' (all Headington dances). It was one of the Espérance Club's first instructional commissions and their two best dancers Florrie Warren and Blanche Payling would have been sent. Charles was pleased to welcome the girls, because of his affinity with the St Pancras area, from which they came. Florrie was the senior girl aged 19, daughter of Thomas and Bridget McCarthy Warren, though it seems she was orphaned early in life. She proved to be a wonderful dancer and teacher, and later accompanied Mary Neal on her trip to America in December 1910. Her romantic story is that she met a young law student Arthur Brown from New Jersey, who broke off a game of golf and took a train to New York to propose marriage to her, just as her steamship was ready to depart for England. But all that was to come for Florrie, as she adjusted to the country air of Minehead and apparently picked up some West Country stepping, which she took to America and called 'The Somerset Step-Dance'. Her co-tutor Blanche Payling was 15, the daughter of William Payling, a laundryman living at 2 Glen Street just off Cumberland Market. It was Blanche who went to Conrad Noel at Thaxted, Essex in 1911 to instruct the first so-called 'revival' morris team in the country.

It was a week or so after the Minehead event (July 5th) that Cecil wrote to Frank Etherington for feedback on the event:

'Do send me a line to tell me how the 'affaire musique' went off last week. CLM never writes except in archaic monosyllables and I am interested. If you can put anything in about the advisability of publishing the morris dances that I could show a publisher, it might help me. I am seeing Novello next week.

Also I want you, if you would be kind enough, some time to send me a letter about the folk songs in your school . . . The educational nobs are obstinate and reactionary and there is nothing like direct evidence of a practical sort with which to convince . . . My banking account is not in a very healthy condition just at the present moment and I am looking around for means, honest and dishonest, by which I can replenish the family coffers. This, of course, between ourselves.'

From these grumpy comments, we can see that Cecil was clearly under pressure, some of which was self-inflicted. He was trying to do too much too quickly. As well as planning ahead for more song collecting in August, he was trying to finalise *Folk Songs from Somerset Series Three,* but Charles was obviously not ready with a preface yet and was distracted by other work.

More significantly, Cecil was caught up in a running feud with the musical establishment over the use of folk songs in schools. The Board of Education had recently issued their guidelines to teachers but Cecil objected to their list of 50 recommended songs in articles to the Press in April and May, arguing that the Board had failed to distinguish between art songs (named composer, uniform tune, printed transmission) and folksongs (anonymous, variety of tunes, oral transmission). Cecil's experience in Somerset had confirmed this distinction in his mind and he took on Sir Charles Stanford and the Folk Song Society itself in the ensuing debate. Like Charles Marson, Cecil launched himself against the establishment, when it would not embrace his progressive ideas. The arguments would continue for the rest of that year. Although Vaughan Williams supported Cecil's stance, their formal resolutions to the Folk Song Society were not supported and Cecil stormed off to write his book *English Folk-Song: Some Conclusions,* which appeared in October 1907. This explains his comments in his July letter about 'educational nobs'.

As if these pressures were not enough, Cecil was further distracted by his new interest in the morris dance. Impressed by Mary Neal's progress at the Espérance Club, Cecil met William Kimber again at the club on May 25th 1906 to note three more Headington tunes. Then during his half-term he went with Neal and MacIlwaine, by invitation of Lady Isobel Margesson, to Foxlydiate House, Webheath (two miles west of Redditch). There he saw the Bidford-on-Avon morris men for the first time. Just as the

Headington Quarry 'side' had lapsed but had reformed, so the Bidford men had revived once before in 1886 and were trying again now. Cecil collected ten tunes to add to the twelve Headington tunes he already had in his new notebook. He also made rough sketches of some of their dance figures but really needed the help of dance experts MacIlwaine and Florrie Warren, if he were to produce proper diagrams for any book on the subject. For he was now keen to write an instruction manual on the dances to meet the growing public interest, but there was as yet no common language to describe the moves and figures. Classical ballet and ballroom dancing had developed their own terminology and teaching methods to perpetuate themselves, but the morris dance was hanging on by the threads of oral transmission and personal demonstration.

⚷

From a highpoint in the late 18th century, there were now just a handful of active 'Cotswold sides' left in the country – 'Cotswold' is the familiar six-person format with hanky or stick styles, traceable to villages in Oxfordshire and Gloucestershire in particular. These few 'sides' had endured partly because they were composed of family members, who passed the dances on from father to son. Cecil was starting to feel the same sense of urgency to collect folk dance as he did for endangered folk song. At this early stage he simply did not know enough about the history and diversity of the morris but set about researching the subject that very month.

Unfortunately he found 'no single work', no definitive answer to the origin of the morris – only 'scraps of information, brief and contradictory'. He was tempted by the exotic theory that the dances expressed pre-Christian ideas like the death and rebirth of Nature and the struggle between good and evil. Puritans like Philip Stubbes (writing in 1583) certainly opposed the dances as being pagan 'abuses'. Some enthusiasts today still propose this 'good luck and fertility' argument. But Cecil, writing in haste, plumped instead for the oft-quoted alternative theory that 'Morris' derived from 'Moorish' (i.e. North African) and that the dance was perhaps brought to England from Spain in the 14th century – the Moors having controlled large parts of Spain until defeated in 1492. There was no real evidence for such transmission, but Cecil had just been told about the 'blackened faces' of the White Ladies Aston dancers near Worcester (what today we call the 'Border' dance tradition), so perhaps thought this news supported the African theory.

In the first edition of his *Morris Book*, therefore, Cecil simply sketches these 'origin theories', lists a bibliography of 21 reference books and then sidesteps the issue, which 'we are content to leave in the hands of the intrepid folk-lorist.' We might note that some modern scholars are so frustrated by the lack of convincing evidence for any of these origin theories that they prefer simply to trace the development of the dances after 1448 (the first written record of 'moryssh daunsers'). Their data trail leads from the 'mourice dance' recorded at Henry VII's court revels in Christmas 1494, through its many references in the pageants of the City Guilds in the 16[th]century, to the wider use of the morris at rural May games and church ales (fundraising events with specially brewed beer). The dance's costumes, characters and performances thus changed over time.

Morris dancers today have their individual ideas of why they do the dance. It combines technical skill with freedom of expression and many dancers simply enjoy it as community entertainment, as perhaps it ever was. Nevertheless the story of the English morris remains somewhat open, with possible lines of enquiry to similar European (and even South American) dance traditions.

William Kemp, one of Shakespeare's actors, morris-danced from London to Norwich in 1600 (the so-called 'Nine Days Wonder'). Note the pipe and tabor man

At any rate Cecil did his best and worked up some draft material to show to the publishers Novello, as his letter of July 5th indicates. Herbert MacIlwaine agreed to be co-author and Florrie Warren would make important contributions too. The new *Morris Book* was dedicated to 'our friends and pupils, the members of the Espérance Girls' Club' and was eventually published in April 1907 with 11 dances including 9 from Headington (4 stick dances, 4 hanky dances and 1 'mock-fight' dance). With more knowledge, Cecil would completely re-write the book in 1912.

Another complication for Cecil at this time was that because Easter was late that year, his commitments at Ludgrove went on right till the end of July. At the end-of-term concert on the 30th, four folk songs were presented by the boys' choir – 'The Keys of Heaven' (which Cecil knew from *English County Songs* but now had two recent versions of his own from Somerset ready for *Series Three*); 'Creeping Jane' (which was in *Folk Songs from Somerset Series 1*); 'The Frog and the Mouse' (which Louie Hooper had sung in 1904 and featured in the new book *English Folk-Songs for Schools*); and a fourth song 'The Tailor and the Mouse'. Cecil was certainly practising what he preached when it came to the educational use of folk songs.

The very last thing to bother Cecil that summer was the happy appearance on July 5th of two workmen, who came to repair the sewer outside his house and began whistling a morris tune 'Belle Isle's March' as they worked! He recognised it because it was the same tune that he had recorded just a month ago from the Bidford dancers, though it was called 'Heel and Toe' by them. The two workmen were William Stagg (aged 41) and his son Arthur (22). They had left Gloucestershire, where they were related to various morris musicians and dancers, to come to Hammersmith in London to find work. Cecil took down brief names and addresses, and resolved to pay a visit to Stow-on-the-Wold in particular, as soon as his busy schedule would allow. Because of illnesses at Christmas to two of his children, however, this would not be till March 1907 – it was a tantalising and frustrating wait meanwhile! He wrote to Etherington on July 9th about the incident but added: 'I am up to my eyes in work and engagements. Committee meetings are the main trouble and such ponderous useless things, many of them.'

$$\circ\!\!-\!\!\sqcup$$

So while Cecil was working flat out in July 1906, what was occupying Charles's attention apart from the political matters already mentioned? The main focus for him in early July was the overdue publication of the 'Report of the Royal Commission on Ecclesiastical Discipline'. The possibility of inhibition or even prosecution was a real one for Anglo-Catholic priests. Just three

259

days after the Minehead folk event, Charles wrote to the Etheringtons jokingly: 'Soon we shall all be booted out and tramping like gipsies, with socialist sermons and portable altars.' He suspected that 'the most compliant clergy will first throw their censers into ponds and then themselves into Rome.' He then took the unusual step of travelling up to London to catch the Press reaction and clerical gossip about the Report. Public opinion was not in fact outraged and there seemed little desire on anybody's part for battle. So, somewhat deflated, Charles returned home to reconsider his part in the folk song project.

As soon as Cecil finished term at Ludgrove, he took the newly opened GWR railway line from Paddington via Castle Cary direct to Langport East, saving a lot of journey time. Eager as ever, he turned up at Hambridge on August 1st and spent several days with Charles doing words, discussing a preface and reading proofs, because *Folk Songs from Somerset Series Three* was at last proceeding. Next he spent two weeks with Revd Sorby at Enmore Rectory, cycling round the Bridgwater area, then on for a week at East Harptree and a week in Devon. It was too late for any of these 46 songs collected to find their way into the new book. On August 7th Charles wrote to Etherington: 'The 3rd Series is labouring under way. My notion of a preface was "Anyone who does not appreciate these songs deserves to be horse-whipped" but Sharp does not like it put quite so abruptly. Yet he is so confoundedly dogmatic.'

It looks like Charles's flippant approach was not appreciated by a hard-pressed partner and it may well be that his own heart was no longer in it. He always enjoyed 'swotting up' on a subject and he did have a longstanding love of folk ballads, but he always held back from an obsessive or specialist approach to subjects. As he observed once at a diocesan conference: 'I have found clergymen well up in athletics, beetles and steam engines, everything except in their own profession – in priestcraft.' Yet Cecil did have that single-mindedness and wrote after his holiday on September 16th to Etherington to thank him for his recent hospitality: 'I am afflicted with nostalgia and want to be back again in Somerset – particularly Minehead. It is nice to be back with one's wife and bairns but I miss the singers and the air and the delight of it all, and feel caged, cribbed and confined! I spent all Friday and most of yesterday in the British Museum where it was quiet and I got through a lot of work . . . I pride myself on not leaving behind me my goods and chattels but on this occasion I cannot lay my hands on my photographs, a cap and a cycle hold-all.' And on the 26th he wrote to Charles, who was having a short break up in Hereford, in between delivering a series of five lectures on Plato at Herd's Hill Langport:

> 'Thanks so much for the quotation. I am in a whirl as usual. I stayed at Minehead for a week and shall pay for it with bad eyes for a while, I am afraid. They are brewing up nastily. I lecture at Bath on Saturday. Do make some enquiries about Morris Dances in the neighbourhood. There ought to be some. Cecil.'

This amount of effort and strain on a man of 47 with some health problems was perhaps starting to tell on Cecil in his occasional forgetfulness and grumpiness. What happened next, however, would be a matter of regret for both men.

22

The break with Cecil Sharp

November 1906 was the month that Charles fell out with Cecil Sharp and it is important to try to see the quarrel from each man's point of view. Cecil had working relationships with several people in his life. He collaborated with Revd Baring-Gould for two books – *Songs from the West* 1905 and *English Folk-Songs for Schools* 1906 – and then with Henry Hammond with *Folk-Songs from Dorset* 1908. Herbert MacIlwaine was his partner in three of the five *Morris Books* (Pt I 1907; Pt II 1909; Pt III 1910); and his most enduring colleague and friend was Miss Maud Karpeles (1885-1976), whom he did not meet until 1909 but who accompanied him on his song expeditions to the Appalachian Mountains in America and was effectively his PA for 15 years. She collaborated in writing the first (1933) biography of Cecil and rewrote it significantly in 1967.

However, the two relationships that ended acrimoniously were those with Charles Marson and Mary Neal. The break-up with Charles was particularly distressing because the two men had been good friends for 17 years. The reasons were threefold – work problems over the next book; financial dispute over profit shares; and injured personal pride.

Although the two men had had one week together that summer to work on the third series of Somerset folk songs, there were still more proofs to check and Cecil had to start back at Ludgrove School for a new academic year's work. The first indication of any real problem between the two men is in a letter from Charles to Frank Etherington dated October 26th 1906: 'Yes! Sharp is a good man and I liked him well. What a pity he's married, for Borneo and its wild men are bad for the domestic life.' The use of the past tense 'liked' is noteworthy; and the unusual reference to Borneo perhaps warns that Cecil's song-collecting trips into the deep countryside might upset his marriage as much as his finances. In fact Connie was always very patient and supportive of all Cecil's expeditions.

It seems that there had already been a tussle over the share of their book profits. Cecil was short of money, and as he had done most of the work for *Series Three*, it might have seemed reasonable to him to request a renegotiation of the royalties. Charles seems to acknowledge as much in a (lost) letter dated November 7th (quoted by Karpeles in her 1967 revised version of Sharp's biography): 'You have done the lion's share of the work and deserve any rewards there may be.' Karpeles furthermore maintained that Cecil did try to change Charles's snap decision to surrender completely his share of the royalties. In a letter to Charles (copied to his own solicitor) dated 30th November Cecil writes: 'you are clearly entitled to some share of the profits, if any accrue. What that share should be, I do not know; but I think that a third would be a fair proportion for you to take.' This offer came too late unfortunately, because Charles had by then decided, according to another lost letter dated November 18th, to break off communications with Cecil altogether. This final letter from Cecil at least confirms his underlying feelings about their working relationship by that time. He had simply lost faith in Charles and in fact on that same November day wrote to invite Frank Etherington to collect morris dances with him in Gloucestershire that December. Cecil was unaware that Etherington was seriously ill and those plans did not proceed anyway.

Charles's version of events, however, is less kind to Cecil. On the same day as Cecil's last letter (November 30th) by coincidence, Charles wrote to his friend Bertha Clarke:

'I am so very busy but Child has passed and Salt (I hope) will next week. But it has cost me no end of work and worry and now old Cole *(vicar of Isle Brewers)* is dead today, so that my horizon seems to be altering. Perhaps the sadder thing is a furious and hopeless quarrel with Cecil Sharp. I ventured upon a frank and careful but friendly criticism of Series 3. In return I had a letter crammed to the muzzle with every insult he could imagine. There is no roguery of which I am not, it appears, guilty. I replied that I should keep his letter and return it in a little, when he would be as much ashamed of it as I was for it. He must then withdraw. I got another bomb to say it was quite deliberate. I wrote then and asked his wife if he were well. She replied that he was very well and wrote what she thought to be excellent letters to me, that she had long held me to be a knave and so would not come here. In that they both agreed. I then replied to him that he was welcome to his opinion but that for

263

17 years I had done my best to serve him with head, heart, voice, pen, wit and loyal trust, and asked why he had accepted my service if he thought so basely of me? I also sent a formal letter making over all my share in the copyrights and said I would pay or help the 3rd series all I could but must ask for my name in future to be withdrawn. He has neither thanked me nor replied. This is my astonishing version.

O don't take gloomy views about life. We are here on campaign duty and must not discharge ourselves from the war, nor expect a smoothe and unbanged lot. In fact it is useless to lose our heads and tempers.'

This letter reveals that Charles is genuinely shocked and surprised by Cecil's reactions. He had obviously been very busy coaching his two pupils through their examinations and clearly had not appreciated that Cecil had also been under great pressure in recent months. So Charles's 'friendly criticism' must have hit some raw nerve. Etherington once said that Charles 'made great demands on the patience of his friends, for he never quite knew the weight of his own fist or the sharpness of his tongue'. It is a pity that Etherington, who knew and liked both men, was not available at this critical time to act as intermediary. He had heart trouble that required a lengthy rest with a locum covering his work.

The tone of Charles's letter also suggests that he tried to be calm over the whole business but was rebuffed. Connie Sharp's intrusion and her comments ('roguery' and 'knave') indicate that matters had got emotional and personal. Cecil Sharp's biographer Fox-Strangways (p32) commented in 1933: 'The actual occasion of the severance was a well-intentioned but indiscreet move on Sharp's part.' It continues that Cecil wrote a conciliatory letter to Charles on November 9th: 'There have, probably, been mistakes on both sides: our tempers are too individual and autocratic for us to run smoothly in harness.' Cecil wrote again three days later, admitting that he may have written clumsily 'but I am not master of the pen like you'. However, the breach was irreparable. Pride was hurt and the two men never saw each other again.

Of the 'indiscreet move' by Cecil, there is little evidence remaining. Maud Karpeles never actually knew Charles but must have gleaned some information about him, directly from Cecil and indirectly later when she had control of Cecil's letters. In 1973 she was interviewed

264

by Dave Bland, librarian at Cecil Sharp House, about the quarrel. His notes record that she said she still possessed some correspondence between the two men but 'had taken advice from several people and had decided to order its destruction on her death – she did not want the correspondence to fall into the wrong hands.' Maud then stated in interview: 'Marson was apparently having an affair with another woman; Sharp didn't approve of this, told Marson so and they quarrelled.' Maud went on that 'Chloe was a "blue-stocking", totally scatter-brained in household matters and undomesticated. The house was always in a mess. But she was highly intelligent and intellectual. I got the impression that she almost sympathised with Marson and didn't altogether blame him for getting his pleasure where and when he could.' Maud thought Chloe must have been very difficult to live with at close quarters. Finally Maud related a story that 'John England's son, a young lad at the time, was passing the vicarage one day when Marson asked him to post a letter for him. For some reason the letter was not posted and later was found to be a letter from Marson to his other woman, who was related to Chloe in some way.'

There is mystery here but we must try to make sense of these statements. As regards the supposed 'affair', we know that Cecil was aware of the tensions between Charles and Chloe back in 1903. Chloe may well have confided her troubles to several women including Connie Sharp. Certainly her own sister Janie and her aunts were off-hand, if not hostile, to Charles. The only 'relative' that continued to act warmly to Charles was his sister-in-law Kitty Powys Marson from Clevedon. She was his fishing companion, to whom he dedicated two of his books; and she was the widow of his dead brother Harry and as such was indeed a 'relative in some way' of Chloe (i.e. sister-in-law also). Kitty was a frequent visitor to Hambridge over the years and there may have been opportunity for a physical affair, but there is no record of a visit by her that summer that might have brought matters to a head that November.

Charles would have felt ashamed, if any physical infidelity had actually taken place and become known to long-standing friends like the Sharps. He might have accepted the break rather sheepishly. But he didn't think he'd done anything wrong, as he wrote to Bertha Clarke on December 26th 1906: 'I hear the poor Sharplets have the scarlet fever, which is bad news. I am almost inclined to write and say "send the well ones down to us" but I suppose it would only call down new artillery upon us if I did and we are (or I am) too debauched to be entrusted with the little rogues.' This joke against himself is either brazen hypocrisy or else a fair claim to innocence.

Bertha Clarke is an important witness to these events because she knew both men well. She was born in 1881 in Bangkok, capital of Siam (now Thailand), where her father Frederick was a timber merchant, trading principally in teak. In the mid-1890s, she returned to Woking to be educated, often visiting her father's sister Frances Gregg in Torquay in the summer months. Frances's husband Revd Edward Pease Gregg had children the same age as Bertha and enjoyed use of a large rectory with several servants. He was first cousin to Dora and Cara Pease, good friends of the Marsons. By their recommendation, Bertha came to stay frequently in Hambridge, studying and helping Charles at his Sunday school classes, learning how to fish and taking up painting as a hobby. When she decided to study art in London in 1904, Charles arranged for her to stay as a boarder along with Mattie Kay at Cecil Sharp's house in Eton Avenue. She stayed there until Cecil resigned from the Conservatoire in July 1905 and had to move to a smaller house.

In an interview with Maud Karpeles in 1934, Bertha recalled Cecil's 'uncertain temper and his fads – at one time no water during meals, at another time he had his food weighed with scales on the table. When he was not in the mood, there was not much talk at table. The children were in the nursery.' She also remembered that he had crazes – Christian Science, metaphysics and Theosophy. When Bertha learned that Revd Etherington was planning to write a biography of Charles Marson, she wrote to him in 1934: 'I am so glad (Marson's) life is to be written and as you say, it is a most appropriate time to do it after Cecil Sharp's has been published. I always resented the latter's attitude towards him and thought he behaved unpardonably.'

Soon after the breakup, Charles protested also to Etherington in a letter dated December 19th 1906: 'As to Sharp, I don't think I have played the Highland Chieftain. I think he is gone daft and rushed on me with a table knife. I have ceded him my whole interest and title, property and work in the books and he does not even thank me and asks for a legal deed of release (at my cost, it is to be). It destroys one's nerve to have old friends run amok.'

Assumptions may have got in the way of the facts here. As Maud Karpeles never even knew Charles, it may be that her confident assertion that there was an 'affair' is based on nothing more than Cecil's or Chloe's assumption that 'something' must have gone on. The story of the letter that was not posted is intriguing but not corroborated elsewhere. There is no actual evidence, then or now, of any 'affair'. Indeed Cecil may never have actually charged Charles with infidelity at all. He may just have been upset if, during his many previous visits to Hambridge, he had seen Charles mistreat Chloe in any way, perhaps with a sarcastic word or disdainful look. Any 'advice' that he may have offered eventually and in the midst of a professional dispute would have been taken badly by Charles out of hurt pride.

The 'lighter charge' theory fits with the memory of Mrs Hazel Wallis, the wife of the last vicar of Hambridge, who entertained and befriended Maud Karpeles in the 1960s. She remembers that, during one visit to Hambridge, Maud 'disappeared up the garden with my husband and ceremonially burned a number of Sharp-Marson letters'. She also recalls Maud saying that she felt 'there was something demeaning over the ending of the friendship' and that it all arose because 'Sharp was very critical about Marson's attitude to his wife.' All this conjecture is important because Charles's personal reputation is at stake. The dispute was conducted entirely by post with no face-to-face meetings, and because most letters have been destroyed, we may never know the real sequence of events.

It is certainly curious that Cecil had hardly spent any time at all that summer at Hambridge, so why he suddenly felt emboldened to offer marriage advice to his old friend is puzzling. If he felt that they could no longer work well together and engineered a rift accordingly, this would be a dishonourable end to their friendship, particularly if he gained monetarily from it. It is perhaps better, and more generous, to conclude that two proud men, who had shared a friendship when both were working against the establishment in their different fields, found that their egos clashed and they could not actually work together in the same field for very long.

From Charles's point of view, his own Christian Socialism was never going to be supplanted by Cecil's new gospel that folk music would revive the spirit of England. His journalistic skills were no longer particularly useful to Cecil and he did not have the meticulous attention to detail (indexing and cross-referencing) that Cecil was showing in the published works. Neither did Charles share the same sophisticated musical skills as Cecil of notating and arranging tunes. He could not and would not continue collecting on his own – Frank Etherington, his likeliest partner in any venture, could not even play the piano. Finally, although he very much enjoyed dancing, he could not follow Cecil's new interest in the morris, because there was none left in Somerset. Churchwarden accounts tell of morris dancers at May games and church ales in Somerset in the early 1600s, but then Puritan suppression was applied from 1624 and little more activity is recorded. In summary, Charles was no longer the right partner for Cecil and they went their separate ways.

So Charles simply submitted a bland and even shorter preface for *Series Three*, and the partnership ended. Several people were upset for Charles and thought that his initial knowledge, enthusiasm and contacts were not given enough credit subsequently. Revd Allen Brockington, vicar of Taunton, summed it up in a letter: 'Sharp talked to me about their break. He said that Marson was indifferent to money. But Marson was not indifferent to *kudos*. Sharp did not give him credit enough. Sharp had only one interest; Marson had many. Sharp was single-minded – almost fanatically single-minded and Marson struck me as shrinking from self-devotion to anything or anyone.' It is instructive too that Conrad Noel, who also knew both men, did not recommend Sharp to his wife Miriam when she needed help in the revival of morris dancing at Thaxted in 1911 but rather turned to Mary Neal's Espérance Club. In his autobiography Noel does refer to Sharp 'in Somersetshire collecting (songs), with the help of Father Charles Marson, who had been in the field long before him.'

It is one of those twists of fate that Charles was near to leaving Hambridge in 1898 to take up a post in Birmingham. If he had in fact gone there, the English folk revival might have been delayed or have developed very differently. Cecil would not have left his bookish research to visit Charles in Somerset and thus discovered the rich living tradition of singers like Louie Hooper and Lucy White.

23

More Upset

Charles tried very hard not to be bitter about the break and quickly wrote to Etherington on December 5th: 'I cannot unlove a man I have loved for 17 years, whatever he does or says.' So he put his mind to other matters, working on an article about the Reformation for a new publishing venture, The Catholic Literature Association. In March 1907 he was invited to give lectures in Oxford and in Exeter, and he generally kept himself busy that spring.

Domestically, daughter Mary, aged 15, had transferred to the Godolphin School at Salisbury and was finding the academic work challenging, while John, aged eleven, was thinking of a naval career. Charles and Chloe seemed to be getting on a little better during these months, perhaps because his attention was not so distracted by the folk project. They took time to write letters to their two children on a regular basis. Chloe's outlook had perhaps improved, because she was doing a little teaching work again – working with a Miss Tindsell on her Greek and Latin, and with George Templeman, the local farmer's son, on all his lessons.

At the end of May 1907, however, Charles was knocked over by another bomb, this time from his bishop. Having survived the Royal Commission Report in the previous year, Charles perhaps thought that he would be left alone but he received a telegram out of the blue from George Kennion, Bishop of Bath & Wells, inhibiting him from taking any more services at Isle Brewers church, because he had 'discovered that vestments were in use' there. Charles had been covering for Revd John Cole, the sick vicar of that parish, for five years now, with the Bishop's tacit consent. When Cole had died at the end of the previous November, however, Charles had just carried on, until a new vicar, Revd Henry Gibbon, was found and was ready to take over. When his churchwardens learned of the telegram, however, they defiantly wrote to the local press to decry the opportunistic and graceless move by the Bishop:

> 'No better man we wish to work with in parish, school or church work; he was most straightforward and punctual in all

269

things; by our Parish Meeting's sanction he made himself heard at the Langport Rural District Council's Board meeting for the benefit of the public generally. We can say that the Revd CL Marson came to us in all winds and weathers; he worked very hard, and we are sorry that he was not allowed to conduct the services on the Sunday before mentioned.' (*Langport & Somerton Herald* June 15th 1907).

The Bishop's blast may well have been a passing shot at Charles, following a letter by him (October 26th 1906) to the *Langport & Somerton Herald* attacking the Bishop for his opposition to Socialism. Fortunately Charles's position at Hambridge church was not threatened by the telegram and the matter died down with no apology expected or forthcoming. It was the last time that the Bishop intruded and he left Charles in peace from then on.

Bishop George Wyndham Kennion 1845-1922

Photo: the State Library of South Australia

These two men just couldn't get on. Charles's nickname for Bishop George Wyndham Kennion was 'Windy', as the following extract from a letter to Bertha Clarke two years later indicates:

'I took Grenfell (*a friend*) to a Confirmation at Brompton Regis. This is a lovely Exmoor place in the hills. We had to footslog for six miles up the Exe valley and found poor Windy at his most odious. He scented an aristocrat in Grenfell and at once wormed slimily up to him and asked him about Lord Peppermint and Lady MacSkullery, his relatives, and if the Duke of Meringues were not his fifth cousin ninth removed. As

270

Grenfell is the secretary of the ILP and a Socialist, he was hugely diverted.' (June 3rd 1908)

The next quarrel that Charles couldn't help but observe with some irony was the tiff between Cecil Sharp and Henry Hammond over the latter's *Folk Songs from Dorset* project. Charles already knew Henry, because the Hammond family were long-term residents of Clevedon and parishioners of his father. Although he was seven years older than Henry and both of them had spent time away at boarding schools, Charles would have met the family many times socially and in church. Henry's father had died young, and over the next thirty years his widow Catherine brought up her five children in three different houses, all very near to the Marson vicarage. Henry went to Oxford University like Charles and his younger brother Robert did likewise, studying theology.

Probably on Charles's prompting, Henry was introduced to Revd Etherington in Minehead and did some song collecting in that area in 1904. He was working with George Gardiner, whom he had previously known as a colleague at the Edinburgh Academy. They were 'trying to collect some of the gleanings of Mr Sharp's harvest' – Cecil's first contacts with Captain Lewis and other singers at Minehead had been in August that year. Guided by Lucy Broadwood, Secretary of the Folk Song Society, however, Henry Hammond left Somerset to Sharp and moved into Dorset in 1905 with his younger brother Robert, collecting 193 songs that autumn. Henry collected the music and Robert the texts. After meeting the impressive Mrs Marina Russell of Upwey near Weymouth, who gave them a hundred songs, they found that in two years they had amassed a huge collection of songs and discussed with Cecil how to arrange and publish a selection. Charles wrote knowingly to Bertha Clarke on June 3rd 1908: 'Sharp has quarrelled with Harry Hammond and seems riding for a fall. Nearly everyone who knows him gropes for a pistol when his name is mentioned. I am awfully sorry he is so very silly.' Three weeks later he writes again: 'The traitor is to have a money presentation this week. Did you hear what he did about Hammond's Dorset Book? He revised the harmonies and put his own name outside the cover instead of Hammond's. HH was mad and thirsts for his gore.'

Cecil's disagreements were by no means over. The most acrimonious quarrel of all was that between Cecil Sharp and Mary Neal. Charles kept well out of it. It was conducted in public through the Press intermittently between 1908 and 1914. It was nothing less than a fight to be the acknowledged authority and pre-eminent leader of the new national folk movement. [*The full detail of the dispute is beyond the scope of this book but a resumé follows – see Bibliography.*]

After the break with Charles, Cecil had achieved a great deal in 1907:-

– recording morris tunes from Gloucestershire fiddlers John Mason and William Hathaway, which would eventually lead him (and others) to reconstruct the dances of Bledington, Longborough and Sherborne (today's 'canon' has 66 dances from these villages alone);

– publishing, without Charles's help, *Folk Songs from Somerset Vol 4*, with the introductory statement, dated December 1907, that 'this volume will, in all probability, be the last of the series';

– collecting more tunes and dances from William Kimber in October in preparation for the Morris Book Part II, although in the end this was held back till July 1909;

– delivering a busy schedule of lectures and performances all round the country with and on behalf of the Espérance Club;

– marketing his books and sheet music through the Espérance Club network.

However, he began to have some concerns when Mary Neal convened a conference at the Goupil Gallery in Regent Street in November 1907. Public demand for the Espérance teachers, she said, required a new and larger organisation to fundraise, promote and deliver folk dancing to the public, particularly through schools and play associations. It was a philanthropic mission rather than an artistic or academic task. In the end, the proposed new 'Association for the Revival and Practice of Folk Music' never really developed a proper constitution nor membership scheme, but worked more as a charity from an office in Kingsway to promote its work and to pay its teaching staff.

It was just at this critical time early in 1908 that Dorothea Sharp, Cecil's oldest child, aged 13, became ill and the whole family was in turmoil, as Connie Sharp explained in a rare letter to Chloe on April 12th 1908. Perhaps the two women were getting in touch again to

272

effect some sort of reconciliation between the two families. She begins:

'My dear Chloe, Many thanks for your letter. It was nice to hear from you again. I have been staying for a week at St Albans which is where we are going to live. I have looked at every empty house there is and we are going over on Thursday to settle on one. I hope we shall improve in health there. We have never been very well in this house. Dorothea is much better and no-one would think there is anything wrong with her. All the same we shall have to be very careful for some years to come. Her spine is not straight and she is having Swedish treatment for it. I am learning how to do it, as it is horribly expensive. The other children are all very well. I mean to make a fortune growing mushrooms in something. Why not? . . . With love, your old friend, Constance.'

It would have been quite uprooting for Cecil to leave Hampstead and his London life; and the 'mushroom' project does sound a rather desperate bid for a new income. In fact they didn't move and Cecil could continue his work, but more trouble hit the family that summer (1908) when they all went to Axbridge, north Somerset for a holiday. Cecil had plans for more songs and he did meet some good new singers like George Say at Axbridge, Jane Gulliford at Combe Florey, Charles Neville at East Coker and Charles Ash at Crowcombe. He collected over 90 songs and had material for another volume of songs but this was all at a cost, as Connie Sharp subsequently explained to Chloe in a letter:

'I had a bad bout of indigestion all the autumn. The result, I suppose, of our alarming summer holiday. We spent it at Axbridge where Dorothea and Charlie got diphtheria. Luckily they had it lightly but my poor brother Walter, who was with us, developed it in London the day after he left us and was five weeks in a fever hospital. Cecil had tonsilitis and ulcerated eyes, and after they were better I got a queer attack of some sort.

'We did not go to St Albans, as you may perceive. The specialist who saw D in the spring said she would do quite well in London except in the winter months; and that if she should take a turn for the worse, she must go into a regular Home to be treated. Well, goodbye, dear Chloe. I don't know if or when

273

we shall ever meet again but in any case I am your affectionate friend, Constance D Sharp.' (letter Jan 26th 1909)

This rather sad letter shows the strain that her family had been experiencing during 1908, and when Cecil returned to London, he found that he was more and more sidelined in Mary Neal's gushing press releases. He reacted badly and began to dissociate himself from the Espérance Club. Herbert MacIlwaine had decided independently to resign from the Club in the previous November, perhaps because on September 19th Mary Neal had invited a representative of the Women's Social and Political Union to talk to the Espérance girls about affiliating to the suffragette cause. Mary Neal was on the WSPU national committee alongside her close friend Emmeline Pethick-Lawrence (her previous co-worker and MacIlwaine's predecessor as Musical Director).

The friction between Sharp and Neal was building up, as Cecil actually learned more about other morris sides. He became convinced that there had to be more rigorous and consistent teaching standards to capture and reproduce the new dances he was finding. He had noted the Winster 'processional' style in Derbyshire the previous June; then in January 1909 he learned about the Chipping Camden dances; in April he visited Sam Bennett of the Ilmington morris (near Stratford), taking rough notes of six dances; and in August he met the fiddler William 'Jinky' Wells of Bampton (near Oxford). These last three 'traditions' would eventually yield 53 dances in today's 'canon'.

By this time Cecil was in open disagreement with Mary Neal, demanding a more 'accurate' approach, which he planned to deliver through his own school of morris dancing based at the South Western Polytechnic at Chelsea. There he lectured and inspired hundreds of teacher trainees, mostly women, among whom was Maud Karpeles, his future assistant, and her sister Helen. They started their own folk dance club at the Canning Town Settlement, out of which grew the English Folk Dance Society (December1911) with Cecil as committee member and then Director.

The Society, in marked contrast to Mary Neal's Association, quickly built a solid membership and a wide branch network. Cecil created his own demonstration 'side', which included the young composer George Butterworth. Between 1911 and 1913 Cecil collected the sword and rapper dances of Yorkshire and

Northumbria, which widened the scope of folk dance still further. These dances convinced him to dump the 'Moorish' origin for the morris and promote the idea of a ceremonial or religious origin. A sacrifice is made to kill (behead) the old king and bring in the new, the swords (or staves) being all that survives of the old ritual. Some scholars very much dispute these Frazerian ideas (*see Bibliography*).

So, as with his break with Charles, Cecil was determined to outpace and outmanoeuvre his rivals and colleagues. Although Mary Neal initiated the morris dance revival with her instructors and spread it widely with her good publicity skills, she never received due credit for this. Like Charles with folk songs, she probably did not have the right skills to take folk dance to the next level – she did not perform the dances herself and was not musically qualified. Her next musical director, Clive Carey, did do good work for her, however, and two *Espérance Morris Books* were produced in 1910 and 1912 but by then Cecil had outdistanced them. He was able to give up his Ludgrove School job in 1910 and devote the rest of his life to folk song and folk dance. He has been criticised because of his personality, his class, his theories and his strategy, but it must be said that he left a solid legacy of tunes, songs and dances – research that was conducted at his own expense and is extensively used today. Charles at least would not have begrudged him credit for that.

24

Ill Health

Charles began the year 1908 with a burst of activity. He wrote to daughter Mary that he had been asked to write for *The Academy* and had received a 'pile of poets' to review. Also he had been lecturing at Clevedon on Dr Johnson, John Parkinson (Charles I's herbalist), Abraham Cowley (17th century poet) and Winthrop Praed (19th century poet). He was still helping Maurice Child with his Oxford degree and was active in the Langport Socialist Group. On June 1st he chaired a meeting, addressed by his old Fabian friend Edward Pease, one of the original founders of that Society and still its Secretary. The Pease family came from the Bristol area and Chloe was a good friend at Newnham with Edward's sister Anna Dorothea (Dora). So no doubt Edward felt at ease and could rely on the Marsons for accommodation that night.

The topic of the meeting was the proposed 'Municipal Control of the Drink Traffic and the Licensing Bill'. The question was whether it was right for government to regulate alcohol to the benefit of the community, even though it might constrict or damage the individual – a familiar and perennial debate! It was a case of 'déjà vu' for Charles, who had caused controversy in Australia nearly twenty years earlier in supporting barmaids against a ban. Charles opened proceedings, saying that 'the proposal to abolish barmaids ought to be opposed, because the young women were engaged in a perfectly legitimate trade, and if their livelihood was taken away from them, they would have to find a living in some other, and perhaps worse, way. He liked his glass of beer and he always found the young ladies who served him very courteous.'

Edward's theme was that some sort of licensing control was reasonable to reduce great drunkenness, as long as the regulator was accountable to the electors. The meeting was not very well attended and was then interrupted by some hecklers, probably from the local pub, who burst into a rendition of 'God Save the King'. Charles wound up the meeting with notice of two open-air Socialist meetings to come in June and July, and he and Edward left for home (or the local pub). As a postscript, only two months later Chloe was very upset by the news of the death after childbirth of Edward's sister Caroline (Cara) Pease, who had married John Bright Clark of Street (near Glastonbury), a Director of Clark's Shoe Company. The Clarks were strong Liberals and Quakers.

Chloe herself was quite productive in 1908, sending in historical material for publication in various magazines. All income was welcome, as she still found the vicarage a difficult place to run, especially in the winter. The coal bill would have been enormous, if they had tried to heat all ten bedrooms. She had just paid (actually her Aunt Agnes had just paid) for a man to install electric bells between Chloe's room and the rooms of Olive and Bessie, the cook and maid. Aunt Agnes not unreasonably supposed that 'running about the cold passages in the winter at 6.30 to wake the servants' was giving Chloe neuralgia! In July Chloe wrote to son John, who was now a boarder at a school in Honiton in Devon: 'I have been very busy over the spring cleaning of my bed-room and dressing-room and have put fresh papers in all the drawers.'

After the summer holidays, Mary went back for her last year at the Godolphin School in Salisbury. She had given up classics to the disappointment of her parents but was progressing well in French and German. She was not shaping up to be a star pupil but seemed to be enjoying school. She and John had just come home for their Christmas holidays, when news came through that Charles's brother Frank had died in London at the age of 39. It was all very sad. He had never broken free of his drug addiction and Charles had not been able to give him support, as he once had when he was near him in London fourteen years earlier.

Frank had been admitted to the Middlesex Hospital in Mortimer Street on Christmas Eve 1908 in an unconscious state. His notes record that he was 'a medical student, very thin and wasted and his forearms are covered with scabs of a hypodermic needle. Patient takes morphia – of late only 3 grains per diem but this is about half his usual amount. His eyes are closed, corneal reflex absent, pupils pin-point, breathing shallow, pulse weak but regular. He was given 1/15 grain of strychnine but it did not revive him. Patient died 2 hours after admission.' The fact that Frank was still a 'medical student' at age 39 indicates that he had never completed his training

277

in all these years. Charles left home immediately to identify the body and register his poor brother's death.

$$\Diamond\!\!-\!\!\pi$$

Having returned home, much saddened, he picked up again the research for his next book, a historical guide to Glastonbury. The work was very time-consuming and he wrote a series of amusing letters to Mary about this. His letter of February 16th contains lovely cartoons and amusing poetry. He said he was sorry he couldn't write better letters but he had no time for anything –
> 'Nothing but abbots hot and abbots cold,
> Abbots young and abbots old,
> Abbots lean and abbots fat,
> Men like this and men like that.
> Danes and kings and pirates too,
> Cloaks of scarlet, cloaks of blue,
> Saints and sinners, salmon catchers,
> Latin writers, knaves and thatchers.'

He was in a rush to put the finishing touches to the book in time for the impending visit to Glastonbury of the Prince of Wales in June 1909. With illustrations and photographs, it's a neat and well-researched book of 100 pages, written without the aid of modern archaeology. It describes the Tor, the Abbey, churches and other buildings of note, drawing on the writings of early historians and monks. It mentions the legend that Joseph of Arimathaea came to Glastonbury and planted his staff there, out of which grew a holy thorn. 'For 14 out of the last 17 years it has decorated St John's altar with its flowers at Christmas.'

Charles describes in detail the rise and fall of the Abbey. It was desecrated by order of Henry VIII in 1539 and its abbot Richard Whytyng was taken to the Tor, where he was hanged, disembowelled, beheaded and quartered. His quarters, boiled in pitch, were displayed at Wells, Bath, Ilchester and Bridgwater.

Although he approved of some aspects of the Reformation, Charles felt that much had needlessly been thrown away – for example, the colour and drama of the rituals, the feast days and Saints' days. This sense of loss comes through in the book: 'Perhaps one of the sadder things of all this desecration is the little stir it made. Men believed that there would be no more taxes, if once the Monasteries were made over to the King. Alas! They were more quickly converted to the truth in that, than in most things . . . The filching and cheap bargains came dear in the end, for the town was nothing without the Abbey.'

The book was a success – the King ordered five copies and by June nearly 1,000 copies had been sold. He had other work lined up too, as he told Mary: 'I've done an article for a Socialist paper and some reviews for the *Daily Mail* and one for the *Sunday Chronicle*. I am doing lots of potboilers to try to make up the mason's bill for John England's house and the rates. The worst of choosing a father, who is a slave to a sort of missionary work, is that you have to share his kicks and poverty.'

He was indeed short of money again and expenses loomed large. First, Chloe went up to London in April 1909 to support Millicent Fawcett in her great preparations for the Congress of the International Woman Suffrage Alliance. There were banquets and receptions to organise, as well as business meetings. The main event at the Albert Hall took place on April 27th and twenty countries sent delegations this time. Chloe would have been a tremendous help with her fluent German and French. Next, Charles set off at the end of June to Donegal via Liverpool and Belfast for a painting and fishing holiday. On his return, however, he faced a heavy bill for 'dilapidations' (i.e. repairs to the vicarage).

His health was not good for most of the summer, as he wrote to Mary (*in joke dialect*) on May 5th: 'I've a-been bad myself, comed out all spotted-like. (Dr) Maidlow he do say I've been a bit blood-poisoned but I be so thankful I be well again and smokin' me pipe as avoor.' On July 31st, however, he wrote to Bertha Clarke: 'I'm at low water. The ladies sent for a leech, who said "bad strain to heart" and that if I do not keep quiet, I shall collapse.'

He did not go with Chloe and the children to Lyme Regis that August but rested at home. However, he became very ill and fainted during early Mass one Sunday. In early September he was still laid up in bed, as he describes to Mary: 'I sit in a chair in the study, with rugs over me, of an afternoon and see people for a bit. I am trying to paint a sunset but it is a hard mess as yet and hideous.'

Chloe received a nice letter of concern from Cecil Sharp at the end of August from his holiday house at Stow-on-the-Wold. He had heard of Charles's illness and asked Chloe to send him details. Connie sent her best wishes too. The decision was soon made for Charles to leave the cold, damp vicarage and go to the warmer atmosphere of Cornwall.

For four months, from October 1909 to January 1910, he exchanged with Father Berry, a genial Irish priest, who enjoyed the swap. St Elwyn's Hayle (near St Ives) is a charming little church and its congregation was welcoming. Charles made a good recovery in the sea air and in January wrote to Mary, who had stayed on in the vicarage with Chloe.

Charles in Cornwall
aged 50

He had always encouraged independence of thought in his two children and released Mary from 'duties' to him, as follows:

'This is just to thank you for your letter and laugh at you for being "too busy" to write, with festivities. Don't ever say such things. They are never true, even when really busy folk say them. It is also unnecessary. I have written very little to you and John, and you less to me since I left. So if any excuse is needed, I ought to make it. But duty-letters are silly and burdensome things, and I find no pleasure in them. So never trouble to write to me unless you really feel inclined and then do not make mangy excuses for not feeling inclined. See?'

He asked Mary to make sure all his clothes and bed linen would be well aired for his return, 'as the doctors have both told me a relapse would mean a certain fizzle out and goodbye to the parsonage for all of us.' On February 1st 1910 he wrote from

280

Hambridge to Chloe's sister Janie: 'Thank you for your kind wishes and the calendar. The change has done me good, for I crawled down to Cornwall with difficulty and left it in as good health as I am ever likely to see again. It is not without its humours to have pulled the whiskers of death and got off. I did not expect to see this place again.' His arrival back in his own parish was a great joy to all the parishioners, who cheered as he drove up in his pony and trap and let off fireworks on the vicarage lawn.

⚿

He felt so much better in fact that within a month he had written some pieces for a new magazine called *The Tramp*, which had been started by his former pupil Douglas Goldring; and he had taken on a new pupil, Lawrence Stuart Dark, aged 13, son of the journalist and author Sydney Dark. Stuart was a clever city boy from Paddington and, by his own admission, had 'found preparatory schools hateful, having decamped from more than one'. He was recommended to go to Hambridge by Revd Percy Dearmer and was immediately surprised by his new surroundings. He became a writer, like Goldring, and in 1934 wrote of his time with Charles:

'He at once started me on a novel method of education. We might do Ovid and Homer in the mornings and in the afternoons I learnt carpentry, horse shoeing and many more practical tasks. Father Marson did everything thoroughly and sensibly: there was nothing of the pedagogue about him. Everything he attempted – and he once told me that he knew "less about more things than most men" – was done from an original, yet sane, viewpoint.

'He and I went to the church daily at 8.30am. Should there be any tramps resting or sleeping in church, as there frequently were, the Church never being locked, I was made to say the responses in a whisper. I was one of his servers and I always carry a happy picture of him in my mind, standing at the altar in his vestments, only to expose a mighty pair of shooting boots when he knelt down.

'During my time with him he bought a grey mare, Bet, which he rode and drove and got great fun. With Bet, he had Ladysmith, the old white pony, Dinah, a donkey and of course

281

Plato, the Airedale. The burden of a huge house was always with him but even this drain he made into a jest. One windy night sitting with him in his study, a tile was blown from the roof. "Another month's stipend gone, Stuart," he laughed.

His battle with his enemy asthma was an unceasing one. He was persuaded to obtain a dispensation to allow him to take some cocoa between the early and the sung Mass on Sundays, but each Sunday there was a fight to make him take it, even on Easter Sunday when he said as many as three early Masses.

Through his tutoring I was able to pass into Tonbridge School with the greatest of ease. The thought of him is ever present with me and those years with him have left an indelible, unforgettable mark on my life. A great friend, a dear priest and an amazing tutor.'

Despite his fragile health, Charles prepared his own hay as usual for his animals that summer from the tithe meadow next to the vicarage. As he explained once to Mary: 'Hay is very important – "now or never" is its motto. If it is not made well, sweet and enough, the beasts get sick and starve, and men are ruined.' Furthermore he did not neglect the village school just because he had a private pupil himself. He still acted as correspondent to the County Council and had achieved many improvements over the years. The children had been using exercise books instead of slates since 1901, and the medical officer, alerted by an outbreak of diphtheria in December 1903, had approved the new sanitation system and better ventilation that Charles organised with Miss Alice Tanner. She had continued as Headteacher after her marriage to John McLennan in 1905. When, however, she was upset that Council Inspectors had complained about the poor state of the cloakrooms in 1911, Charles rose to her defence that money should not be diverted to that purpose:

'The hats and jackets are now housed in a lean-to shed which is unpretending but watertight. This building seems to awaken the fierce animosity of your agents, who aspire to lordlier housing for the vacant garments and apparently would like us to build something in the Corinthian or Ionic mode. Consequently we are asked to spend considerable sums that the hats of our children may be more luxuriously housed than their heads. We can but reply that we are convinced of no such necessity and decline to undertake any such work.'

282

The Inspectors did not pursue the matter. Charles was never afraid to tangle with the authorities. Another complaint that came to him was from the Bishop of Salisbury, who urged Charles in forceful tones to change the word 'Mass' (written in large letters) on his parish notice-board and use instead 'Holy Communion' or 'Lord's Supper'. Whenever Charles wrote to friends, he would invariably head his letter with the name of any Saint's Day or feast day rather than just the day of the month. Noticing that it was 'Michaelmas Day' on his calendar when he sat down to make reply to the Bishop, he headed his letter 'MichaelLord's Supper-Day' and said that, at his Lordship's suggestion, he had substituted the word 'mass' but didn't like the sound of it. He hoped his Lordship did, however. The Bishop never replied to the letter and never troubled him again.

Charles may have recovered his old spark after returning from Cornwall in 1910, but his relationship with Chloe was unfortunately not improved that year. The issue of women's suffrage was the focus of their division this time. The national debate was continued in their drawing-room, as in so many others. Although Chloe's loyalty lay with the moderate suffragists led by Millicent Fawcett, Charles irritated her by labelling her opinions and actions as 'suffragette'. This was not right. The Women's Social & Political Union (WSPU), begun in 1903 and led by Emmeline Pankhurst and her daughters Sylvia and Christabel, constituted the 'suffragette' movement. Initial public sympathy and financial support had flowed to the WSPU, whose members were seen as heroic victims when arrested for heckling or petitioning in the years 1905 to 1907. By 1908, the WSPU's income was over £20,000 (equivalent to over £1 million today). A larger staff of 70 could now be paid in London and in the provinces to organise meetings and publicise the cause.

However, some of this public support was lost by the WSPU's change of tactics after 1909 – namely, to promote incidents of window-smashing, crowd incitement and personal attacks on politicians. Hunger-strikes and imprisonment issues (like forcible feeding) complicated and fuelled the propaganda war. Finally, the bombing and arson campaign, which followed Parliament's rejection of a Franchise Bill in January 1913, led to further recalcitrance on both sides.

The WSPU certainly quickened the pace and changed the public perception of women during this period, but Millicent Fawcett's National Union of Women's Suffrage Societies (NUWSS) was the alternative pressure group, which continued its surge in popularity from just 16 societies in 1903 to 70 by 1909 and to 305 by 1911 with 26,000 members. By 1914 the NUWSS was spending £45,000 a year on its campaign. The Great War brought everything to a temporary halt, but Chloe was in London with the Fawcetts at the victory celebrations on March 13th 1918 for the Act that gave women over 30 the vote.

For several years, therefore, Charles and Chloe read the London newspapers and discussed all these developments, deepening their different conclusions.   Despite his early support for women's education and votes, Charles now felt unable, at the age of 50, to adapt some of his ideas. Perhaps the Victorian *paterfamilias* image, originally provided by Prince Albert, still held sway. For example, Charles wrote to a friend Edyth Bryen on July 5th 1910:

> 'You ask why a vote should breed strife between man and wife? Partly because we are none of us quite reasonable and partly because a voting wife would challenge the headship of the husband. Headship is a tiresome and burdensome thing but a "free union on equal terms" means slavery for the woman and a smash up for the children. I never qualified to vote till I was over 30 but have spent untold energy in preaching Socialism. The feminine vote in New Zealand and in Australia has been very disappointing. It has done nothing to lessen the immoralities in big towns nor to stop sweating and low wages.'

He did feel other issues were a more important priority, as shown in a letter to Revd Paul Stacy dated January 17th 1913: 'The Socialist Movement is being choked by feminism – like a tree with ivy.' In fact that year Charles resigned from the Fabian Society after 28 years 'owing to the feminisation of the Society'.

The truth is that he and Chloe were just irksome to each other now and finding fault over every little thing. He wrote to Douglas Goldring in March 1910: 'Madame is well on the war trail just now, so the devotion of Holy Week is somewhat chilled.' Again on June 4th: 'Madame freezes me, when she sits white and vindictive below the pulpit, hoping for a split infinitive or a howler.' To Bertha Clarke he confided on January 30th 1912: 'C is worse and worse. I hope to find grace in the great day because I have neither flogged nor strangled nor beheaded her. She is wild with wrath today because I will not drive her to a Suffragette meeting but I am going for a ride in the opposite direction.'

Chloe looking very tired and strained.

Photo taken by Lady Agatha Russell at Hambridge in 1913

The friction thus went on for years. Chloe summed up her feelings in a letter to her sister Janie on October 26th 1912. She had recently visited Janie and, scatterbrained as usual, she had left some clothes behind:

'Thank you for the parcel. I was tremendously glad to get them back. As I never have any money over to buy new clothes, my old nighties and combies get most dreadfully shabby. Now I am sitting alone in the dining-room by a very nice fire, which I made up myself before going out to pay the bills. I am only incommoded by Tuckles who will purr and force her nose in under my arm. This has been an awfully sad lonely week. Now I know that C detests me, I feel I have much more leverage towards altering that feeling of his, if I humour it in every way I can. Perhaps one day if he gets an inkling of my philosophic tolerance of his not altogether unreasonable dislike, he will change his mind and think there's something endurable in such a hoary old abuse as me!'

In another letter, written to Etherington later in 1938, Chloe wrote:

'It is terrible to plunge again into those years of agony. You see Charlie would not tell _me_ things. I wrote in my diary each day whether I'd kept control of my feelings or not – given way to despair or lost my temper.'

They were two intelligent and sophisticated people, unable to find their way out of their emotional predicament. Perhaps the stress hurt Charles more than he knew, because he was ill again and exchanged with father Berry in Cornwall for another two months from April to May 1911.

Whenever he went away, he could always rely on John England to keep his house and church in order. Miss Sophy Pedder wrote that when Charles got back from Cornwall the previous time, 'He found that all had been done and carried out, as though he had been present. "Well done! Good and faithful", he said and the poor factotum's eyes were wet with tears.'

John England, 40, Charles's gardener and sexton. The Vicarage Hayloft is in the background with stables adjacent

Photo: EFDSS

John England had been a wonderful help to Charles as gardener, handyman, parish clerk and mainstay of the choir. It was so appropriate that he should have been the first one to sing for Cecil Sharp and start the folk song project. John was a wise counsellor and adviser on village matters. He knew everyone. He was born in Westport in 1865, the only child and son of Joseph England, a farm labourer, and Mary Anne Edmonds, a glover. Joseph came from Isle Brewers village where his father and grandfather, both called Samuel, lived before him. He was therefore no close relation of Louisa England (Hooper), whose family came from the Barrington and Shepton Beauchamp villages.

John was just four years old when his father died but he was brought up in the house next door to his grandfather Henry Edmonds, a fruiterer. It was a natural progression for John to take the occupation of gardener, first to Revd Grueber, then to Charles at Hambridge Vicarage. In June 1886 he married Rose Morris (*another perfect name, given their future link to folk music*), and they had eight children over twenty years. Although Charles had obviously paid John as best he could and helped him with his housing repairs, John was still struggling to make ends meet. In 1907, for example, he was a recipient of coal charity gifts at Christmas. In 1911 he made the decision to emigrate to Canada and the family made preparations to leave, as Rose England later described:

'I shall never forget our last days in England after we had our sale, he would have us stay there with all our children and eat at the same table as they did, and the night Mrs Marson and Miss Mary put all our children to bed and Mr Marson made me sit in the Study with him in the easiest chair and put cushions at my back and told me to rest, and anyone that wanted to see me had to go there, for I wasn't to move again, and I believe that was the first real hour's rest I had had for a month, and I will never forget our last talk. No-one knows better than we do what a dear Friend as well as Master he was to us all the years he was at Hambridge right up to the time we came away.'

Charles kept in touch with the family, during the time they worked in the Milestone area of Saskatchewan, before they bought land at Paddockwood, near Prince Albert. It was very cold there in the winter months (more than 20 degrees below Centigrade), but they were all resourceful people. John lived into his 70s and Rose into her 90s.

Deprived now of his right-hand man, Charles had also lost the services and company of his daughter Mary at Easter 1911. She had been at home for most of the previous eighteen months and he had got used to her cheerfulness. She was nearly 20 now and had gone to Clevedon to work at Miss Porter's academy as a teacher trainee. She was homesick at first and Chloe had 'rushed over in a fine hysteric frenzy and brought back no news and great incoherence', according to Charles. 'It is the girl's great chance,' he wrote to Etherington, 'and her mother is doing her utmost to unsettle her.' He then wrote a series of charming and uplifting letters to Mary over the next two years, as she tried her hand at teaching. She found it hard at first, but he encouraged her in a letter dated July 3rd 1911: 'Do not be weary. Everything worth learning is hard. To mind children is very hard – but glorious, so it needs, I expect, years of learning and not weeks . . . I am rather sick with asthma and insomnia and am inclined to howl but I don't. So don't you!' At the bottom of the letter he sketched two cartoons of Bet, the horse and Dinah, the donkey. Mary would have been cheered by such a letter. She completed eighteen months in Clevedon and then went to do more training at Winchester. John meanwhile had progressed to Sherborne School for Boys in 1910 for three years, before going to Glasgow University to study naval architecture, so the house was quite empty again.

Charles embarked on a final fling of writing in the autumn of 1911. First, he had 18 books to review in September and then began work on his own translation from the Greek of Plato's 'Apology' and 'Crito'. Plato was Charles's hero. He quoted him and followed his ideals and principles in his life. Plato (428-348 BC) was a student of the philosopher Socrates and wrote a number of dialogues – conversations that establish certain philosophic points or principles. The 'Apology' is one of these dialogues and is basically Socrates' defence at his own trial. He was accused of 'not believing in the gods of the state' and thereby corrupting his pupils. Socrates begins his long and eloquent defence by saying that the true philosopher's starting-point is to admit that he knows nothing. Charles often repeated this line to his own pupils! Eventually, however, Socrates is found guilty by a narrow margin and is condemned to death by drinking hemlock.

In the 'Crito' dialogue, Socrates is visited in his death cell by his friend Crito, who offers him the possibility of escape from his fate, because he can bribe the gaolers to set him free. Crito argues that because Socrates' trial was unjust, it would be no shame to escape. All his friends were asking him to take his chance for freedom. However, Socrates argues that even if the State makes a mistake, its citizens are bound to follow its laws because they have enjoyed its protection. It's not difficult to imagine Charles going through the Greek text line by line in his study and feeling inspired by the stoicism described in Plato's work. He could easily apply it to his own trapped situation. His translation was published in 1912.

The second piece of work from him that year was completely different. It was a one-act comic play called *Just like Nettie*, which was put on at the Clavier Hall, Hanover Square, London in May by The Black Kat Club. Unfortunately the text, featuring just three characters, has not survived among his papers. It was the 'warm-up' piece before the main fare – a revival of the successful play *The Passing of the Third Floor Back* by Jerome K Jerome, who personally directed its performance. This was the most successful of Jerome's many plays, written in 1905 long after *Three Men in a Boat* had secured his fame in 1889. It's the story in three acts of a mysterious stranger who comes to a rundown boarding house in Bloomsbury Square. His selfless and kindly behaviour transforms all the cynical characters around him. It was a religious allegory and this may explain why Charles was asked to contribute a companion piece.

The two men probably met through journalism and found that they had a few things in common. For example, they were the same age, born within a fortnight of each other in 1859. Jerome's father began as a West Country preacher – a dissenting minister in North Devon, as compared to an Anglican clergyman in Somerset, but a slight link. His father then lost family money through bad investments and ended up in the East End of London scrabbling for a living. So Jerome grew up in poverty in Poplar, and Charles could relate to that from his Whitechapel days. Jerome had to fend for himself at 16 and did a variety of jobs as an actor, railway clerk, journalist and schoolteacher. With fame, in the 1890s he edited and wrote for various periodicals, which is no doubt when he met Charles (*there is an entry in Chloe's 1894 diary about JKJ*). He was interested in socialism, but his own struggle for survival led him to doubt the role of a benevolent and intervening State. His witty essay *The New Utopia* (1891) may not have supported Charles's socialist stance but both men had a good sense of humour and would have enjoyed this theatrical experiment together. It set Charles up for his final phase of writing.

25

Odds and Ends

Cheered by his theatrical venture in London, Charles returned to Hambridge to work on another book. As many thoughtful people do towards the end of their working lives, he wanted to assemble, articulate and share his thoughts and experiences – about the Church, the priesthood and the wider world. The title of the book was to be *God's Co-operative Society* and it was to be three things – a frank justification of Anglo-Catholicism; a fervent appeal for the Church to reform and modernise itself; and a bold affirmation that Socialism was the next and necessary phase, but that it would be useless without Christian values. The book is teeming with ideas and opinions but perhaps lacks directive argument. It's a firework display rather than a careful candle. Typical of Charles – it's what drew people to him.

In the first two chapters, he looks back to the Reformation and the emerging Church of England with its degraded ritual and heavy reliance on an infallible Bible. As a child, Charles had reacted against the evangelical strictness of his mother and would not hold back now:

> 'We did not promise at our Baptism to believe the Bible. The Church is not founded upon it. It is not the one thing needful. It was written, composed, gathered, preserved, and translated by Churchmen and for Churchmen. Many of the dead in Christ never knew there was or would be a New Testament at all . . . The Church has the right to contradict the Bible. The proud ignoramus, who thinks that a Bible in his knapsack makes him master of the highest wisdom, is in a perilous condition indeed. No wonder the ever-worshipped Bible becomes the object of the utmost contempt and derision. Often the earnest youth, trained in bible adoration, ends as the most bitter detractor of what he ought never either to adore or burn.'

The 'earnest youth' is clearly himself, and this looks like simple scepticism, which today might raise an easy cheer in the pub but seems unworthy of a clergyman of the time. However, Charles had thought through his faith very deeply and in a really modern way, for he paid no great deference to his 'superiors' or to accepted wisdoms. He had big vision and had studied (but not always agreed with) ideas from different cultures and different eras – from Plato and the ancient Eastern Religions to the newer ideas of Spiritualism and Theosophy. He understood that in all religions people construct sacred spaces, venerate holy scriptures and argue over fine doctrines. These human constructs sometimes act as signposts and sometimes act as roadblocks; but to understand the limitations of human thought and behaviour is not to diminish or ridicule them. Charles enjoyed life and loved the human mind – its great insights and noble art and poetry – but he was also able to laugh at its stupidity and selfishness. Having lost his faith as a young man and tested alternatives, Charles now exudes courage and confidence in his final faith.

In subsequent chapters he goes on to discuss what we would call multi-faith issues. He questions, for example, the value of Christian missionary societies, who insistently press Bibles on all nations, as if that was enough to grow faith. There is no sensitivity or respect towards the recipient: 'Pathans find (*Bibles*) in their forts, Arabs in their burnouses (*cloaks*), sailors in their bunks and Esquimaux in their igloos. The recipients do not profit by them. They sometimes only light pipes.' In short, Charles understood the two-way nature of communication. Obliging others to adopt Christianity through gifts or 'aid' did not seem right to him. Equal engagement and honest persuasion were better ways.

Next he considers the present need for Church reform in various areas, reworking some of his earlier essays ('Huppim and Muppim'; 'And Ard'; 'The Church and Democracy'; and other leaflets). He calls for better training for the clergy, greater involvement of lay people and disestablishment of the Church from State. As regards religious education, he is anti-intellectual: 'the knowledge which saves is small and easily gotten. It is not God's will that all His people should climb the steep heights of logical difficulty or ford the deep streams of learning and research.' In their daily work, Charles would advise the clergy to listen more and talk less. He always tried to keep in touch with the instincts and emotions of religious experience and gives a small example from his work as a country parson:

'The harvest festivals are the people's desire, often actually disliked and discountenanced by the clergy, some of whom have boldly declared that the house of prayer shall not be turned into a greengrocery, although the Father of all good gifts has not been squeamish about filling His world with kindly fruits. But it is an outward symbol of labour endured, of the skill of a thousand years, the embodiment of men's lives. That is what they feel and what they want to say.'

In the final chapters of the book, he looks forward confidently to the future, hoping that the Church will become more flexible and responsive to the needs of its people. First and foremost, the Church must deal with the problems of the real world – hunger, poverty, injustice. He chides the Church for acquiescing to the land grabs of the Enclosure Acts and the exploitation of the displaced industrial masses. The clergy, he said, 'became the toadies and servitors of the rich and insolent'. He saw the clergy's silent support for 'individualism' as an essentially 'Protestant' trait, whereby the individual soul is alone and apart, working and accumulating wealth to demonstrate the virtuous rewards of self-discipline. Charles preferred the 'Catholic' emphasis on the community of believers, into which the individual is submerged. He quotes from the leaders of the early Christian communities of the Near East (such as St Ignatius of Antioch) and of North Africa (St Augustine in Algeria and St Clement of Alexandria, Egypt), all of whom spoke up against usury and private property. St Augustine, for example, wrote: 'It is because of private possessions that lawsuits, hatreds, discords, wars among men, riots, civil dissensions, scandals, sins, iniquities and homicides arise.' Or St Ambrose: 'How far, ye rich men, will your mad greed be strained? The world was created for all men and you, the rich minority, try to claim it for yourselves.'

Charles wanted the Church to take the lead again in social discourse, saying that the clergy 'are not only negligible in politics, ineffective in the City, impotent in all great movements, unheard upon all great questions of the day, and only half accepted, as a kind of game, by the people who profess to support them. That is why the air is full of quackery, of Nonconformist substitutes, of Christian Science, Theosophy, Buddhism, and Labour Churches, of religions of golf and motoring, of new theories to support old sins.' This unexpected tirade nearly rings true of today's consumerism and

292

spiritual confusion, but its language is somewhat out of tune now and the book as a whole is not easy to read. This is no more than he would have expected, as he says at one point: 'The past is the past, because it was outgrown.'

$\mathfrak{O}\!\!-\!\!\mathbf{g}$

No sooner had he finished this book but he started on the next one entitled *Village Silhouettes*. There are eight sketches of various village characters, complete with pseudonyms and their own black paper cut-out profiles. This last skill he practised with the school children, who loved his dexterity with the scissors. The first sketch, for example, is that of John Moore, the village musician, whose name in reality was James Marsh, the village poet. The final four chapters are articles about rural life, reprinted from various magazines.

***Example of
Charles's
Silhouette Art***

'Village Inns' is from *The Tramp* magazine, edited by his former pupil Douglas Goldring. There is a paragraph that perfectly explains Charles's sense of freedom in country pursuits and pleasures:

> 'You stand your rod against the porch and what a shilling's worth of delight and mercy you get from the comfortable landlady in 5 or 10 minutes! You go forth again to the gurgling,

plashing waters . . . these fish, good sneering sir, are no trout nor salmon but saucy silvery dace in the stickles, and we are armed with no more flies than black gnat, coachman, a small palmer or two, and perhaps a blue upright. No keepers ask for tickets, rod licences and tips. We take what the unguarded waters bring forth abundantly . . . we shall soon be spinning for pike along the oozey banks, as then the inn will shine red in the grey evening and we shall have hot cider with ginger in it before we go home. Will the welcome there be as warm? Never mind, we have lived today.'

'Voices in Nature' is a charming piece about birdsong ('what are the birds really saying?'), and 'A Whiff of Ireland' is full of stories and observations of his Donegal holiday a few years before. He finished the preface for this book in October 1913 and wrote to daughter Mary that same month that 'there was not much news and we are rattishly poor'.

It had indeed been a difficult year financially. In April his son John, aged 17, had started a training in Naval Architecture in Glasgow and needed support. Moreover his review work dried up over the summer, although it came back in a hectic string of deadlines in the autumn. He wrote to Etherington in early September, inviting him over for a spot of fishing: 'I live very near the margin of the bankruptcy court but the great spice of life to sparrows seems to be to escape the cats' claws and mine are the claws of the official receiver. It is fun in its way. Can't you come and do a day's chub and jack fishing here? I usually keep Mondays for such. We could wander up the Yeo or drive to Thorney on the Parrett.'

By December, however, he was ill again with bronchitis and retreated to Clevedon to be looked after by Kitty, who had the added responsibility of nursing her aged mother Mrs Ker at the same time. He would miss the Hambridge choir supper after Christmas but wrote to Mary to specify the guest list and sundry arrangements that she would organise with Joseph Ree (John England's replacement). 'I am slowly getting better,' he wrote, 'and have given up bedroom fires and walk out in the warm of the day like an October bluebottle. It is unusual to be so feeble and languid. I usually hurry up when I mend.' On December 31st he wrote to his friend Miss Kiddle, teacher at Isle Brewers:

'I am really mending at last. A lump of congestion in the lung refused to budge but is now budging, so that I am to be alive and kicking yet. I have had a terrible time (i.e. one that scared me), for they supposed I was to fall into that nasty ditch between the worlds where a man neither lives usefully nor dies neatly. But kind folk have hauled me out and I am being refitted for another run, I am thankful to say, and am beginning to find how delightful it is to be alive.'

In January 1914 Mary went back to Winchester for one more session of teacher training. Charles wrote to her on Friday February 27th to say that this would in fact be her last term: 'So come home at the end of this term with horse, foot and artillery, and see if you can subdue the spiders here!' This was the last letter he ever wrote, for just five days later on Tuesday March 3rd he died quite suddenly. He was 54. According to newspaper reports:

'He was busy about the village all day Tuesday but in the evening he complained of being unwell. Dr William Maidlow, of Ilminster, was hastily summoned. On his arrival Mr Marson was given every attention. Seeing no immediately dangerous symptoms, the doctor left to procure a nurse but before he returned, Mr Marson had passed away, the cause of death being angina pectoris. Mrs Marson and the vicar's sister Miss Marson were with him to the end, which came with peaceful suddenness.

'The news of his death created a profound impression of sorrow in the parish and throughout the district, Mr Marson having been much beloved by his people and numerous friends on account of his devotion to the Church, his great sincerity, and his unfailing good humour.'

The funeral took place at Hambridge Church on Saturday March 7th. Sixteen members of the clergy attended. Revd Frank Etherington conducted the service and Bishop Kennion addressed a few words, frankly admitting that he had not agreed with Charles on many issues but praising 'the consistency of his character, the devotion of his life and the fearlessness with which he spoke out'. Notable among the congregation was Cecil Sharp, who came to pay his last respects to his old friend. Other family members came to support Chloe and the children on the day: Charles's two sisters Annie and Grace, and sister-in-law Kitty; and Chloe's brother Charles, who had recently retired from the Indian Civil Service where he had ended as Chief Secretary to the Government of Burma, and who came down from Beckenham to represent the Bayne family. Conspicuous by their absences, however, were Chloe's sister Janie and her oldest brother Ronald.

Chloe felt she had to leave the vicarage straightaway but did not have many options as to where to go and how to support herself. Charles had tried and failed to obtain life insurance cover for himself when they got married in Australia but may have taken out a policy on return to England. There is no mention of any pay-out, however. Chloe may have received some help from the Women's Friendly Society in the neighbouring village of Drayton. It was the only female society in Somerset at the time. Any help would have been short-term and her longer prospects were not good. Even though John immediately returned to his training in Glasgow, Mary, at age 23, did not really have employment skills to offer. Chloe had been doing a little more teaching recently – in 1912, for example, she had done some part-time work at Roedean, the private girls' school in

296

Brighton, and could perhaps produce a testimonial, but at age 48 she might struggle to launch a new career.

As to where to live, her sister Janie was in London but couldn't help. She lived as a lodger in a house in Bethnal Green, where she was a church worker. Her two older brothers did offer help. Charles Bayne was in Beckenham with his wife Augusta. He was retired now and had a comfortable house with plenty of room, because his son was away at naval college. However, Chloe did not want a suburban setting and turned instead to brother Ronald in South London, sending Mary to him in the short-term. He had married again and had three children, but only one was then at home. Chloe herself disappeared down to Southampton, where her step-aunt Constance was desperately ill and actually died three weeks later at the age of 72.

In the midst of all her current distress Chloe was desperately trying to stay in control of all the various suggestions coming from Charles's friends – ideas about memorial services, tributes and publication of his letters. She wrote to Frank Etherington on March 21st:

> 'I am very anxious to collect Charlie's letters up to 1898 myself, and I have an idea of getting his and Miss Pedder's great friend Archibald Constable, who lived at Clevedon till two years earlier, to edit the later letters, with my power of veto for anything I wished left out. Mr Constable is a man of immense judgement and delicacy. I must have those later years in my full control. Please dear Frank, do understand how it makes my poor heart bound with terror to think anyone* publishing letters that would break my heart and injure Charlie's best real life.'

[*There is a handwritten code in her letter to Etherington which indicates that she did not want C# (Cecil Sharp) in particular to have access to certain letters.]

Chloe was naturally very sensitive to any public exposure of the rocky state of their marriage in their later years – 1898 is given as a dividing line – but she was clearly reconciled and forgiving about that unhappy period. She wanted the best part of his life to be portrayed fairly and with due consideration. She confirmed that Canon Scott Holland had volunteered to write a memorial, which did actually appear in 1915 as a preface to the reprint of some of Charles's best articles. For various reasons, including the outbreak of war in August 1914, Charles's letters were never published. Just as Maud Karpeles used selective quotes from Sharp's letters and even burned some of them, so Chloe probably protected Charles's reputation by destroying some of his.

Her loving reactions to his death were somewhat checked by a letter from her brother Ronald dated 28th March, in which he wrote:

'I have been thinking over your letter; and if Canon Scott Holland approaches me, I will do anything he may wish in the way of answering any questions but I do not personally feel that I am called upon in any way to promote a reunion of your Husband. Quite apart from his dealings with you, I am not of sympathy with his two most conspicuous activities – his particular way of presenting socialism and his particular way of presenting High Churchmanship. I am against him on both lines, especially on the latter.

'His death on the whole makes me feel that I might have quarrelled with him more, instead of merely keeping quiescent. Now it is too late and I will not make up for it by any attempts to present his case, to explain his personality to the world. For five and twenty years I have been so far away from his confidence, from any knowledge of his aims and actions that I cannot bear any useful witness. His published work repelled me as much as it attracted. I cannot pretend that I have no bitterness in me for what I consider your married life of unnecessary and cruel suffering. With much love, your affectionate brother Ronald.'

This is a bitter letter indeed and it must be remembered that these two men had once been such good friends – at Oxford and in the slum work in Whitechapel. Realising the nature of her brother's feelings, Chloe felt she could not stay under his roof and began to look round for her own house and employment.

26

Chloe's new life

If she could not stay with her sister or brothers in London and the Fawcetts were 'full up' at 2 Gower Street, Chloe really had to set up independently somewhere. She found a rented house at 86 Oakwood Road, Golders Green, and Mary joined her there. Her old friend Philippa Fawcett, who was now Principal Assistant to the Director of Education of the London County Council, no doubt was influential in helping Chloe to find a part-time job as a teacher at Tufnell Park – a job that she held for the next eight years.

She continued to correspond with Revd Etherington in Minehead over his plans to write Charles's biography. She sent him facts and figures, trawling through letters and checking details, but nothing was committed to paper for two reasons – firstly, Etherington in his early 40s was still a busy parish priest and couldn't find time for research; secondly, and most shockingly, Chloe received news in August 1915 that her dear son John had been killed at Gallipoli, fighting against the Turks. Aged just 19, he was a Lieutenant in the 8th 'pioneer' battalion Welsh Regiment that embarked from Avonmouth (Bristol) on June 15th, bound for Lemnos in the Eastern Mediterranean and from there to the Gallipoli peninsula, a finger of land 40 miles long and as narrow as 5 miles across at points. John fell within a few days of his arrival, and all around him thousands of men would die – if not from battle, then from disease. The conditions were dire. The terrain was either thick jungle vegetation in the valleys, which were steep and exhausting to climb, or else rocky and scrubby expanses on the hills, where it was difficult to find or dig out suitable cover. In the heat of battle, corpses, left out in the open, became bloated and stank. The flies were atrocious, the summer heat was appalling, and poor sanitation led to outbreaks of dysentery and fever. Water was scarce with rations of just one pint per man per day. Nothing further removed from the peaceful wetlands of Somerset could be imagined for poor John to end his short life.

Given the stalemate in trench warfare in France, it had been Winston Churchill's idea as First Lord of the Admiralty to open a supply route through the Dardanelles Straits, past Istanbul into the Black Sea, and thus boost the Russian fighting on the eastern front against Germany. But the Turks had come into the War on the side of the Germans in October 1914 and resisted both the naval attacks on the Straits in March 1915 and then the landings of ground forces on the Gallipoli peninsula on 25th April. The British and French troops became bogged down in trench positions at the southern tip, while the Australian and New Zealand troops made their base at Anzac Cove on the western side.

John Marson's battalion (part of the British 13th Division) was called up as part of a major push in August 1915 to break out from Anzac Cove and climb up the ridges and gullies that led to the central hill position at Chunuk Bair. This move would cut the supply line to Turkish troops further south and take out their artillery and sniping positions, which were pinning down the Allied troops below. John arrived at Anzac Cove by boat under cover of darkness on Wednesday August 4th. The whole beach, just 600 yards long, was a hive of activity with men heading off hurriedly to camouflaged camps and mules carrying supplies away to storage. The next day, John busied himself in preparation for battle but watched the hardened Australians and New Zealanders, most of whom had by now spent more than three months holed up here, swimming in the sea despite the occasional sniper fire, because there was simply no spare fresh water in which to wash.

The fighting began soon enough just after midnight of the new day August 7th. Under the command of Brigadier-General Cox, John moved his men up behind New Zealand, Australian and Indian troops across the ravine called Chailak Dere. General Sir Ian Hamilton's Third Report to the War Office (which was later published in the *London Gazette* on January 6th 1916 and read avidly by poor Chloe) takes up the story: 'The surprise was complete. Two Turkish officers were caught in their pyjamas; enemy arms and ammunition were scattered in every direction. The grand attack was now in full swing but the darkness of the night, the density of the scrub, hands and knees progress up the spurs, sheer physical fatigue, exhaustion of the spirit caused by repeated hairbreadth escapes from the hail of random bullets – all these combined to take the edge off the energies of our troops.' But by 9.30am they had thrown the enemy back and established a holding position on a spur, just 500 yards short of the Chunk Bair summit.

At 4.15am of the following morning of Sunday August 8th, John's battalion joined the Auckland Rifles, the New Zealand and Maori Infantry, and the 7th Gloucestershire Regiment, as they attacked the south-west Chunuk Bair ridge. The fighting was particularly brutal then, as the Turks resisted fiercely against surrender of such a key piece of their territory. Bayonet charges and hand-to-hand fighting ensued. The 7th Gloucesters, for example, lost every single senior officer either killed or wounded. It was during this phase of the battle that John was killed. By

2ND-LIEUT. J. C. MARSON.
8TH WELCH REGIMENT
BORN APRIL 15TH. 1895
KILLED IN ACTION ON THE SUMMIT OF CHUNUK BAIR.
GALLIPOLI PENINSULA. SUNDAY. AUGUST 8TH. 1915
"BETTER DEATH THAN DISHONOUR"

that night 800 men held the summit for the Allies, sleeping in pathetically shallow trenches without wire protection. Unfortunately the hard-won gains were lost in the violent counter-attack of the next two days and the summit was surrendered. The 13th Division, which included John's Welsh battalion, had (according to Hamilton) 'lost 6,000 out of a total of 10,500 and 10 commanding officers out of 13 had disappeared from the fighting effectives'.

The eventual evacuation of all troops from Gallipoli that Christmas was carried out successfully, and with very little loss of life, but the failure of the campaign as a whole led to military sackings, political demotion for Churchill and loss of confidence in the Prime Minister Herbert Asquith, Lloyd George taking over in December 1916.

Chloe actually heard quite quickly about John's death, because casualty lists were telegraphed home and her brother had read of John's death in the newspaper on August 19th 1915 and written immediately to his sister that day:

'Dear Clotilda, I am afraid John is gone by the list in this morning's paper. He would be in the thick of it and would expose himself fearlessly. I do not know how to help you to bear it, dear! I know you will feel that your John has died as a brave man should; has gone to God strong and brave and innocent. You and your husband are one, more absolutely than perhaps you ever were while he was with you. And now in your worst grief it may come to you that God wills that John should be with his father: you and Mary will find strength and help in one another. Cannot you all come here for a bit? . . . Your very affectionate and mourning brother, Ronald.'

Chloe must have been desperate for proper news of John's death and eventually received a letter from Major Lynn Stevens of the Welsh Regiment written on October 20th from the Convalescent Hospital, Alexandria, as follows:

'Dear Madam, Only yesterday did I receive your letter of Aug 23rd, asking about your boy. It went to the Peninsula and has come back to me here. Yours is a pitiful loss and there is little or nothing that I can say that will help you to bear it, I fear. It will, however, be some consolation to you, and, later when you can think of him more calmly, a source of never-ending pride, to know that your son died fighting most gallantly in a hand-to-hand attack upon the enemy at the summit of Chunuk Bair. He would not suffer restraint, but charged forward outstripping everybody in his resolve to do his duty. It was a gallant death, dear lady, and you must feel proud to have been the mother of such a son. He was full of work, ardour and happiness during the whole time since we landed at Lemnos. None so keen or more hard-working. His heart was in his job. I cannot tell you how sorry I am for you and for his young sister; it is easy to read from your letter how dear he was to you. Please accept my deepest sympathy.'

The Dardanelles Commission Report of 1919 blamed bad planning, and recent historians have highlighted the very poor state of military maps, which meant that several units got lost or encountered unexpected terrain. The campaign was a defining moment in the national consciousness of the ANZAC troops, many of whom lost confidence in the leadership of the mother country.

The mood was somewhat different for Chloe, who would not countenance the idea that John had died in vain and so threw herself into war work. She joined the War Office as a reader, using her languages to scan and review reports on war progress in the Foreign Press. She kept the letter that she had received from Alice McLennan, the Hambridge schoolteacher for the last 20 years. Alice had written on August 13th 1915, not knowing of John's death: 'I heard from Frank Marsh and Harry Priddle from the Dardanelles' base. They both say how hot it is there and that they are waiting orders to go into action. I also heard from Harry Marsh. He is in France. We have now 48 of Father Marson's old boys on the roll of honour and 23 of them on active service. Isn't this grand? Much love to Mary and yourself, Alice.'

It is easy to see from this letter how deeply the war penetrated into even tiny rural villages. The patriotism and subsequent hurt were felt keenly and the War Memorial erected right opposite the vicarage records that 18 village lads lost their lives in the war – Harry Priddle and the Marsh boys actually survived. Hambridge quickly set up its own branch of the Comrades' Association (which merged into the new British Legion in May 1921) and raised £100 to bring an army hut from Salisbury Plain to the village to serve as a Legion Hall. It was one of the first locations in the whole country to make such a move.

After the war, Chloe undertook paid research work at the British Museum and at the old Public Record Office in Chancery Lane. Later in 1934, prompted no doubt by the new biography of Cecil Sharp, Chloe resurrected with Etherington the idea of a biography about Charles's life. This time they involved Maud Karpeles at the planning stage, because she now had control of Sharp's letters. A draft book was prepared but never published.

Chloe's life, however, really revolved around Mary, who got married in August 1921 at the age of 29 to a confirmed bachelor Stanley Gaster, a bank clerk 23 years older than her. Their two children Isabella Mary Gaster (born 1922) and John Marson Gaster (born 1924) became Chloe's main focus until she died on December 20th 1952 in St Andrews Hospital, Cricklewood, aged 87. In her will she wished to be cremated and then buried with her husband Charles in Hambridge. She left all Charles's letters, manuscripts and book copyrights to Revd Frank Etherington.

27

Legacy

A person's life can be summed up in less than a page by simply listing their 'achievements', apparently solid and enduring gains chalked up by historians and biographers with wonderful hindsight, in which case Charles Marson's contributions would seem slight and evanescent. Alternatively, a life can be told in much more detail with its flaws and hesitations and bravery too. In this case, with the help of the reflections of those who knew him, we can see that Charles had much more influence than we first imagined.

In the sphere of Church Reform, he was thoroughly modern in his irreverent challenges to authority. Peter d'A. Jones in his book *The Christian Socialist Revival* wrote that 'men like Stewart Headlam, Charles Marson and Thomas Hancock were alive to the need for eradicating class consciousness, snobbery and elitism, and for smashing the upper-class Tory image of Anglicanism'. Maurice Reckitt continues in his book *For Christ and People*: 'His books were never widely circulated and are now almost unobtainable; they tended to be either too fiery or (on rural themes) too placid for most readers to welcome or cherish them. This was a man who lived most vividly in the memories of those who knew him best, and these are now dead. The causes he so vigorously espoused were generally highly unpopular then, while now they may seem unimportant because they have so largely become victorious. He showed unfailing courage in the face of adversity and hostility and contempt. In his self-denying and deeply charitable devotion to the oppressed, the weak and the simple, he manifested throughout his life some truly saintly qualities.'

Gilbert Binyon wrote in his book *The Christian Socialist Movement in England*: '(Marson) compelled attention, as much by his caustic wit as by the cogency of his arguments. But new ideas cannot become current until the old ones have been displaced and it was here that Marson excelled – in ridiculing ideas and habits out of existence.' Douglas Goldring, his former pupil, wrote: 'Marson was a man who, in the largest crowd, would have arrested attention. He was dark-haired, tall, broad-shouldered, with humorous twinkling eyes and a magnificent Roman nose. In cassock and beaver, snuff-box in hand, shoulders thrown back, he looked like a Cardinal who had retired from the hierarchy to become a comedian. It was customary to say that that his was a "wasted talent" because his ecclesiastical superiors, who strongly disapproved of him, kept him exiled in a remote corner of a backward county. So magnetic was his personality, however, that he was able to get away with anything he chose to do in the parish, and he was not the kind of man to let his talents go to waste for lack of exercise.'

In the field of politics, Charles's name is not often mentioned in the annals of the socialist movement, but he was an important reporter and supporter of events and ideas in the 1880s in England, as well as a real catalyst for the development of the South Australian Labour Party in the early 1890s. He was a member of various Christian Socialist groups but was a far better speaker and writer than he was an administrator and organiser. He was no "Champagne Socialist" either. Lord Arthur Ponsonby, a Liberal then Labour MP of many years' standing, met Charles in 1903 but made this reminiscence in 1934: 'He was content in his small corner to try to live consistently with his ideals and he regulated his sense of proportion through his sense of humour. I regard him as a fine figure untouched by any craving for publicity, one of those people who in a quiet way exercise far more influence than they are aware of. I delighted in him but I saw how difficult he found it to lead his ideal socialist life personally in a capitalist society.'

As regards the English Folk Revival, he took an early interest in folk ballads and encouraged Cecil Sharp in that direction. He not only introduced Sharp to a number of singers but also taught him a proper respect for those individuals, whom he had come to know so well as their priest. Charles's hospitality and enjoyment of the songs made the whole project a pleasurable experience rather than a dry scholarly task. Because of his own photographic hobby, he probably persuaded Sharp to buy a camera to take pictures of the singers too, so that a wonderful gallery of faces is available to us to go with the songs.

The first folk revival was checked by the onset of the First World War and thereafter by the arrival of jazz and recorded sound. The second revival in the 1950s and '60s (Electric Folk) did recall

Marson's name but due to his quarrel with Sharp, his contribution to folk music has largely been under-played or misconstrued, whereas it is clear that Sharp valued his friend's role immensely in those early years. The stone plaque laid at Hambridge Vicarage by Maud Karpeles on June 10th 1961, along with a commemorative plaque in the church itself, remind us of their close collaboration.

Charles's personal life was extraordinarily unsettled. Including locum posts, he had 14 different jobs in 12 years, none for longer than three years until his last spell of 19 years at Hambridge. He had romantic (though platonic) affairs with Lady Agatha Russell and Edith Nesbit, before a marriage that had both sweet and sour times. He loved his own children but revelled too in the local children, whom he taught and entertained with his faery stories. Just as he made his sermons lively and his services sensual and full of mystery, so he talked to children of a magic world just behind the veil of ordinary life. It was part of the charisma that drew everyone to him. A tribute preached in Hambridge church by Revd Hilder 50 years after his death to many who remembered him in the parish said that he brought 'colour and life and value into human relationships. There was a great love of fun and he enormously enjoyed humanity, with all its quirks and oddities.'

Above all perhaps, he believed in the shared community, as he explained in his last book: 'The absolute inefficiency of the individual to help himself by himself, the consequent need of a society, a club, a country, a church'. That would be his only warning today in the face of rampant consumerism and individualism. He would have loved the easy communications and progress in living standards that we enjoy today. In fact he would slot in quite easily to the modern world, because he was really ahead of his time then. He wasn't always sure of his own progress, however, and a letter that he wrote to his daughter Mary in March 1909 might be a fitting end to our investigation into his life: 'It will be nice, when we are dead, to have it said "they scrabbled to make the world juster and to help the poor". It does not seem much juster yet for my scrabblings, I must admit, but I think it is better and going on the right way, but oh so slowly. If I were a big angel, I would kick it along – like a football. But perhaps they know better?'

Charles Marson Literary Output:

1883-88 occasional articles for *Church Reformer, Pall Mall Gazette* and *To-Day* newspapers

1884-86 Editor of the *Christian Socialist* (monthly) newspaper

1891 *Faery Stories* pub E.A.Petherick & Co of Adelaide; nine original stories about trolls, fairies and dwarves, set in Australia

1894 *Psalms at Work* pub Elliot Stock; selection for clergy and lay people, with notes

1894 Article 'Social Teaching of the Early Fathers' in *Vox Clamantium (Gospel of the People)* Ed Andrew Reid pub London: Innes

1895 *The Following of Christ*, a selection from modern writers arranged by Marson, pub Elliot Stock

1897 *Turnpike Tales* pub Elkin Mathews

1901 *Hugh, Bishop of Lincol'*, a short biography of Bishop Hugh (c1140-1200)

1901 Article 'Huppim and Muppim' – a few words upon the sore need for better religious education in schools, published in *The Commonwealth*, a Christian Social magazine (July) ed Canon Scott Holland

1904 Article 'And Ard', a satirical comment on the recruitment, training and role of the clergy in the modern world, pub in *The Commonwealth* magazine (November) ed Canon Scott Holland. Subsequently reprinted by Mowbray 1906.

1905 *Super Flumina, angling observations of a coarse fisherman*, pub John Lane

1909 *Glastonbury, a historic guide to the English Jerusalem*, pub Gregory (Bath)

1912 *Apology and Crito*, a fine and original translation of Plato

1914 *Village Silhouettes* pub Soc of St Peter & Paul

1914 *God's Co-operative Society'* suggestions on the strategy of the Church, pub Longman, Green & Co (preface dated St Luke 1913 Oct 18th)

Acknowledgements

Many people have helped in the making of this book. In no particular order I would like to thank: my brother Roger for his good advice; David Lawrence who has done a wonderful job preparing all the old photographs for modern printing; my daughter Amy and husband Tim Dawson who have been brilliant with computer advice and designing the website with David Bradshaw; David Rabson and other members of Taunton Deane Morris Men who have goaded me on till the work was done; Andrew and Margaret Swift who have been superb in their editorial support and great desire to see this book published by their company.

Further afield, Malcolm Taylor and Rebecca Hughes at the Vaughan Williams Memorial Library in London have been of outstanding help and I'm truly grateful to them. Other librarians I must thank include Rose Wilson of the State Library of South Australia; Robert Pryor and Dieuwke Jessop of the Holdfast Bay History Centre (Glenelg); Sandra Bonnett, Archivist of the Diocese of Adelaide; the National Library of Australia in Canberra; Anne Thomson, Archivist Newnham College, Cambridge; Robin Darwall-Smith, Archivist University College, Oxford; Mike Heaney of the Bodleian Library, Oxford; Annie Lindsay, Archivist University College Hospital; Sue Donnelly at the London School of Economics Library; Bonny and Cynthia Sartin at Halsway Manor library; staff at Lambeth Palace Library; Laurina Deacon of Langport Library who sourced so many books for me and read my manuscript; Tom Mayberry, County Archivist, and his staff at the Somerset Heritage Centre in Taunton.

Others who have given important help are: Revd Alan Mills who originally allowed me access to the Marson Papers; Revd Alan Ellwood, current vicar of Hambridge; Jane Lilly for her invaluable help with Clevedon History and Mary Walters of St Andrews Clevedon for finding the photograph of Marson Senior; Daisy Parsons who helped to edit the manuscript; Eddie Upton of Folk South West for introducing me to folk music properly; Byron Joce for his friendship and for singing Somerset songs with me; Sally Pizii for her advice on fishing; the villagers of Hambridge and Westport for being interested in their village history. My former colleagues at Hambridge nursing home certainly deserve my thanks not only for their important work but also for their patience over my folk affairs.

Perhaps the biggest vote of thanks is to my wife Lesley for persuading me to start the project in the first place and for her encouragement all along the way.

Bibliography and Sources

This book is not designed as an academic work and I have tried to tell the story by identifying precise sources within the main text. Listed below, however, are the main books and reference points used in my research, so that readers may follow up matters of particular interest. These are grouped together under the most appropriate chapter but, of course, some sources overlap and are important throughout the book.

Of particular value are the 440 letters and papers, which until recently were in the care of Revd Alan Mills, former vicar of Minehead, but are now deposited at Somerset Heritage Centre in Taunton. They are referred to as the 'Marson Papers'. Revd Mills inherited these documents from Revd Roger Wallis, vicar of Hambridge; he in turn had inherited them from Revd Frank Etherington, a personal friend of Charles & Chloe Marson. After Charles's death, Chloe appealed in national newspapers for any of his letters to be returned to her, so that a biography of his life could be prepared by Mr Etherington. In some cases he made typed copies of these letters and returned them; in others he kept the originals. His biography never came to full fruition and he died in 1961.

Etherington's draft biography was in turn the main source for a 19-page booklet on the life of Marson, written by Reg Groves and published in 1985 by The Jubilee Group (held at the University of Warwick Modern Records Centre). In addition the Halsway Manor Folk Library in Somerset and the Vaughan Williams Memorial Library (VWML) at the English Folk Dance and Song Society (EFDSS) in London were excellent resource centres.

I have quoted pre-decimal currency without conversion (e.g. £3-10-6d is three pounds, ten shillings and sixpence). To convert to current prices, multiplication by 60 times is approximately correct but the website www.eh.net/hmit is more precise in this regard.

I freely acknowledge that I consulted Wikipedia on the internet to open avenues of research and endeavoured to check any information so gathered. Likewise I used www.ancestry.co.uk to check certain family histories. Finally Crockford's Directory was most helpful to check the clerical careers of many players in this story.

Chapter One: First Impressions
- Marson, CL, dates from 1863 to 1914, unpublished letters & papers preserved at Somerset Heritage Centre.
- Etherington, Revd Frank, Unpublished biography of C.L.Marson (no date) transcription held at VWML, London.

- Marson, CL, *The life of Amos Peterson* (no date) unpublished fragments of autobiography, Marson papers.
- Marson genealogy traced with help of Birmingham and Midland Society for Genealogy and Heraldry.
- Woolley genealogy via www.cityark.medway.gov
- Lilly, Jane *The Shops of the Old Village* 1999 Clevedon History.
- The Clevedon trains linked to Yatton Station on the Bristol-Taunton (GWR) line. Clevedon was a victim of the Beeching cuts in the 1960s. See www.clevedon-civic-society.org.uk

Chapter Two: Oatmeal and Grapes
- Barnett, Henrietta, *Canon Barnett – His life, work and friends* 1918 pub John Murray.
- Watkins, Micky, *Henrietta Barnett in Whitechapel* 2005.
- 1881 census Whitechapel North enumeration districts 9 to 14
- 1882 Reynolds map 'London and its suburbs'.
- 'An autumn evening in Whitechapel' from Littell's *Living Age* November 1888: courtesy of East London History Society.
- Booth, Charles 1886-1903 *Inquiry into the Life and Labour of the People in London*, maps and notebooks held at the London School of Economics (www.booth.lse.ac.uk)
- The Whitechapel Wash House is now the Women's Library, part of London Metropolitan University.
- The Children's Country Holiday Fund is based today in Hassocks West Sussex www.childrensholidays.org.uk

Chapter Three: Pen or Pulpit
- www.workhouses.org.uk a website run by Peter Higginbotham
- Webb, Beatrice, *My Apprenticeship* 1926 Longmans *p182*.
- Briggs, A & Macartney A., *Toynbee Hall The First Hundred Years,* 1984 Routledge & Kegan Paul.

Chapter Four: The Lady and the Bishop
- Edited MacCarthy, D, and Russell, A, *Lady John Russell: A Memoir* 1910 Longmans.
- 1881 census for Richmond District Union Workhouse.
- Aglionby, FK, *The life of Edward Henry Bickersteth* 1907 Longmans.
- Durey, Dr Jill, *The Evangelicalism of Bishop Anthony Wilson Thorold* 2004 Edith Cowan Univ Perth, Australia.
- Simpkinson, CH, *The Life and Work of Bishop Thorold* 1897 Isbister.
- Scotland, Dr Neil, article 'Evangelicals, Anglicans and Ritualism in Victorian England' 1997 Churchman periodical.
- Letters at Lambeth Palace Library ref: Benson 15 ff215-258.
- Image of Westcott on www.anglicansonline.org

Chapter Five: Without a Cure
- Letters at Lambeth Palace Library ref: Benson 15 ff259-262.

- 1891 census Shoreditch South enumeration district 8.
- *The Christian Socialist* newspaper 1883-91 in 4 vols: Bodleian Library, Oxford.
- O'Connor, Sheila *History of Christchurch, Cinder Hill* www.christchurchcinderhill.com Babbington colliery closed in 1986.

Chapter Six: Fabians and all the rest
- Shaw, GB, *The History of the Fabian Society* 1892 Fabian Tract.
- MacKenzie, N&J., *The First Fabians* 1977 Weidenfeld & Nicolson.
- Reckitt, M (ed)., *For Christ and People* 1968 SPCK.
- Jones, P d'A., *The Christian Socialist Revival* 1968 Princeton University Press.
- Bryant, Chris, *Possible Dreams* 1996 Hodder & Stoughton.
- Bagwell, Philip, *Outcast London* 1987 Epworth Press.

Chapter Seven: The Matchless Orinda
- 33 letters from Charles to Edith Nesbit survive among the Marson papers in Somerset Heritage Centre.
- Briggs, Julia, *A Woman of Passion: The life of E.Nesbit* 1987 Rowan & Littlefield.
- Marson papers: Letter from CLM to Edith Nesbit Sept 24 1887 re Ruckinge church poem.
- Nesbit, E. 'Man-size in Marble' story in *Grim Tales* 1893 Innes.
- Marson papers: Letter from Mrs Harold Bryen, former schoolteacher at Orlestone, 29 Apr 1934 re Nesbit's catholic conversion.

Chapter Eight: St Mary's Orlestone
- Letters to Archbishop Benson at Lambeth Palace Library ref Benson 49 ff46-55.
- Marsh, Jan, *Back to the Land* 1982 Quartet Books.
- 1891 census Kent Orlestone Enumeration District 6.
- Clevedon Mercury 22 Sept 1888 re mother's funeral.

Chapter Nine: The Bayne of My Life
- Information on Newnham College and Chloe's time there courtesy of Newnham College Archives (Anne Thomson).
- Oxford Dictionary of National Biography *Peter Bayne* by Ronald Bayne, courtesy of University of Aberdeen Library.
- GRO Death Certificate: Klothilde Bayne,12 Dec 1865 Staines.
- Flanders, Judith, *The Victorian House* 2003 Harper Collins.
- Booth, Charles 1886-1903 *Inquiry into the Life and Labour of the People in London*, notebook ref BOOTH/B/221 pp182-195 Library of London School of Economics.
- Robinson, Jane, *Bluestockings* 2009 Penguin.

Chapters Ten to Thirteen (Australian period)
- Bayne, C. *Diary 1889-90* Nat Lib of Australia Ms2733 Canberra.

311

- Lee, John *History & Directory of Glenelg 1883*, held at State Library of South Australia.
- Anon, *A short history of the church of St Peter's Glenelg* 1943, held at State Library of South Australia.
- Manning, Geoffrey *A Social History of Glenelg 1836-1936* held at State Library of South Australia.
- Vestry minutes St Peter's Glenelg ref SRG 94/A37 State Library of South Australia.
- *History of St Jude's Church, Brighton 1853-1987* by Lochee Andison, held at Holdfast Bay History Centre, Brighton, SA.
- Anderson, Hugh 'Virtue in a Wilderness: Cecil Sharp's Australian Sojourn 1882-92' *Folk Music Journal* vol 6, number 5, 1994.
- Fox Strangways, A.H *Cecil Sharp* 1933 OUP (written in collaboration with Maud Karpeles).
- Australian Dictionary of National Biography vol 15 p6 for life of Prof David Kelly.
- *Quiz* newspaper records on microfilm at State Library of South Australia, Adelaide.
- Palmer, Roy 'Veritable Dunghills' article in *Folk Music Journal* vol 7 no. 2 1996.
- *Pioneer* newspaper records on microfilm at State Library of South Australia.
- Jaensch,D, 'South Australia' in *The Emergence of the Australian Party System* Eds Loveday, Martin & Parker 1977 Sydney: Hale & Iremonger.
- Murphy,DJ, *Labor in Politics: the State Labor Parties in Australia 1880-1920* 1975 Univ of Queensland Press.
- Mathews, Race, *Australia's First Fabians* 1993 Cambridge University Press.
- Jackman, M, *The visit of Henry George to Australia* 1983 Univ of Melbourne.
- Marson, CL, *Faery Stories* 1891 EA Petherick, Adelaide. Copy at Australian Literature Resource, Brisbane, www.austlit.edu.au
- Asylum story courtesy of David Buob, Principal Clinical Psychologist, Southern Mental Health, Adelaide
- Vestry Minutes of St Oswald's Parkside held at State Lib of South Australia ref SRG 94/A81.
- Mattingley, Christobel *Survival in our own Land* 1988 Wakefield Press, Adelaide.

Chapter Fourteen: Back to London Town
- Durham Mining Museum www.dmm.org.uk
- Marson, CL *Psalms at Work* 1894 Kegan Paul.
- Letter from Lilian Purdon (nee Heppel) Sept 1931 held at VWML, London re Heppels family life.

- Letter April 9th 1934 from Henry Maskell re Marson's visiting.
- Letter July 1998 to author from Mike Price of University of Leicester re Heppel's mathematical career.
- Information about Ludgrove School Wokingham obtained during author's visit there 1998 with kind permission of the Headmaster Mr Barber. It is the school that was attended by Princes William and Harry.

Chapter Fifteen: Cabbies' strike

- Marson, Clotilda *1894 Diary,* typescript by author, copy held at Somerset Heritage Centre.
- Marson, Charles *The Following of Christ* 1895 SS Peter & Paul
- Box file on St Mary's: Camden Local History Library.
- Bagwell, Philip *Outcast London'* 1987 Epworth Press.
- Pethick-Lawrence, Emmeline *My part in a changing world* 1938 Victor Gollancz.
- Moore, Henry Charles, *Omnibuses and cabs* 1902 Chapman and Hall.
- For coverage of cab strike, microfilm MLD10 *The Daily Chronicle* (May 14 – June 12 1894) British Newspaper Library Colindale.
- Marson, Charles, 'The Case for Omnibus and tram-men' File X, Marson papers, Somerset Heritage Centre.
- Re 'the monthly robe' gift to baby Sharp I am grateful to Vicky Dawson, Museum Consultant for information that at that time new babies were dressed for their first two months in long robes 'before being shortened'.
- Leslie, Shane, *The film of memory* 1938 Michael Joseph.
- Schofield, Derek, 'Sowing the Seeds' 2004 article in *Folk Music Journal* Vol 8 pp484-512 for Cecil's teaching role.
- Boulton, Harold & Somervell, Arthur, *Songs of the Four Nations* 1893 Cramer.
- Chappell, William *A Collection of National English Airs* 1840. Sharp's own copy of this book is preserved at the English Folk Song & Dance Society library with a date stamp in flyleaf saying 189- (final digit unfortunately not completed) but its spelling for the song 'The Leather Bottèl' is identical to that used in the Ludgrove concert programme rather than the later 1893 edition of Chappell's *Old English Popular Music* which has 'Leather Bottle'.
- Sharp, Cecil *A Book of British Song for Home and School* 1902 Curwen.
- 'School Notes', Ludgrove School, Wokingham April 1st 1896 – author's visit to Ludgrove July 1998.

Chapter Sixteen: Poor Frank

- 'The Keeley gold cure for inebriety' *British Medical Journal* July 9 1892 pp85-86.

- Sanders, Mark 'Inhalation Therapy: an historical review' *Primary Care Respiratory Journal* (2007).
- www.inhalatorium.com for Himrod information.
- Re Sharp's use of Himrod as asthma treatment: His letter to Chloe Marson August 28th 1909: Marson papers, Somerset Heritage Centre.
- Marson's challenge to Headlam in Jones, Peter d'A, *The Christian Socialist Revival* pp 139-149 1968 Princeton University Press.

Chapter Seventeen: Marson the Parson
- For CS Grueber treatises see Crockford's 1874 + Google. Account of his funeral www.oldhambridge.com
- Censuses for Hambridge & Westport 1841-1901. Typescript and analysis by author. Details in website above.
- Collinson, John *The History and Antiquities of Somerset* 1791
- Hambridge School Diary 1895 includes reports on Charles's evening classes (author's visit to school).
- Massingham, HJ, *Country Relics* (re gloving) 1939 CUP; the Yeovil Town Football Club is nicknamed 'The Glovers'.
- Kelly's Directory of Somerset 1875, 1883 and 1906.
- Body, G & Gallop, R., *The Parrett Navigation* 2002 Fiducia Press
- Somerset Archaeology Society 'Somerset's Industrial Heritage' 1996 refs to shirts and collar factories in Somerset.
- www.somertonmuseum.org.uk for collar factory.
- Author's interview with Maurice Paull 1998 re demolition of workshop. Mr Paull owned the house and workshop.
- Author's interview 2003 with Ken Masters of South Petherton re his reminiscences of his grandmother Mary Duck of Burrow Hill and her gloving.
- Dale, Peter, *Somerset's Lost Railways* 2001 Stenlake.
- Bayne, Ronald *Oxford Dictionary of National Biography: entry for Peter Bayne* re his father's death.
- Horn, Pamela *Labouring Life in the Victorian Countryside Appendix A* 1976 Alan Sutton.
- *Royal Commission on Labour Vol 5 1894* for agricultural wages.
- Information on coal charity and school minutes from Somerset Heritage Centre. Poor relief part of records of Langport Union.
- Bearman, Dr CJ 'Cecil Sharp at Marlborough House' article in *English Dance & Song* magazine Summer 1998.

Chapter Eighteen: Trouble and Strife
- Report on pub sign: *Somerset County Gazette* October 23 1926.
- Report on Hambridge Friendly Society: *Langport & Somerton Herald* June 15 1901.
- Miss Pedder's accounts of CLM's ministry and family life are part of the Marson papers lodged at Somerset Heritage Centre.
- Marson, Charles *Turnpike Tales* Elkin Mathews.

- Hutchison, Revd CW letter dated 22 Feb 1934 re Sharp's earlier visit to Hambridge. His photo of the church choir is reproduced in this book. Marson papers, Taunton.
- Marson, Charles *Hugh of Lincoln* 1901 Edward Arnold.
- Marson, Charles 'Huppim and Muppim' 1903 Mowbray.
- Some experimental photos that Marson took of his children dated April 1901 are among the Marson papers at Somerset Heritage Centre. Also a letter dated May 31st 1906 referring to Marson's son John buying his own camera 'and developing the films himself', so there was a darkroom at the vicarage.
- Tottle, Margaret *A Brief History of Isle Brewers* 1993 St Andrews Press, Wells.

Chapter Nineteen: Discovering Folksongs
- Examples of folk melodies in classical music: Brahms Hungarian Dances 1869; Tchaikovsky Russian Folk Songs 1869; Dvořák Slavonic Dances 1878.
- Grant, Bob *'When Punch met Merry'* article *Folk Music Journal* 1999 vol 7 no. 5. Note: Sandfield Cottage was demolished in 1965 but a plaque exists in its place in Horwood Close, junction of Sandfield Rd and London Rd.
- Bearman, Dr CJ 'Kate Lee and the Foundation of the Folk-Song Society' 1999 *Folk Music Journal* vol 7 no. 5 re Elgar story.
- Schofield, D., 2004. 'Sowing the Seeds' article 2004 *Folk Music Journal*, EFDSS vol 8 no.4 for a full account of the first collecting visits.
- Newall, WA 'In the Footsteps of Cecil Sharp' article in *English Dance and Song* magazine April 1943 for 'doughnuts' story and also information about William Spearing.
- Re: The Oak and the Ash song (Roud 269). Cecil's final text for this song is in his Folk Words p27. The Roud Folksong Index is a database of over 21,000 songs, compiled by Steve Roud. It can be accessed by going to www.efdss.org and selecting VWML online (search indexes option).
- Sharp and Marson collected fragments of tunes and words from many singers. When reference is made to songs (numbers, titles), information is taken from *Cecil Sharp's Collection of Folk Songs* edited by Maud Karpeles 1974 OUP. The fullest details can be retrieved from Sharp's notebooks – the originals are at Clare College, Cambridge but facsimiles are at VWML library in London.
- Will of James Sharp, probate 19th January 1904.
- Bearman, Dr CJ 'Who were the folk?' 2000 *The Historical Journal* 43 CUP re Spearing and other singers.
- Bearman, Dr CJ *'Cecil Sharp at Marlborough House'* article in *English Dance and Song* magazine 1998 re royal tutor post.

- Fabian News July 1904 for CLM's talk on folksong; Langport & Somerton Herald Dec 10th for his ballads talk.
- Sharp's photos can be seen online www.library.efdss.org Click photo gallery option. His negatives are Kodak 6x9cms. Mike Yates in email to author believes Sharp used a Kodak No.1 folding pocket camera 120 roll film, which is confirmed by expert Michael Pritchard, research fellow Dept of Imaging & Communication Design, De Montfort University, Leicester. Further proof is in a letter by AN Brown, former Ludgrove teacher, to Fox Strangways Oct 7th 1931 VWML.
- *The English Hymnal* 1906 featured 5 tunes collected by Cecil Sharp (hymns 355, 389, 498, 656 pts 1 & 2). Louie Hooper was particularly proud that her tune was used for the hymn 'There is a land of pure delight' 498, surprisingly listed as 'Mendip' tune. Her letter March 11th 1934 (VWML) refers.
- Letter to Miss Trask is a typescript by Revd Etherington of an original letter now lost.
- Sharp, CJ & Marson, CL *Folk Songs from Somerset* 1904 Barnicott & Pearce, Taunton.

Chapter Twenty: Under Investigation again

- Harker, Dave *Fakesong: the manufacture of British 'folksong'* 1985 OUP.
- Bearman, Dr CJ 'Cecil Sharp in Somerset' 2002 *The Folklore Society* pp11-34.
- Boyes, Georgina *The Imagined Village* 1993 Manchester University Press.
- Marson, Charles *Super Flumina* 1905 John Lane.
- The Report of the Royal Commission on Ecclesiastical Discipline July 1906: Lambeth Palace Library 25 vols.
- Scotland, Nigel 'Evangelicals, Anglicans and Ritualism in Victorian England' 1997 *Churchman* magazine 111/3.
- Sharp's income details for 1910 Box 9 Sharp Miscellaneous at VWML.
- Mary Clara Sophia Neal (1860-1944): Dictionary of National Biography. See also www.maryneal.org
- Pethick-Lawrence, Emmeline *My part in a changing world* 1938 Victor Gallancz.
- Judge, Roy 'The relationship between Cecil Sharp and Mary Neal in the evolution of the English Folk Movement' 1989 article in *Folk Music Journal* vol 5 no.5.
- Notes of interview re Mary Neal: Helm 61 486-7 efdss library re St Christopher's club.
- For MacIlwaine's writings go to Australian Literature Resource: www.austlit.edu.au

-   Re MacIlwaine's time in Australia: author's emails with Dawn Bopf of Townsville City Libraries.

Chapter Twenty One: Conflicts of Interest

-   Eton story quoted from Revd Baverstock letter to Etherington (Feb 28th 1934) in Marson papers at Somerset Heritage Centre.
-   Marson, Charles 'And Ard' *Commonwealth* magazine November 1904, reprinted 1906 Mowbray.
-   Strachey, Ray *Millicent Garrett Fawcett* 1931 John Murray for letter to Chloe p177.
-   Langport & Somerton Herald May 12th 1906 for report on Charles's sermon in Bristol; and July 21st 1906 for the Langport Socialist Group.
-   Letter Feb 1979 from Professor John Saville, Dept of Economic & Social History, University of Hull for the Dictionary of National Biography project. Modern Records Centre, Univ of Warwick Reg Groves papers mss.172/CS/3/1-13.
-   Noel, Conrad *An Autobiography* 1945 JM Dent (for Thaxted morris reference p105).
-   Forrest, John 'The History of Morris Dancing 1458-1750' 1999 University of Toronto Press. A comprehensive account of the morris dance in royal revels, church ales, guild processions, may games, the theatre etc.
-   Heaney, Michael 'The Earliest Reference to the Morris Dance?' 2004 article in *Folk Music Journal* vol 8 no. 4.
-   West Somerset Free Press Sat June 30th for report on the Minehead Folk Event. Actual programme is among the Marson papers in Taunton.
-   Krause, Rhett 'American Morris Newsletter' 2005 vol 25 no. 4 for information about Florrie Warren. I am grateful to Rhett for sharing his research. Florrie's solo performance of the 'Somerset Step Dance' was given in Hartford Connecticut in May 1911 'Hartford Daily Courant' 20 May.
-   Sharp, Cecil *English Folk-Song: Some Conclusions* 1907 London Simpkin
-   Burgess, Paul 'The Mystery of the Whistling Sewermen' *Folk Music Journal* 2002 vol 8 no. 2 for a full account of the Staggs' family connections to morris musicians and dancers.
-   Judge, Roy 'Cecil Sharp and the Morris 1906-09' *Folk Music Journal* 2002 vol 8 no. 2 for full account of Sharp's dance collecting trips to the Cotswolds.
-   Chandler, Keith *Ribbons, Bells and Squeaking Fiddles* 1993 Hisarlik Press.
-   Sharp, Cecil and MacIlwaine, Herbert 'The Morris Book Part I' 1st Ed 1907, 2nd Ed 1912 Novello.

Chapter Twenty Two: The Break with Cecil Sharp
- Sharp's letter about the profits is in Sharp Correspondence Box 4 Folder 1 in VWML. My thanks to Dr Chris Bearman for drawing it to my attention.
- Etherington quote about Marson is in Maurice Rickitt book *For Christ and People* 1968 SPCK.
- Bland, David *Notes of his Interview with Maud Karpeles Sept 27th 1973* Dave Bland Collection Box 5 VWML. I am grateful to Dave Bland, former VWML librarian, for permission to use this material.
- Wallis, Hazel, letter to the author November 14th 1999. In a prior telephone conversation with the author Mrs Wallis, who died in Feb 2010, said that her husband Revd Roger Wallis was once deep in conversation with Maud then they both went up the garden and burned some letters. No date given for this event.
- Letters from Ethel Spilsbury Aug 30th 1931; from Bertha Clarke Feb 21st 1934; and from Revd Brockington June 3rd 1934. Marson papers at Somerset Heritage Centre.
- Interview with Joy Etherington 1989 re her father's musical skills. Part of the Bob Patten archive. I am grateful to Bob & Jacqui Patten for sharing this information with me.
- Hutton, Ronald *The Stations of the Sun* 1996 OUP for references to morris dancing at Wells and Poyntington p255.

Chapter Twenty Three: More Upset
- Mary Neal's archive of papers, photos and letters is now kept at VWML. View online www.maryneal.org Roy Judge's article on Mary Neal in Folk Music Journal 1989 is best starting-point for the whole dispute, which is beyond the scope of this book.
- Crawford, Elizabeth *'The Women's Suffrage Movement'* p443 for Mary Neal and the WSPU.
- Bearman, Dr CJ *'The Societies'* extract from his MA thesis, Hull University 1999.
- Bacon, Lionel *A Handbook of Morris Dances* 1st Ed 1974 The Morris Ring (2nd Ed 1986) contains 319 morris dances from 32 locations, of which 67 are stick dances, 158 are hanky dances, 21 handclap dances and 61 (solo) jigs.
- Transcript by Alex Helm of notes by Margaret Dean Smith (Nov 1957 VWML) re start of the English Folk Dance Society.
- Frazer, Sir James *The Golden Bough first 2 vols* 1890. This influential study of myth and ritual led Sharp to see the morris as a quasi-religious business, whereas Neal saw the dances as the 'hoydenish' expressions of the working-class: 'There must be nothing in this revival which cannot be done by the average boy and girl. I am afraid of the hindering touch of the pedant, of the professional dance and music teacher.'

Chapter Twenty Four: Ill health
- Langport & Somerton Herald June 6th 1908 for report on Socialism meeting.
- Patient notes for Frank Marson released to author by University College Hospital Archives.
- Strachey, Ray *Millicent Garrett Fawcett* 1931 John Murray.
- Crawford, Elizabeth *The Women's Suffrage Movement* 1999 Routledge.
- Bearman, Dr CJ 'An Examination of Suffragette Violence' 2005 *English Historical Review* vol CXX OUP.
- Purvis, Jane *Emmeline Pankhurst* 2002 Routledge.
- Pedder, Sophy *'Some notes on a Country Parson'* handwritten notes, part of Marson papers.
- Letter from Rose England March 26th 1914. Marson papers.
- Author's correspondence with Saskatchewan Archive Board 1998 re John England's family in Canada.
- Notes on Plato: Marson Papers Box A File X.
- Programme for Black Kat Club event May 1912. Marson papers.
- www.jeromekjerome.com (Jerome K Jerome Society); his play 'The Passing of the Third Floor Back' first performed at St James' Theatre London Sept 1st 1908 (pub by Samuel French 1905).

Chapter Twenty Five: Odds and Ends
- Marson, CL *God's Co-operative Society* 1914 Longmans.
- Marson, CL *Village Silhouettes* 1914 SS Peter & Paul.
- *The Tramp* magazine 1910-11 British Library ref 02855573.
- Record of Chloe's life: Newnham College Archives: correspondence with author 1998.

Chapter Twenty Six: Chloe's New Life
- Maj Stevens' letter reported in Langport & Somerton Herald Nov 13th 1915.
- Sir Ian Hamilton's Third Report on Gallipoli Campaign was dated Dec 11th 1915 and published in *The London Gazette* January 6th 1916.
- www.1914-1918.net/welsh.htm for information on the Welsh Regiment.
- Sunday Times article 'Bad maps led to carnage of Gallipoli' March 21st 1999.
- Hambridge British Legion Branch minutes 1920-21.
- Will of Clotilda Marson dated 27/7/1944, proved in London 1953.

Chapter Twenty Seven: Legacy
- Binyon, Gilbert *The Christian Socialist Movement in England* 1931 SPCK.

About the Author

I worked for 20 years as manager of the nursing home based at the old vicarage in Hambridge and thus saw evidence of Marson's life and work all around me. By chance I then discovered that I am related to one of Cecil Sharp's singers – Charles Neville of East Coker – and this deepened my appreciation of folk music. A regular member of Taunton Deane Morris Men for 17 years, I now lead two community choirs (in Isle Abbotts and Ilminster). My research into Marson's life began over ten years ago and I feel strangely destined to produce this book – my first biography.

Like Marson, I am the son of a clergyman. I studied theology and then sociology with psychology at Cambridge University – a curious combination but perfectly suited to a two-year posting as a VSO teacher in the Highlands of Papua New Guinea! There (like Marson in Adelaide) I met some very kind Australians as well as missionaries and mercenaries. Adapting to a new culture and finding the right messages were big challenges for me – more similarities with Marson – as the school prepared its pupils for their country's imminent independence. I taught social studies, English and business studies, starting up the school's co-operative store where pupils learned retail skills.

Teaching in England was not for me after such exciting ventures. Jobs with OXFAM and then the British Council helped me to refocus, before I eventually learned patience and some management skills in Somerset. It was a great pleasure to lead a skilled and committed team of people there.

I still live in Somerset with my wife Lesley who is a doctor. Our two children have left home – Amy is a chemistry teacher and Thomas is a West End actor in musical theatre.

David Sutcliffe
Somerset
November 2010

Index